To: Frank

Best wishes to a longtime
Tennessee fan and a wonderful
friend with close UT ties.

Go Vols!

Haywood Harris

Frank Manning

SIX SEASONS REMEMBERED

The National Championship Years of Tennessee Football

Haywood Harris and Gus Manning

The University of Tennessee Press / Knoxville

Library of Congress Cataloging-in-Publication Data

Harris, Haywood, 1929–
Six seasons remembered: the national championship years of
Tennessee football / Haywood Harris and Gus Manning – 1st ed.

p. cm.
ISBN 1-57233-317-0 (hardcover: alk. paper)
1. University of Tennessee, Knoxville—Football—History.
2. Tennessee Volunteers (Football team)—History.
3. Tennessee Volunteers (Football team)—Interviews.
I. Manning, Gus, 1923–
II. Title.

T

In memory of Margaret and to Sammy,

Meg, Joe, Chad, and Elizabeth

—Gus Manning

To Carolyn Jo, Carol, Jimmy, Mike, Kaye, Debbie, Matthew,

Jennifer, Cody, and Jeffery

—Haywood Harris

Contents

Illustrations

Chapter 4   1951

Chapter 5   1967

Chapter 6 1998

Foreword

When I heard that Gus Manning and Haywood Harris were writing a book on the University of Tennessee's national championship teams, I immediately thought this was an assignment that only they could accomplish. After all, they have nearly 100 years of Tennessee football watching between them, Gus since 1951 and Haywood since 1961.

Their book covers Tennessee football through championship teams in the 1930s, the 1940s, the 1950s, 1960s, and 1990s. They've interviewed many of the players and coaches from these teams and added their own unique perspectives on what makes Tennessee championship football so special. Not only have they followed the teams, but they've also known the players and been there for the great moments. It's a wonderful and evolving tradition, and they've been an integral part of it.

For Gus and Haywood, this has been literally a labor of love—for their alma mater and for its football program.

In these pages, you'll review success in Orange and White, from the days of Bob Neyland, through Doug Dickey and the more current days with Phillip Fulmer.

You'll grow to appreciate the history and heritage of Tennessee football, regardless of when you saw your first game, as you leaf through *Six Seasons Remembered: The National Championship Years of Tennessee Football.*

I know I did.

Michael E. Hamilton
University of Tennessee Director of Athletics

Acknowledgments

From the beginning, when the idea of a book about Tennessee's national championships was broached, Jennifer Siler encouraged the authors every step of the way. As the director of the University of Tennessee Press, she was generous in giving valuable advice to a couple of guys who were totally unfamiliar with the complicated process of publishing a book.

For her patience, expertise, and all-around assistance we are grateful to Jennifer, who was chief among many whose help made it possible for us to put together the finished product. On Jennifer's recommendation, we obtained the services of Gene Adair to serve as our editor. Gene went beyond the call of duty not only with his deft copyediting but also by making suggestions for additional information that would result in a better-rounded publication. He recognized and brought to our attention gaps that needed to be closed.

Support from top leaders within the Athletics Department has been everything we could ask for. Mike Hamilton, in the 11 years at UT leading up to his appointment as director of athletics, developed an appreciation for UT's his-

tory and tradition that fits well into his otherwise excellent qualifications for the job. And the man he followed into the A.D.'s office, Doug Dickey, also gave full backing to the project along with helpful guidance on how best to proceed.

Dr. Rob Hardin is a UT assistant professor in sport management. And, we hasten to add, a huge Tennessee Vols fan. He helped in ways too numerous to catalog here, but a couple deserve special mention. In the early stages of the process, Rob spent hours in the library with the authors selecting material from endless reels of microfilm containing the newspaper stories of each game. It was from such raw material that we reconstructed the six national championship seasons.

Since neither of us qualifies as an organizational wizard, we are especially grateful to Rob for procuring and keeping track of the dozens of photographs that allowed this to become a "coffee-table" publication. With his vital assistance, we were able to return photographs to the people who submitted them. We hope all reached their respective owners in good condition.

By supplying photos from his vast collection of Vols lore, Arthur L. (Bud) Fields did everything in his power to get us to print. Our gratitude knows no bounds. We extend thanks also for their help in securing pictures to Pat Shires, Betty Moeller, Dr. Andy Kozar, Nick Showalter, Ed Morgan, Ed Cifers, Leonard Coffman, Hank Lauricella, Dick Williams, Doug Atkins, Janie Hill, and Bert Ackermann.

Special appreciation goes also to Russ Bebb, partly for the exhaustive documentation he provided about UT football in two superb books he wrote on the subject, *The Big Orange* and *Vols*. In addition, Bebb, who has the eyes of a hawk when it comes to spotting errors, took time to proofread the entire book, offering numerous useful suggestions.

People like Bebb, Kozar, Ben Byrd, the highly respected sports editor of the old *Knoxville Journal*, longtime Vol statistician Bill Petty, and former Voice of the Vols John Ward possess an encyclopedic knowledge about Tennessee and SEC football that the authors drew on frequently as this book was being assembled. Syndicated "Grammar Gremlin" columnist Don Ferguson was never too busy to field questions concerning sentence structure or anything else related to word usage.

Bud Ford, a master of compiling historical data as UT's hard-working and earnest associate athletics director for media relations, runs an office that is second to none when it comes to being helpful. They came to the aid of a couple of old-timers beyond measure, meeting every request with a smile on their youthful faces. Ford came up with many photographs and made the services of his assistants available to the often hard-pressed authors.

Special thanks to the always cooperative Tom Mattingly, Susie Treis, Nathan Kirkham, Dustin Mynatt, John Painter, Jeff Muir, Craig Pinkerton, Lori Cate, Douglas Blair, Accalia Wombold, Josh Pate, Amber Scarbro, Tom Satkowiak, and Hillary Burress. They are the backbone of a sports information office that has made Tennessee's a model for publicity organizations throughout the nation.

Most of all, our appreciation goes to the dozens of Vols and their coaches who generously gave their time and granted the interviews that brought to life the national championship teams of 1938, 1940, 1950, 1951, 1967, and 1998. 🏈

Introduction

University of Tennessee football fans are justifiably proud of the national football championships won by the Volunteer teams in 1951 and 1998. But whether they know it or not, they have reason to be even prouder.

Make that four reasons. In fact, Tennessee teams were also awarded national titles by recognized ranking systems for the seasons of 1938, 1940, 1950, and 1967. History has largely overlooked those great teams, mainly because they were not ranked first by the best-known ratings systems, which were the Associated Press poll in 1951 and the Bowl Championship Series in 1998.

This book was written partly in an effort to highlight those four champions, too many years afterwards. But better late than never.

The years 1938, 1939, and 1940 formed the richest era in UT gridiron history, three consecutive unbeaten and untied seasons that owed a huge debt to the coaching of the legendary Robert R. Neyland. The '38 team, captained by All-America end Bowden Wyatt and boasting such other Tennessee immortals as George Cafego and Bob Suffridge, was awarded the national title by no fewer than seven recognized ratings entities, including the highly regarded Dunkel System (which, as its current managers like to boast, is older than the AP poll).

A case could be made that the '38 team was as good as any the school has ever fielded since the beginning of the university's football program in 1891. The 1938 Vols went on to beat Oklahoma in the Orange Bowl, and for 60 years they remained the only Tennessee team to go through both the regular season and the postseason with a perfect record.

Oddly, the 1939 team—the last team in college football history to complete a regular season unbeaten, untied, and unscored-on—was passed over by all the ranking systems. This was probably more of a tribute to the universally recognized national champion, Texas A&M, than to any lack of appreciation for the '39 Vols. But in 1940, the last of the three perfect-record years of the era, UT was awarded the national crown by two ratings systems, including the Dunkel group.

Bob Neyland's 1950 team lost an early game to Mississippi State but went on to fashion a 10–1 regular-season record, including a memorable battle in the snow with previously unbeaten Kentucky. Six systems, including Dunkel, proclaimed those Vols national champions. And, of course, in 1951 Tennessee was an overwhelming choice, and for the first time the school won the Associated Press's number-one ranking.

It should be noted that postseason results did not count in those days; the final polls were taken at the end of regular season play. That same situation was still in effect when Doug Dickey's 1967 team posted a 9–1 season record and was recognized as national champ by the Litkenhous ratings, one of the oldest of all the ratings systems.

By 1998 the Bowl Championship Series format had been put in place, and Tennessee's win over Florida State in the Fiesta Bowl won Phillip Fulmer's team an undisputed title. But it should be kept in mind that there is not, and has never been, any such thing as an official NCAA Division I national championship. Until an NCAA playoff system is put in place, as seems inevitable someday, there will never be one.

But the Volunteer teams of 1938, 1940, 1950, and 1967 laid legitimate claims to the mythical title, and they deserve to be remembered with the same respect as their more celebrated brothers of 1951 and 1998.

In the pages that follow, we are proud to recall Tennessee's six national championship seasons through pictures, game-by-game recaps, and the reminiscences of players and coaches who experienced the action on the field firsthand. 🏈

SIX SEASONS REMEMBERED

The 1938 Vols

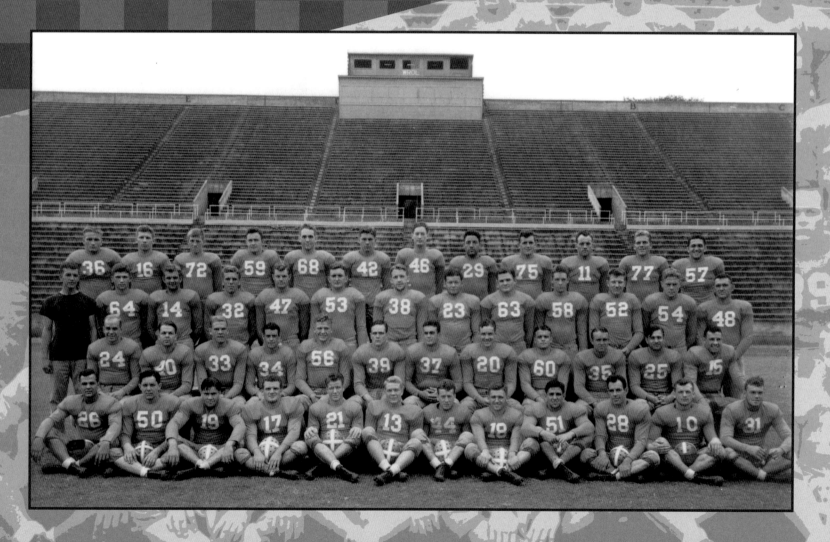

Chapter 1

Bob Neyland transformed the ancient rite of "poor-mouthing" into an art form. He had no peer when it came to explaining why the Volunteers were about to take a drubbing, regardless of the opponent. And this from a coach who was already something of a living legend: His UT teams, by 1938, had won a total of 88 games in 11 seasons, while losing only 12 and tying only eight. In fact, it was during Neyland's one-season absence from coaching—in 1935, when the Army sent him to Panama—that the Vols had gone 4–5 and had the fans clamoring for his return. Everyone knew his sob stories were an act.

Nevertheless, in 1938 Neyland exceeded even his own wide boundaries of how far he would go to paint the Vols as underdogs. A man who despised making speeches before civic clubs, he was at his best decrying Tennessee's chances with a preseason talk before the Downtown Rotary Club. Conceding that he had a more gifted team than in 1937, Neyland quickly added, "Inasmuch as the opposition appears to be even more improved, our record might not be as good as last year."

The 1938 coaching staff included, from left, Head Coach Bob Neyland, Murray Warmath, Bill Britton, Hugh Faust, and John Barnhill.

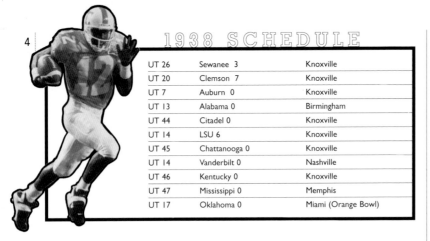

1938 SCHEDULE

UT 26	Sewanee 3	Knoxville
UT 20	Clemson 7	Knoxville
UT 7	Auburn 0	Knoxville
UT 13	Alabama 0	Birmingham
UT 44	Citadel 0	Knoxville
UT 14	LSU 6	Knoxville
UT 45	Chattanooga 0	Knoxville
UT 14	Vanderbilt 0	Nashville
UT 46	Kentucky 0	Knoxville
UT 47	Mississippi 0	Memphis
UT 17	Oklahoma 0	Miami (Orange Bowl)

Considering that Tennessee had lost three games in 1937, a 6–4 record in 1938 (which, in effect, he was predicting) would not have been pleasing. "I'll never lose three games in one season again," Neyland had told the Vols during the 1937–38 off-season.

Neyland's crocodile tears were even more evident before the eagerly awaited midseason joust with LSU. His lament became so exaggerated that *Knoxville Journal* columnist Tom Anderson urged the head coach to refrain from further commentary. Anderson reasoned that it would be nice if the Vols could go into the game thinking they had at least an outside hope of winning.

Until the 1998 Vols came along to become the undisputed national champions, a sizable segment of public opinion thought the 1938 team was the most deserving UT aggregation of all. That opinion was based on the team's perfect record, including the bowl game.

Vols 26, Sewanee 3

As 10,000 Knox County schoolchildren, admitted as guests of the UT Athletic Association, lifted their voices in approval among the crowd of 20,000, Tennessee handily disposed of

Sewanee, 26–3, in the 1938 season opener. After posting three first-quarter touchdowns, the Vols apparently concluded that Sewanee was done for, as they never regained their early form.

Not that it mattered. There would be larger fish to fry as the season moved along. The best that could be said for the UT victory was that it was "workmanlike," an adjective that could have been joined by "uninspired."

UT's first possession resulted in a touchdown, attributed in part to the deft ball-handling of blocking back Sam Bartholomew, who frequently fooled the visiting Tigers with the sleight of hand he employed before shoveling the ball elsewhere.

For all practical purposes, the opening touchdown settled the issue. George Cafego and Bob Foxx figured prominently in the 72-yard excursion, which began with Cafego bring-

Called a "super backfield," the 1938 contingent included, from left, wingback Bob Foxx, fullback Leonard Coffman, tailback George Cafego, and blocking back Sam Bartholomew.

ing the ball back to the 28 on the kickoff. Foxx covered the final 30 yards, employing a well-planted stiff arm to discourage Sewanee's last would-be tackler.

Captain Bowden Wyatt put the outcome beyond question on Sewanee's ensuing possession when he blocked a punt and then pounced on the ball in the end zone. Fullback Joe Wallen dazzled the crowd with a 16-yard run that allowed Coach Neyland to relax and play reserves for much of the remaining time.

Sewanee made some inroads against the UT defense later in the game, picking up its only points with a field goal in the last quarter, but by that time the Fighting (or Purple, if you prefer) Tigers might as well have headed for home.

Sewanee	0	0	0	3	3
Tennessee	20	6	0	0	26

UT   Foxx, run 30 (Wyatt kick)

UT   Wyatt, fumble recovery in end zone (Wyatt kick)

UT   Wallen, run 16 (kick blocked)

UT   Duncan, run 3 (pass failed)

S   Higgins, field goal 12

Ed Cifers Remembers

"Back in those days, almost all major colleges had warm-up games, and this was the warm-up for the University of Tennessee. Also, Neyland said he could tell in the first game who was a ballplayer and who wasn't.

"Neyland had a way of padding his schedule with breathers. He always had one for the opening game, and he had one just before Alabama. All three years I was there, we had a breather before Alabama.

"He told the squad before every game the same things he would tell the press, even though we knew we weren't playing a topflight opponent. He would make Sewanee and Wofford and The Citadel sound like top-10 teams. He had his coaches talking the same way.

"I remember telling [Assistant] Coach Bill Britton, 'Coach, there's no way this can be a good game or even a good scrimmage.' And Britton told me, 'Oh yeah, go on out there and play like they are a great team.'

"You know, there was a lot of difference between the employment of the backfield back then and how it was done in the '50s. The blocking back was lined up sideways and could receive the snap direct. He could then run with it or hand it to the wingback, coming around.

"But I believe 1938 was the last year we snapped to the blocking back. We were getting away from that and didn't use it at all in 1939 or 1940. Our substitution then was done by teams.

"To show how things have changed as far as play-calling was concerned, it was actually done by the tailback, not by the coaches. The rules said a substitute had to stand on the side of the field until the huddle broke. That was so he couldn't run in there and call a play.

"I remember Cafego looking at his sleeve for the plays. Certain things were understood between the coach and the tailback, such as what you will do at a certain place on the field, but mostly the tailback was on his own.

"Another interesting thing from back then was that they didn't have hash marks. If you got tackled a yard from the sideline, that's where the ball was snapped for the next play."

Vols 20, Clemson 7

A man whose name was seldom heard in an era that was dominated by George Cafego, Bowden Wyatt, and Bob Suffridge emerged as the hero of Tennessee's 20–7 victory over Clemson.

Bob (Breezer) Andridge lined up at wingback on the play that allowed Tennessee to bounce back from a 7–0 deficit in the second quarter to even the count with the Tigers and set the stage for UT's hard-earned triumph.

Andridge ran 59 yards on the next possession after Clemson had drawn first blood with a 64-yard scoring march. He took the ball on a reverse around left end, found a wall of blockers at the 25, shook off a couple of tacklers, and crossed the goal with the tying touchdown.

With tongue extended, in his famous style, George Cafego ran, passed, and punted his way into the National Hall of Fame.

As one newspaper report lamented, there were so many blocks made on Andridge's run, it was impossible to catch the names of the men making them. But that was the way Neyland coached football, so there should have been no surprise at the sight of a phalanx of blockers dispatching the Tigers into oblivion.

George Cafego, whose passing and kicking were below his usual standard, ran the ball with his customary aplomb, netting 150 yards on the ground, or 1 more yard than all the Clemson backs combined. It was Cafego's double-duty stint at defensive back, however, that set the stage for a go-ahead touchdown after the half ended with the score deadlocked at 7–7.

A Clemson pass tipped by Leonard Coffman ended up in Cafego's hands, who returned it from his 21 to the 43. A pass to Bob Foxx, a Foxx reverse, and a short pickup by Cafego put the ball at the 1-yard line where Coffman plunged across for the score.

Fondly known as "Old Double X," Foxx provided an insurance tally when he took an interception and ran 23 yards to the northeast corner of the stadium. Apparently, he had recovered pretty well from a charley horse that had put his participation in doubt at midweek.

As the preceding paragraphs suggest, Clemson was no slouch. Coach Jess Neely's Tigers were formidable enough that newspapers from throughout the South had their best writers covering the game.

Clemson	0	7	0	0	7
Tennessee	0	7	7	6	20

CU	Willis, run 4 (Pearson kick)
UT	Andridge, run 59 (Cafego kick)
UT	Coffman, run 1 (Cafego kick)
UT	Foxx, interception return 23 (kick failed)

Norbert Ackermann Remembers

"We only played Clemson on rare occasions, but it was always a tough opponent for Tennessee. During the Condredge Holloway and Larry Seivers days, back in the '70s, Tennessee had some really tough games with Clemson.

"Jess Neely, the coach at Clemson, would fool you. He'd just sort of lull you to sleep by doing things very routinely. Then all of a sudden, he would pull some kind of trick on you and catch you off guard.

"Neely had coached at Vanderbilt and later coached at Rice. He was very well respected. Breezer Andridge was a fine runner on a team that had many outstanding backs.

"Of course, Cafego was one of the best when it came to running. But it would be a mistake to overlook the value of George's defensive play. He was a tough and determined tackler and a very good defensive back."

Vols 7, Auburn 0

Auburn was another of those invading powerhouses Neyland insisted deserved the favorite's role against the Vols, but a budding sophomore star with the unusual first name of "Buist" made the UT mentor a poor prophet once again.

But first, it took a standout defensive play to give the Vols a chance to post the only score of the game in the fourth quarter. That was when Jeep McCarren scooped up an Auburn fumble at the visitors' 25.

Frustrated by numerous squandered opportunities earlier in the contest, the Vols turned deadly serious, knowing that they might not have another chance that late in the game. Buist Warren, UT's gift from Miami, Florida, picked up

5 yards from the tailback slot, then fired a pass to Bob Foxx that covered 15 yards. Warren plunged ahead in two tries to put the ball at the 1, and from there Joe Wallen dived across the goal line.

Auburn had some chances earlier, just as the Vols had. A bevy of Tiger backs penetrated well into UT territory, but the Tennessee defense stopped the drive at the 19. The Vols, behind George Cafego, moved inside the Auburn 10 in the first half but failed to score.

Penalties put Tennessee behind an eight ball from which it couldn't emerge, and with this turn of fortunes, the Plainsmen managed to hold the Vols at bay until McCarren's fumble recovery and Warren's smart direction provided the game's lone touchdown.

Overall, the Vols were treading dangerous waters. Penalties and below-average kicking had given a strong opponent some good opportunities. That Tennessee hung on under these adverse conditions and won the game was a tribute to the quality of Coach Neyland's players.

Substitute tailback Buist Warren breaks loose against Oklahoma in the Orange Bowl.

With Alabama lurking on the horizon, the Vols were pleased to escape their tough challenge from Auburn with a victory of any size or shape.

Auburn	0	0	0	0	0
Tennessee	0	0	0	7	7

UT   Wallen, run 2 (Wyatt kick)

Coach Murray Warmath Remembers

"That year I was helping John Barnhill, who was the line coach. I also did some scouting of opponents that season. We had a lot of Tennessee boys on that team, native Tennesseans. This team had a lot of sophomores and some awfully good players from inside the state.

"Bob Suffridge was a Tennessee boy, a guy who had it all. He had the best burst of speed off the ball I ever saw. I knew a lot of coaches who worked around him at UT, in the service and in pro ball. They all looked on him just the way I did. I've never seen anybody as fast and quick, and that's what they all said about him. He had great speed and great instincts and just loved to play.

"Bob made All-America in 1938 when he was a sophomore. We had a team that played well and beat everybody, and Bob was the tiger on it. That's how you explain him making All-America in his first year. People talk about his defensive abilities, but he was also very good as an offensive guard.

"Buist Warren was a passer who played spot duty at tailback. Back then, there wasn't much passing because we tried to ram the ball down everybody's throat. Cafego, of course, would run over people. Buist was smart and directed the team well.

"Joe Wallen was the fullback who ran the ball in for the only touchdown of the game. He was another Tennessean who was called on a lot to make short yardage when we needed it.

"Neyland's teams emphasized avoiding penalties because they hurt your field position. There were a number of penalties against Tennessee in this game, but remember one thing: Aggressive teams are going to get penalized. That happens when you carry the fight to them.

"But Neyland told the team, when you get a penalty you're helping the other team because you're doing something that they haven't forced you to do. He worked very hard on that, but he knew an aggressive team will get penalized.

"This was a low-scoring game, but there were quite a few six- and seven-point games, something you don't see much anymore. It was unusual that Tennessee played Auburn and Alabama on consecutive Saturdays. Normally we played Chattanooga before Alabama because they used the same kind of offense that Alabama did. Scrappy Moore was a good coach down at Chattanooga, and it helped us against Alabama to play Chattanooga on the previous Saturday."

Vols 13, Alabama 0

Sniffing a bid to the Rose Bowl and riding a 21-game regular-season winning streak, Alabama fans could point to a book's worth of statistics to predict victory when their Red Elephants took on Tennessee at Legion Field in Birmingham.

But Bob Neyland's teams were never ones to put much faith in statistics. Thus trained, the 1938 Vols thoroughly routed the Crimson Tide, much to the chagrin of 25,000 partisan spectators anticipating a feast of orange blood.

While George Cafego recorded his usual spectacular game, outgaining the entire Alabama backfield, it was the Volunteers' vicious line play that inspired Tennessee sports-

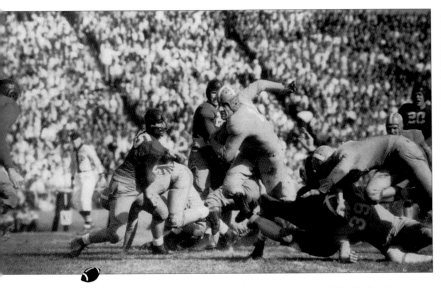

Blocks from Bob Suffridge, Sam Bartholomew, and Ed Molinski spring Leonard Coffman against Alabama.

writers to lyrical heights. One wrote: "The underrated Tennessee line trounced their vaunted opponents in the front trenches to a frazzle. From the outset the UT forewall outcharged Alabama. Frequently, crimson-shirted linemen were knocked back into the laps of the ball-carrier. It was known by one and all that Neyland had a plethora of excellent backs, but until today no intimation had been had of the latent power of his primary."

Tennessee scored touchdowns in the first and third periods and dominated the game so thoroughly that disappointed Tide fans departed the stadium thankful the outcome hadn't been even more lopsided.

Leonard Coffman negotiated the final yard of both scoring drives, the first with Babe Wood at tailback and the second with Cafego back in his customary starring role. Cafego had yielded to Wood temporarily when he was in-

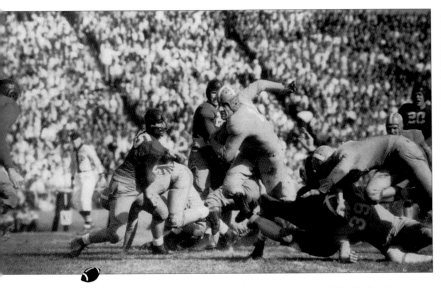

jured during the initial scoring drive but returned to inflict his usual brand of punishment on the Red Elephants.

Tennessee's defense was as stellar as the offense, only once permitting the Crimson Tide to get as close as the UT 29 but then bowing up to prevent further incursions. After the game Coach Neyland said, "We were greatly surprised to win. All my boys played well and made few mistakes. I was overly impressed with the way our line opened the way for the backfield."

Tennessee	6	0	7	0	13
Alabama	0	0	0	0	0

UT   Coffman, run 1 (kick failed)
UT   Coffman, run 1 (Wyatt kick)

Leonard Coffman Remembers

"I scored the two touchdowns, but George Cafego did most of the running. I handled the ball a lot on the spin plays. I would carry about 10 percent of the time, but handed off either to the tailback or wingback. It was the 70 series. On 77 I went right over center. I did it in the Rose Bowl, first play, and went about 12 yards.

"We prepared for Alabama during spring practice, working on how we would go against them on defense. We spent much more time on defense than offense. It was a big ball game. We didn't have any idea we could beat them. We were always preparing for Alabama.

"The line Neyland talked about was made up of Bob Suffridge and Ed Molinski at guard, Abe Shires and Bob Woodruff or Boyd Clay at tackle, Joe Little at center, and Bowden Wyatt and George Hunter at end. Amazingly, the second team was about as good as the first team. Guys like

Tom Smith, Ed Cifers, Bill Luttrell, Norbert Ackermann, Jimmy Rike. That Ed Cifers was about as tough as anybody I ever knew. I know, because I had to go against him on punt formation.

"But after a game Neyland didn't say much to the press or to us. He would just call us together and say, 'Good game.'

"[Fullback] Marion Perkins, from Chattanooga, was a tough guy. Thought he was tough, anyway. One time I had gone into the training room when I was a freshman. Perkins said, 'Hey, rookie, you are not supposed to be in here. This place is for the big boys.' I said, 'Well, the big boys are right here.' That's the first time I ever saw him back down on anything. But Perkins was a good guy, really.

"Alabama had this long winning streak, but we didn't pay much attention to that. Tennessee fans always traveled well to see us, people like Dr. E. R. Zemp and Ray Jenkins. The team took the train quite a bit, but for Alabama, we rode buses.

"I knocked out the best player Alabama had, a man named Fred Davis, or Killer Davis, they called him. He

George (Bones) Hunter was an accomplished end on the opposite side of All-America Bowden Wyatt.

All-Americas Abe Shires, center, and George Cafego, extreme right, gather with some fellow students, including blocking back Sam Bartholomew, third from right.

played tackle, and I broke his nose. I told him after the game I was sorry I broke his nose, but he ran into my elbow.

"This was the first game anybody used the dive play for short yardage. Neyland put it in a year earlier. He told me to dive over the center onto some dummies during practice. I could get two or three yards easy. We used that effectively against Alabama."

Vols 44, The Citadel 0

Coming between headline showdowns with Alabama and LSU, the 1938 game with The Citadel attracted minimal interest. The paid attendance was only 8,000.

That day anyone who even approached the Tennessee bench made it into the game, as Coach Neyland turned to his reserves for most of the dramatics in a 44–0 white-washing of the Cadets.

Among the unexpected Big Orange heroes were Bob (Doc) Sneed, who was credited with passing, running, kicking, and just about everything else, and wingback Pryor Bacon, who ran the Cadets ragged by both catching passes and running reverses. Bob Foxx accounted for two touchdowns. Bacon, Sneed, Joe Wallen, and Lloyd Broome registered the other scores for Tennessee.

Sunday newspapers, scarcely noting the fireworks the previous day at Shields-Watkins Field, were already looking ahead to the forthcoming LSU game. A page-one story called attention to the fact that the LSU game the following Saturday would draw governors from three states: Tennessee, Louisiana, and Kentucky, the latter sending the venerable A. B. (Happy) Chandler, a big fan of college football.

The Citadel	0	0	0	0	0
Tennessee	7	27	0	10	44

UT	Wallen, run 2 (Barnes kick)
UT	Foxx, run 7 (Cafego kick)
UT	Foxx, run 12 (kick failed)
UT	Bacon, pass from Sneed 16 (Sneed kick)
UT	Broom, run 1 (Bacon, pass from Sneed)
UT	Sneed, run 23 (Broom kick)
UT	Wyatt, field goal 8

Coach Murray Warmath Remembers

"I was out scouting that weekend. I'm sure Neyland wouldn't try to run up the score. Doc Sneed had a good game, and he was

a good tailback, but I don't believe he ever played with the first team. He was an excellent triple-threat back who would have started for a number of other schools.

"With guys like Cafego, Coffman, Foxx, and Bartholomew, you could be a good player and still not be a starter. Pryor Bacon was a lot like Sneed in that he was an excellent high school player who made a good replacement player but wasn't on the starting team. Pryor was more a blocker than a receiver.

"Our quarterback, like everybody else, had to be a two-way player, as capable defensively as he was offensively.
—Murray Warmath

"Our quarterback, like everybody else, had to be a two-way player, as capable defensively as he was offensively. When it came to defense, probably Leonard Coffman and Bob Foxx were the best we had.

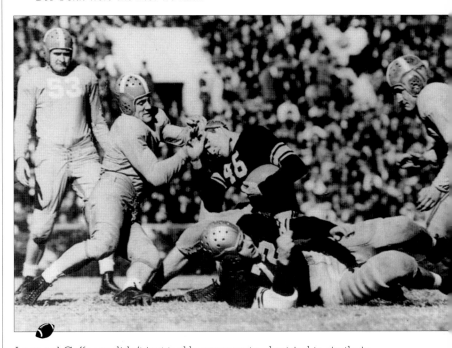

Leonard Coffman didn't just tackle opponents—he tried to rip their heads off. Many ranked Coffman the "toughest Vol" of all.

1938

"Coffman was our most underrated player. He was the key to the team. He played well offensively, he played well defensively, he played well in the clutch, and he carried the fight to the other team. His attitude was, 'Come on guys, let's go get them.'

"We knew LSU, a good team, was coming up, so we probably didn't have our minds completely on The Citadel. But Neyland did everything he could to make sure we didn't overlook anybody. But The Citadel wasn't as good as Chattanooga."

Vols 14, LSU 6

LSU made the long-awaited match-up with UT a festive occasion, bringing its Mike the Tiger mascot to Knoxville along with 2,800 ROTC cadets from the Baton Rouge campus, but it was the Tennessee fans who celebrated into the wee hours of Sunday after the Vols pasted a 14–6 drubbing on the Bayou Bengals.

A Knoxville newspaper described it as "the greatest gridiron spectacle ever presented hereabouts," and one writer was so carried away by the scope of the event that he compared it favorably with Barnum and Bailey's three-ring circus.

True to his gracious nature, Coach Bob Neyland said that the host school was "lucky" to emerge victorious, but it was a judgment to which the national press on hand for the game didn't subscribe.

The "ruthless" Vols, as *Knoxville News-Sentinel* sports editor Bob Wilson described them, put together a 72-yard touchdown drive to open the game and never gave up the lead after that. Leonard Coffman, from Greeneville, Tennessee, made the sensational play of the drive, exploding for 39 yards—on 10 of which three Tigers dangled from his neck.

After a 17-yard carry by George Cafego, Coffman needed two plunges from the 1-yard line to dent the powerful LSU

defense for the touchdown. End and captain Bowden Wyatt kicked the extra point. Massive bedlam broke out among the 36,000 fans, excluding, of course, the LSU loyalists who had invaded Knoxville by train.

LSU's great end, Ken Cavanaugh, snagged two passes, including one for a touchdown, as the Tigers stormed back to cut the margin to 7–6. A failed extra-point kick allowed Tennessee to maintain its narrow lead. Cafego added a second touchdown in the third period, and with Wyatt adding the extra point, the Vols were out of danger. In that era, the two-point conversions that coaches today so flagrantly misuse were unknown.

LSU	0	6	0	0	6
Tennessee	7	0	7	0	14

UT   Coffman, run 1 (Wyatt kick)
LSU Kavanaugh, pass from Simes 21 (kick failed)
UT   Cafego, run 2 (Wyatt kick)

Bill Barnes Remembers

"I don't remember the LSU students coming up for the game as much as I remember them bringing Mike the Tiger, their live tiger mascot. That always intrigued me a little bit, carrying a damn tiger around. They had him in a cage down there at the end of the stadium, as I remember it.

"That game was an awful big one, for them and for us. It was LSU's biggest game, except for Tulane. It was a very good ball game. Other than the fact that Alabama, Vanderbilt, and Kentucky were our traditional opponents, that was the biggest game as far as anything out of our normal schedule was concerned.

"Kavanaugh, of course, was a great player. I had played against him in high school. He was at Little Rock Central while I was at Memphis Central, and our schools met during the season. He was a big guy for back then, about six-four. He was a year ahead of me in school, and he came to see me about following him to LSU.

"The General [Coach Neyland] had us all pumped up for that game. We only gave up 16 points all season, and LSU had six of them.

"I remember Leonard Coffman scoring that touchdown on the 77 play. That was off the spinner series. The General would run the spin series, where they would run the wing-back on reverses. And this was a counter off it. Fake the reverse, and Coffman would run up the middle. We'd trap the guard. Coffman dragged three guys in there with him.

"Coffman was a great player, absolutely great. He could do everything. He could block, he could run, and he was a lot better runner than people thought. He was a big, old strong guy, and he was quick. I was very high on him, and I still am. He came by and visited me in Los Angeles once. He and Abe Shires both did.

"But most of those guys are gone now. Bob Woodruff tried to hire me down at Florida. Later I dealt with Woodruff when he was A.D. at Tennessee and I was head coach at UCLA. I called him in 1963 about scheduling a game between the two schools, and we agreed to play in Memphis in 1965. That turned out to be quite a ball game.

"At UCLA, we ran Tennessee's offense, the single wing. The only difference was the blocking back wasn't underneath the center. He was out, with his hand down, sort of like the fullback.

"That LSU game was a big one. General Neyland always complimented the opponents, both before and after the game. He was always gracious. The only time I ever saw him get mad was one day out on the practice field when he grabbed Bob Suffridge because he hit

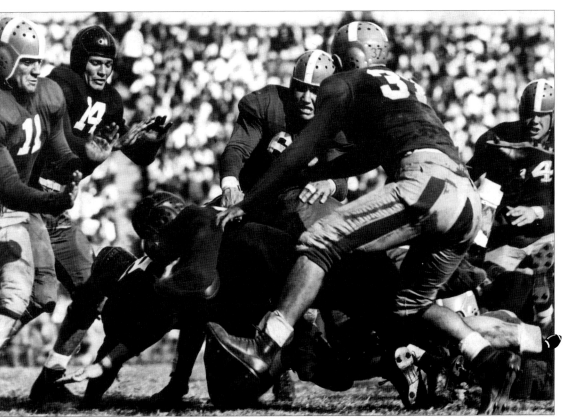

Defensive starters zero in for the kill, including Leonard Coffman (11), Butch Rike (64), Bowden Wyatt (37), and Abe Shires (54).

Bill Nowling in the nose with a forearm. He shook Suffridge like a rag doll.

"The General was a big, tough guy, but he was mild-mannered. He was a gentleman. He was smart and had a great personality. I never knew him to gloat."

Authors' Note: The reader will notice that Coach Bob Neyland is variously referred to as "the General" or "the Major" in these pages. These weren't honorary titles. A 1916 graduate of West Point, where he had played end on its football team, Neyland had a career as a U.S. Army officer that paralleled a significant portion of his coaching career. In fact, Neyland first came to the University of Tennessee in 1925 as ROTC commandant and assistant football coach; he became head coach a year later. An Army engineer, he was promoted to brigadier general during World War II.

Vols 45, Chattanooga 0

Little Chattanooga was hopelessly outclassed by the Vols, who might have been due for a letdown, but in case they had one, they still managed to pound out a 45–0 triumph over the punchless Moccasins.

Things were in such fine shape that the contest turned into a display of finesse by Bowden Wyatt, the squad's beloved captain and end. Wyatt accounted for the first 19 points, scoring three touchdowns and one extra point. The only complaint against the handsome product of Kingston, Tennessee, was that he missed the extra points that followed two of the touchdowns.

But in a 45–0 massacre a point here and there doesn't matter a great deal.

Judging by attendance figures, UT devotees weren't expecting much of a contest. Only 7,000 were in attendance, a far cry from the audience of 36,000 that had come to Shields-Watkins Field a week earlier for the LSU game.

More interesting than the lackluster exhibition on the field was a comment that Tom Anderson, the perceptive sports editor of the *Knoxville Journal,* made during the Chattanooga game week about Coach Neyland: "A reader wants to know what has impressed me most about Major Neyland's coaching. Well, everybody has known for years that the Vols boss ranks with the country's greatest mentors. There is, or used to be, the opinion elsewhere that his attack lacked deception. I accepted that report at ear value until closer observation broke me from sucking eggs.

"The Vols get more deception into fundamental maneuvers than most teams do in concealed ball plays mixed with 14 lateral heaves. The notion that Neyland's stuff was old-fashioned probably grew out of the fact that he did not go haywire when the razzle-dazzle craze struck the country. It is interesting to note that the hocus-pocus is dying a gradual natural death."

Chattanooga 0	0	0	0	0
Tennessee 13	0	18	14	45

UT	Wyatt, pass from Warren 41 (Wyatt kick)
UT	Wyatt, pass from Wood 46 (kick failed)
UT	Wyatt, pass from Wood 12 (kick failed)
UT	Andridge, run 11 (pass failed)
UT	Broome, run 3 (pass failed)
UT	Bacon, pass from Sneed 13 (Sneed kick)
UT	Sneed, run 12 (Sneed kick)

Ed Cifers Remembers

"Scrappy Moore, the coach at Chattanooga at that time, was considered as good a coach as you would find in the

Southeastern Conference. In fact, in the '50s he was offered the job as head coach at LSU. He was starting to get a little age on him and turned it down. He put the T formation in real early, and he had a good offensive ball club.

"The players we had didn't have trouble getting up for a game. We had a bunch of individuals, and sometimes you wondered how they could beat anybody. But everyone on the team had a lot of pride in doing the job.

"The coaches had a way of dealing with the situation. Some of the guys would be bruised up after a physical game like LSU. So Neyland might hold a bunch of them out of practice until Wednesday or Thursday. Then, he'd gather them all up and say, 'Look, fellows, this is going to be a tough game, and we better get ready for it.'

"He was a great motivator. He could remember every mistake everybody made and what they needed to do to have better results. Neyland had a good man in [Assistant Coach] Bill Britton. The reason he was never a head coach is that he didn't want to work at it. He just never wanted to do the things you needed to as head coach. I liked Bill Britton. He was my friend.

"He was a tremendous scout. Neyland didn't have a lot of coaches. At that time, he had Britton and John Barnhill and Murray Warmath, and that was about it.

"The crowds varied a lot. But on games like Chattanooga, UT would have Band Day and let the band members from local high schools in free. We might have 15,000 people, counting the bands.

"Teams like Chattanooga were outmanned. They may have had 10 players who could make the UT squad. What Scrappy did was take players who hadn't made it at Tennessee or Alabama or Georgia and put them on his team.

"Bowden Wyatt accounted for the first 19 points because he caught three touchdown passes and was the extra point kicker. Bowden was a good college player, better on offense than defense, but Neyland used the subs a lot that day against Chattanooga."

From left, Abe Shires, Bob Suffridge, Bowden Wyatt, George Cafego, and Babe Wood prepare to leave for an out-of-town game.

Vols 14, Vanderbilt 0

When Bob Neyland substituted a homegrown Middle Tennessean, Babe Wood, for All-America tailback George Cafego late in a scoreless deadlock with Vanderbilt, many UT partisans suspected that the old Army warhorse had flipped his lid.

They should have known better. They should have realized that whenever Neyland did something unexpected, there was a reason. And when Babe Wood scored two touchdowns to win the game in the fourth quarter, they knew the strategic substitution was soundly conceived.

Wood ran all over the Commodores in the final period after Cafego had been held in check through the first half and into the third period. With the score 14–0 only a short time into the final quarter, Neyland substituted freely, aware that no team was going to overcome a two-touchdown deficit against the stingy defense led by Bob Suffridge.

"As had been the case all year," said one newspaper story, "Suffridge was the man to halt the exploits of the opponents."

The Vanderbilt staff was also full of high praise for Suffridge. "That Suffridge is the greatest guard I have ever seen," said Ray Morrison, the Commodores' head coach.

The Vols were taking pride in the ultimate test of a defensive team—stopping the opposition from chalking up points. The last time Tennessee's goal line had been crossed was in the LSU game. Suffridge and his teammates were getting a taste of what it would be like in 1939 when no regular-season opponent would score a single point against them.

Tennessee	0	0	0	14	14
Vanderbilt	0	0	0	0	0

UT   Wood, run 2 (Wyatt kick)
UT   Wood, run 4 (Wyatt kick)

Ed Cifers Remembers

"Vanderbilt was always a big game, one of the biggest we had. George Cafego played most of the first half and part of the second. But Babe Wood was from Middle Tennessee, and Neyland put him in looking for him to have a big day.

"Cafego softened them up a little bit, and then Wood went in. The game was scoreless at that point. Part of Neyland's plan was that Babe would be fired up by playing in front of his hometown crowd. Babe was a good runner.

"Ray Morrison, the coach at Vanderbilt, had his boys ready to play. Bob Suffridge made All-America that season. He had a knack for getting off on the snap, sometimes before the snap, which resulted in a penalty. He was very fast, which was important since he only weighed about 195 pounds.

"At that time, Vanderbilt was still considered a tough opponent, one of the most successful programs in the SEC. They were one of the four or five top teams in the conference year after year at that time.

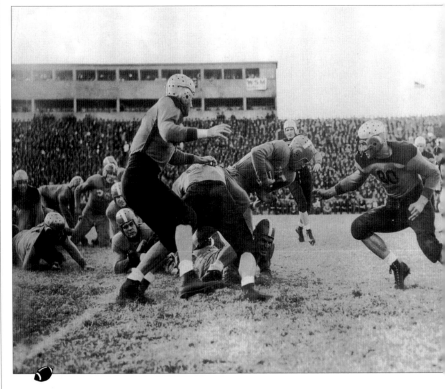

Bob Foxx, who divided time between tailback and wingback, gains yardage against Vanderbilt.

"We were always trying to be at our best defensively, because Neyland told us there were more ways to score on defense than on offense. A year later when Vanderbilt was threatening to score, with Tennessee going through the season unscored-on, Neyland put several of us starters back in late in the game to make sure Vanderbilt didn't score. But posting a shutout was never mentioned as being a goal."

Vols 46, Kentucky 0

Snow fell throughout Thanksgiving morning, helping give rise to the continuing myth of "typical Tennessee–Kentucky football weather" as the Vols and Wildcats met under treacherous playing conditions at Shields-Watkins Field.

By the time the game ended, the field was a quagmire of slush and mud, and Tennessee was a 46–0 victor, one of the most lopsided margins in the history of the border-state rivalry. Even on a slow track, the Vols' speed and depth were too much for Ab Kerwin's Wildcats to handle.

In an era when running up a score was held in contempt—the Bowl Championship Series and its margin-of-victory idiocy were still six decades away—Coach Neyland did everything he could to hold down the tally. He played his starters for only one period and turned the proceedings over to the third team for most of the second half.

But these efforts couldn't suppress the slaughter. The orange-clad benchwarmers enjoyed a field day. The combined Tennessee units amassed 321 total yards, compared to 32 for the Wildcats.

Tailback Bob Sneed, with ball, saw Orange Bowl action against Oklahoma. The Vols drilled the Sooners, 17–0.

Bob Foxx planted his cleats in the snow and took off 19 yards for a touchdown on UT's first possession. The drive inspired one reporter to the following: "No Tennessee eleven in history ever showed more power, deadly blocking and expert passing than the Vols did as they drove 58 yards in four plays to score their first touchdown."

Before the afternoon ended with the field a sea of slush, Jimmy Coleman, Bob Andridge, Bob Sneed, and Buist Warren had assumed the hero's mantle normally worn by George Cafego and Leonard Coffman.

Twelve seniors made their final home appearance that day: Bowden Wyatt, Cheek Duncan, Joe Little, Gerald

Hendricks, Babe Wood, James Cowan, Jeep McCarren, Bob Sneed, George Hunter, Ralph Eldred, John Bailey, and Bob Woodruff.

Kentucky	0	0	0	0	0
Tennessee	12	19	6	9	46

UT   Foxx, run 24 (kick blocked)

UT   Cafego, run 2 (kick failed)

UT   Andridge, run 15 (kick failed)

UT   Wallen, run 3 (Coleman, pass from Warren)

UT   Coleman, pass from Sneed 19 (kick failed)

UT   Duncan, run 19 (kick failed)

UT   Safety, ball out of back of end zone on punt snap

UT   Bacon, run 27 (Whitehead, pass from Sneed)

Ma Brann, extreme left, who ran the training table for the Vols, has a hearty meal prepared for Captain Bowden Wyatt, standing next to Mrs. Brann, and several of Wyatt's 1938 teammates.

Norbert Ackermann Remembers

"Playing conditions in Knoxville were about as miserable as you could imagine. Lots of snow, cold, and you've got to remember that was the time before tarpaulins covered the field to protect it.

"That 1938 game was of historical significance because it marked the end to the tradition of playing the Tennessee–Kentucky game on Thanksgiving. We were all kind of glad about that because it meant we wouldn't be spending a week and a half getting ready for the next game.

"Thanksgiving was special to us because we knew we would have a great dinner that night prepared by Ma Brann [director of the UT training table for athletes]. We didn't have a lot of bad weather during football season, but it seemed the Kentucky game was always played under foul conditions.

"Neyland substituted a lot in that game, as was his custom. It was a good win and made everybody happy to see our seniors bow out on their home careers with an impressive showing.

"Kentucky was always at its best against the Vols. The Kentucky teams weren't especially good back then, partly because they changed coaches a lot. But there were plenty of times they gave Tennessee a fit."

Vols 47, Mississippi 0

An Orange Bowl invitation already in their pockets, the Vols made quick work of the Ole Miss Rebels at Crump Stadium in Memphis, 47–0, wrapping up the first perfect season in Tennessee history.

Fearful that an Oklahoma scout might be sniffing around for clues about what to expect in Miami's postseason classic,

Coach Bob Neyland had his troops stick to a basic bread-and-butter script against the Rebels.

There was nothing fancy in the offensive-game plan, nor in the defensive scheme for that matter. The object was to render the Rebels' All-America back, Parker Hall, impotent. His two pass attempts were incomplete, part of a first half that was so personally frustrating that Hall never returned to the lineup after halftime.

For Tennessee's offensive stars, however, the afternoon was anything but frustrating. Leonard Coffman scored twice, while George Cafego, Bowden Wyatt, Joe Wallen, Buist Warren, and Bob Snead each posted a touchdown.

Press reports underlined the fundamental soundness of Neyland's coaching. Of Leonard Coffman's 52-yard touchdown run in the third quarter, one newspaper reported that every Mississippi player was knocked to the ground at least once. "That's perfect blocking on any field," the newspaper reported.

Although Neyland didn't dwell on statistics, consistent with his "bend-but-don't-break" defensive philosophy, it would be remiss not to note that while the Vols were chalking up 415 yards, Ole Miss was being held to 79.

Mississippi	0	0	0	0	0
Tennessee	14	7	19	7	47

UT	Cafego, run 2 (Cafego kick)
UT	Coffman, run 1 (Wyatt kick)
UT	Wallen, run 1 (Cafego kick)
UT	Coffman, run 52 (kick failed)
UT	Wyatt, interception return 34 (Cafego kick)
UT	Warren, punt return 85 (kick failed)
UT	Sneed, run 6 (Sneed kick)

Leonard Coffman Remembers

"We had heard a lot about Parker Hall, Mississippi's great back, but I knocked him out on his return of the opening kickoff. He got back in the game but didn't do much the rest of the day. I was always pretty quick getting downfield.

"The scouting report on Hall helped. It told us Parker would fake one way and then go the same way. I was waiting for him.

"I think we voted on whether to accept the Orange Bowl bid, but we knew Neyland wanted it. What he wanted, he got.

"We stuck to the basics because we didn't want to help Oklahoma prepare for us.

"The key to our success was that we ran the same play over and over and over in practice. On the 10 play, our main play, Sam Bartholomew and I would block the end. The wingback and end would block the tackle.

"Neyland was a great man. He took care of me a lot. I got in trouble one time, though. I took off and went home to see my girlfriend. When we were dressing for Monday practice, Neyland asked me how far it was to Greeneville. I told him 72 miles. He said, 'Okay, that will be 72 laps around the track.' Dink Eldridge, our manager, counted them off."

Vols 17, Oklahoma 0 (Orange Bowl)

George Cafego of Tennessee and Waddy Young of Oklahoma had been the focal point of ballyhoo ever since the Tennessee–Oklahoma Orange Bowl match was set up, with the drumbeaters paying homage to the Vols' triple-threat tailback and the Sooners' all-everything end.

Wingback Bob Foxx advances the ball while Sam Bartholomew, trailing him, looks for someone to block.

So, it was a matter of some significance when Cafego, delivering a crushing block to Young to set up a run by Bob Foxx, put the Oklahoma star out of the game in front of the largest crowd ever to see a football game in Florida up to that time.

With or without the gifted Young, however, the Sooners were overmatched against a Tennessee team described in one glowing account as "a football machine as splendid as any that ever yanked off a sticky sweat sock after a day's work well done."

Tennessee's 17–0 triumph over Tom Stidham's squad brought an end to a year that saw the Vols march through the regular season unbeaten and then dominate a bowl game in such a fashion that no Sooner was left demanding a recount.

1938

T

Components of the scoring were touchdowns by Bob Foxx and Babe Wood, a field goal by Bowden Wyatt, and extra-point kicks by Foxx and Wyatt.

The statistics were even more lopsided than the score. Tennessee led in first downs, 15–6; in rushing yardage, 205–25; and in total yardage, 268–94. One sports columnist, suitably impressed, wrote, "I have never been more thoroughly mistaken in my life if that array of Vols would not have been too much for any football organization in existence today."

Unfortunately, displays of poor sportsmanship marred this postseason contest between two fine teams. Slugging, kicking, heckling, and wrangling with the officials went on throughout the afternoon, a sorry sight that alienated many of the 32,191 customers in attendance. Joe Little, inserted by Neyland with instructions to calm things down, was himself ejected on the first play after he was assigned the role of peacemaker.

Babe Wood, a Tennessee native who had transferred to UT from Oklahoma, stole Cafego's thunder against his old alma mater. Cafego played well, but Wood electrified the crowd with his spectacular running, passing, and kicking. Wood picked up 67 yards on the ground to Cafego's 38.

Cafego's block of Young, Ed Cifers's blast that knocked over three Oklahoma defenders, and blocking back Sam Bartholomew's aggressive play exemplified the hard-hitting tactics the Vols employed to overcome the size advantage enjoyed by the Sooners.

Oklahoma	0	0	0	0	0
Tennessee	7	3	0	7	17

UT   Foxx, run 8 (Wyatt run)
UT   Wyatt, field goal 22
UT   Wood, run 15 (Foxx kick)

Coach Murray Warmath Remembers

"We didn't get the invitation to go to the Rose Bowl that year like we felt we deserved. And just about everybody else felt the same way. But we did get an opportunity to play a very fine Oklahoma team in the Orange Bowl. As I remember it, we were the only two undefeated teams in one bowl game that year.

"That game pretty much made the Orange Bowl.

"Waddy Young was the Oklahoma leader who was later killed in the war. An outstanding leader and football star. If I'm not mistaken, it was a block by Cafego that injured Young. It was a hit in the shoulder by Cafego that caused the injury.

"Cafego only weighed about 170 pounds, but he hit like 270. I think it was a play in which Cafego set up a run by Foxx down the sidelines by making a great block of Young.

"Both sides were heated up, which led to the brawl. It was a rough game, and they had to stop play for a while to cool things down. Our offensive linemen had some boxing experience in the Golden Gloves. They believed in defending themselves.

"I know we sent Joe Little in to cool the game down, and he got penalized on the next snap himself. After Cafego got hurt, Babe Wood came on and played very well. Babe was a tough, aggressive football player, and he could do everything you wanted from a single-wing tailback.

"That was an amazing thing about Neyland, that he coached so well while commuting on another job with the Army engineers."

—Murray Warmath

"We felt we should have been in Pasadena that day, but we also felt Oklahoma was about as good a team as we played all year or maybe any other year. Tom Stidham was a big-name coach who had his team ready for a physical game, just as we were.

There were few cordial moments associated with the 1938 team's appearance in the Orange Bowl with Oklahoma, but All-America Bowden Wyatt, left, hit it off on a fishing trip with Sooners great Waddy Young.

"Barnhill was a well-thought-of coach. Players came to him with their problems because Neyland was gone a lot, holding two jobs, including his Army engineering duties. That was an amazing thing about Neyland, that he coached so well while commuting on another job with the Army engineers.

"I think he was probably the best coach ever, but then I have to say I'm prejudiced, so maybe it wouldn't be fair to some of the others."

Authors' Note: Murray Warmath's reference to Neyland's performing two jobs pertained to his U.S. Army service at the

same time he coached football at UT. In 1930 he was assigned by the Army to Chattanooga as district engineer in charge of Tennessee River navigation. Three years later, he was named district engineer at Nashville in charge of Cumberland River navigation. Reassigned to the Panama Canal in 1935, Neyland retired from the Army less than a year later—only to be called back into service during World War II.

1938 National Review

When Tennessee sailed unscathed through the 1938 season and ripped Oklahoma, 17–0, in the Orange Bowl or ("Orange Brawl" as some press-box pundits dubbed it), the Vols were trying to ward off more than only an unbeaten TCU team for the national championship.

They were also fighting the legend of TCU's Davey O'Brien. Standing five feet seven inches and tipping the scales at 150 pounds soaking wet—small even by 1938 size standards—O'Brien was the glamour boy of college football. He led Coach Dutch Meyer's Horned Frogs to their first unbeaten season and was awarded both the Heisman and Maxwell Trophies. O'Brien passed for 1,457 yards, astronomical in that age, setting a Southwest Conference record that stood for 10 years.

In the Sugar Bowl encounter with Carnegie Tech—then a powerhouse in college football—O'Brien led TCU to a 15–7 victory. Another All-America that season for the Horned Frogs was center Kyle Aldrich, who, like O'Brien, is a member of college football's Hall of Fame.

Until 1965 bowl games were not taken into account in wire-service polls. The Rose Bowl, nevertheless, provided one of the most memorable postseason games in the history of college football.

Heroes of 1938: Coach Bob Neyland with tailbacks George Cafego, left, and Babe Wood.

Third-ranked Duke was facing seventh-ranked Southern California in the Pasadena classic. The Blue Devils were unscored-on in nine regular-season games. But the Trojans won, 7–3, when reserve quarterback Doyle Nave hit Al Krueger with a 14-yard touchdown pass in the final minute.

The only other team besides TCU and Tennessee to receive a first-place ranking was Notre Dame under Coach Elmer Layden. The Irish, who didn't play in a bowl game, compiled an 8–1 record, losing only to Southern California, 13–0, in the season finale.

Pittsburgh, led by Marshall Goldberg, started the season ranked number one by the AP, but the perennially strong Panthers stumbled against Carnegie Tech at midseason and ended the year with an 8–2 record.

The 1940 Vols

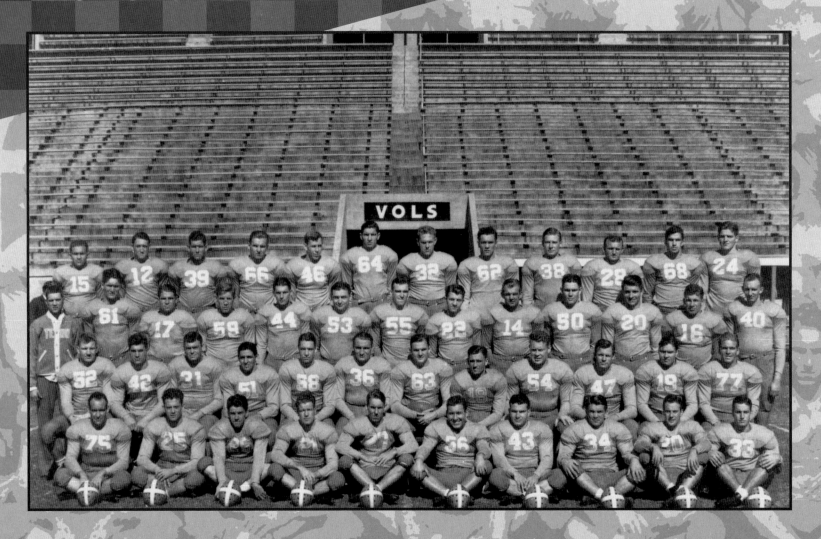

Chapter 2

1940

The first thing Tennessee fans may wonder about as they peruse these pages is this: Whatever happened to 1939? Considering that back in those distant days national champions were selected at the end of the regular season, how could a team that shut out all its foes fail to wind up at number one?

All we can say is that Texas A&M must have had a spectacular team to garner more votes than the unsullied Vols in the final polls. Not one of the so-called experts judged Tennessee as best squad in the land, despite the fact that all 10 regular-season foes were denied so much as a safety or a field goal.

With that kind of season, Neyland's forces must have wondered in December what you had to do to impress voters. The Rose Bowl was another story. Without their great tailback, George Cafego, the Vols were shut out by Southern California, 14–0.

Still, for a single-wing team to play without its tailback is comparable to a T-formation team foregoing the presence of its star quarterback—even more so. The reason is that a single-wing tailback not only did the passing; he was also the primary runner and the team's punter.

The 1940 coaching staff. On the front row, from left, are Hugh Faust, and Bob Woodruff. On the back row, from left, are John Barnhill, John Mauer, Bill Merrill, Bill Britton, and Head Coach Bob Neyland.

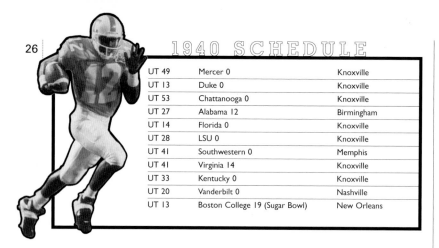

UT 49	Mercer 0	Knoxville
UT 13	Duke 0	Knoxville
UT 53	Chattanooga 0	Knoxville
UT 27	Alabama 12	Birmingham
UT 14	Florida 0	Knoxville
UT 28	LSU 0	Knoxville
UT 41	Southwestern 0	Memphis
UT 41	Virginia 14	Knoxville
UT 33	Kentucky 0	Knoxville
UT 20	Vanderbilt 0	Nashville
UT 13	Boston College 19 (Sugar Bowl)	New Orleans

On the field for Tennessee as the season began were Ed Cifers and Jimmy Coleman at end, Abe Shires and Bill Luttrell at tackle, Bob Suffridge and Ed Molinski at guard, Norbert Ackermann at center, Foxx at tailback, Bob Andridge at wingback, Ike Peel at blocking back, and Bill Nowling at fullback.

In 1940 the Vols forged back into the championship picture, ending the year at the top of the polls as selected by the Dunkel and Williamson services.

Neyland said before the season started that sophomores would hold the keys to the Vols' success. The youthful newcomers he was counting on included Bill Nowling, Billy Meek, Al Hust, Billy King, and Leonard Simonetti.

Vols 49, Mercer 0

Mercer wasn't much of a test for Bob Neyland's 1940 team, but the opening foe gave service as guinea pigs to help the UT coaches figure out how well their revamped lineup of players would work.

The experiment they watched most closely occurred at tailback, where Bob Foxx was assigned the task of replacing the legendary George Cafego. Foxx and his teammates acquitted themselves well enough to club Mercer into submission, 49–0. After the game, jurors still debated whether Foxx should stay at tailback or should return to his tried-and-true wingback slot.

Jim Coleman, standing, and Ed Cifers were outstanding ends with the 1940 Vols.

One of the largest season-opening crowds in UT's history, 20,000, attended the event, the figure padded generously by the 5,000 local schoolchildren who attended as guests of the Athletic Association, as the UT Athletic Department was known at the time. The kids consumed enough popcorn and Coca-Cola to allow UT to turn a profit despite the fact that they came through the gate on complimentary tickets.

Few among the record mob guessed that they were watching a national championship team in action. The less-than-overwhelming reaction wasn't due to a lack of appreciation for what Neyland's 45 athletes accomplished as much as it was an awareness that Mercer didn't offer much opposition.

Foxx and second-teamer Johnny Butler directed touchdown marches in the early going. Mercer was so worn down by the Vols' superior numbers that their touchdown gates opened wide for Tennessee incursions as the contest wound down during the second half.

A better gauge of Tennessee's strength would come a week later when the much-feared Duke Blue Devils were scheduled to arrive in Knoxville from across the mountains of North Carolina.

Ed Cifers Remembers

"Opening the season against a team like Mercer allowed Neyland to play everybody and help determine how he would use the team's depth the rest of the season. This was another of those warm-up games.

"There wasn't a big drop-off in quality between the second and third teams. There were plenty of good football players on this team. While Neyland wouldn't run up the score—he never did intentionally do that—he wouldn't tell the subs not to score. That wouldn't have been right.

"We didn't have the wide-open offense the way they do now. That achievement of the 1939 team in never giving up a point couldn't happen again today, not with field goals so routine and with the great passing games that you see today.

"Abe Shires was a good college football player who probably didn't get all the credit he deserved. He was tough, not quite the size who could have played pro ball lately, but a very valuable member of our team. And, on top of it, one of the greatest guys you'd ever hope to meet. I think Abe was the best tackle during the years I played at Tennessee.

"Some of the writers got on Tennessee because of its schedule, talking about teams like Mercer and Southwestern. But sometimes a team would be scheduled and then decline in its football strength before the game would be played."

Mercer	0	0	0	0	0
Tennessee	7	7	21	14	49

UT	Andridge, run 4 (Foxx kick)
UT	Butler, run 14 (Newman kick)
UT	Foxx, pass from Butler, 16 (Foxx kick)
UT	Andridge, run 21 (Webber kick)
UT	Steiner, blocked punt return 15 (Warren kick)
UT	Hust, pass from Thompson 10 (Thompson kick)
UT	Powers, run 8 (Aurelia kick)

Vols 13, Duke 0

The magnitude of the Duke game was apparent to everyone from the fact that Bill Stern and Ted Husing, the eminent radio broadcasters of the pre-television era, called the contest for NBC and CBS, respectively.

Duke's great coach, Wallace Wade, had pointed to the 1940 match as the game in which he believed he could get

TENNESSEE

VOLUNTEERS

The cover for the 1940 media guide featured Norbert Ackermann, in center of layout, and, clockwise from top left, Bob Foxx, Johnny Butler, Bob Suffridge, Ed Molinski, Abe Shires, Buist Warren, Ed Cifers, and Fred Newman.

the best of Bob Neyland. It didn't work out that way, however, for the Blue Devils' mentor.

Tennessee pushed across two touchdowns in the second period and then played stout enough defense the rest of the day to make the 13-point margin stand up.

Newspaper accounts chalked the UT victory up to Neyland's ability to prepare his team for a specific assignment. Ever since spring practice, Neyland had devised plays that he felt would work against the Blue Devils. He also concentrated on producing a mental attitude that would help bring forth the Vols' best effort.

All the scoring was concentrated in the second period, which meant that large portions of the game were dull to anyone looking for a thrill a minute. But that's the way Neyland liked it, and no one complained, unless it was the Duke faithful who had made the trip across the Smoky Mountains.

Tennessee marched 63 yards for its first score, with Bob Foxx at tailback in the single-wing formation. Foxx passed to Al Hust for the first score and then barged into the end zone himself for the second.

The Vols were so dominant that Wade's charges, who had come to Knoxville confident they could take the measure of the orange squad, managed to penetrate Tennessee territory just once. A crowd estimated at 42,000 filled all the seats in the stadium and overflowed onto the terrace at the south end of the field.

While Knoxville had experienced some gala weekends leading up to big games, none of the predecessors could match the pomp and circumstance that attended the scuffle with the dreaded Blue Devils, according to one local newspaper writer.

Duke	0	0	0	0	0
Tennessee	0	13	0	0	13

UT   Hust, pass from Foxx 33 (Foxx kick)

UT   Foxx, run 1 (kick failed)

Van Thompson Remembers

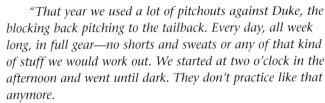

"This was the game where Wallace Wade, a great coach in his own right, paid Coach Neyland the highest compliment I have ever heard. Wade, of course, was the Duke coach and a highly successful man in his profession.

"On Sunday, after the Duke-Tennessee game, Wade said, 'Neyland can take his and beat yours, or he can take yours and beat his.' Imagine somebody saying that about his archrival after losing to him. Neyland was smart. There were no two ways about it.

"I didn't play a lot in this game. I became first-team tailback in the LSU game at midseason and started the rest of the year. One game I especially remember was the Southwestern game of 1940. I got hit twice on one play, losing some teeth on one hit and injuring my eye on the other.

"We went back in the huddle, and Ike Peel asked who it was that got me. I told him I thought it was the end. A few plays later, Peel knocked the end out of the game. When we got home and looked at the film, we found out it was the linebacker who had done it. But Ike was trying to take care of me. We all took care of each other. We were a close-knit group. Not like it is today.

> "Neyland got a two-touchdown lead and sat on it. He knew that was a safe margin the way Tennessee played defense."
>
> —Van Thompson

"As far as my teeth were concerned, I'm still going to the dentist today about them, having to get new bridges every once in a while.

"Bill Britton was the smartest scout in the country. He would come back from a scouting assignment and tell Neyland where the opponent's weakness was and what would work against them. Then we would practice the play all week. Over and over and over.

"That year we used a lot of pitchouts against Duke, the blocking back pitching to the tailback. Every day, all week long, in full gear—no shorts and sweats or any of that kind of stuff we would work out. We started at two o'clock in the afternoon and went until dark. They don't practice like that anymore.

"Bob Andridge and Bob Foxx were different kinds of players and did different things when playing wingback. Andridge was the fastest man on the team, but had an awful bad back. Foxx had good hands and caught the ball better. Not many people realize Bob Foxx played a year at the University of California before coming to UT, even though he was from Knoxville.

"The Duke game was huge. There were people everywhere. Everybody who could squeeze into the place did so for that game.

"Neyland got a two-touchdown lead and sat on it. He knew that was a safe margin the way Tennessee played defense. Once

Ferocious blocking, as seen here freeing Bob Foxx in 1940, was a staple of the teams coached by Bob Neyland.

Bob (Breezer) Andridge was a speedy wingback who shared duties with Bob Foxx in 1940.

he had a two-touchdown lead, he would kick on first or second down. He'd play for a fumble or an intercepted pass; in other words, let the other team make the mistakes."

Vols 53, Chattanooga 0

The excitement of the Duke game would have to suffice for an extra week as the contest with Chattanooga didn't require the Vols to work up a sweat. That isn't to say Coach Neyland didn't do his usual competent job of building up the visitors on the sports pages and over the radio airwaves.

Scrappy Moore, the quotable and popular Moccasins coach, came up with a unique strategy to counter the Vols, but if it accomplished anything at all, it was in the area of first downs.

Moore started his second unit against the Tennessee regulars, a questionable tactic, to say the least. Later Coach Neyland pitted his subs against Chattanooga's first team. For the day, the visitors amassed 11 first downs to UT's nine,

which turned out to be little consolation for the thoroughly outclassed but not outgamed visitors from Hamilton County.

But the game goes to those who chalk up the most points, and here the Vols enjoyed a striking advantage, 53–0. The Mocs had one distinction to their credit. They drove all the way to the Tennessee 1-yard line, the first time a regular-season opponent had gotten that close since Vanderbilt arrived at the same marker in 1939.

The excursion went for naught, however, when Junior Orend passed incomplete and then was halted inches short of the goal on a fourth-down run.

Six Vols scored touchdowns, including two apiece by Van Thompson and Fred Newman. Al Hust, Bob Foxx, Bob Andridge, and Leo Simonetti posted single six-pointers.

Chattanooga	0	0	0	0	0
Tennessee	14	6	20	13	53

UT	Foxx, run 14 (Foxx kick)
UT	Andridge, run 12 (Foxx kick)
UT	Thompson, run 3 (kick failed)
UT	Hust, pass from Butler 12 (kick failed)
UT	Thompson, run 33 (Thompson kick)
UT	Newman, run 3 (Aurelia kick)
UT	Simonetti, blocked punt return 18 (kick failed)
UT	Newman, interception return 69 (Newman kick)

Ike Peel Remembers

"Scrappy Moore started his second team that day because he would do anything to aggravate Neyland. They were good friends, but Scrappy got a big kick out of it when he could do something to give Neyland a problem once the game got under way.

"Scrappy started his second team, thinking his first team could move the ball against Tennessee's second-quarter team, as it was called. Neyland didn't think in terms of starters and reserves. He would use one unit the first quarter and another unit the second.

"What Scrappy didn't take into account was the fact our second-quarter team was composed of a very good bunch of football players, even though it included a lot of sophomores.

"When Chattanooga reached the 1, everybody on our team got excited and determined not to let them score. On fourth down, they couldn't have crossed the goal if they were using a tank. It was a massive defensive play. The entire team took pride in our string of shutouts. I guess Al Thomas at guard was more responsible than anybody else for the tackle.

"But we were all there, all ganged up trying to help. I was in there at the time, but the play had been stopped by the time I reached the pile.

"We played Chattanooga every year before the Alabama game, and it was understood that they would run Alabama-type plays. It was sort of a gentlemen's agreement between the two schools that helped us get ready for the big game with Alabama."

Vols 27, Alabama 12

In 1939, Johnny Butler made a snake-like touchdown run against Alabama that the famed sportswriter Grantland Rice called the greatest he had ever seen. Playing the Crimson Tide had the superlative tailback's juices flowing again in 1940.

Knoxville native Johnny Butler was one of the most dangerous open-field runners in UT history.

For Tennessee's 27–12 victory at Birmingham's Legion Field, the Volunteers were indebted again to Butler, the scat-back who exhibited extraordinary skills and energy any time he saw the crimson jerseys of arch-foe Alabama.

Early in the second period, with Tennessee trailing by six points, Butler circled right end and dashed for 68 yards to the Alabama 11. He then fired a touchdown pass to Al Hust. UT moved into the lead on Fred Newman's kick.

An even more spectacular run a few plays later kept the Vols on the path to their impressive victory. Snaring a punt at the Alabama 49, Butler went 20 yards down the right sideline, then veered inside for the final yardage as Alabama defenders grasped in vain for the elusive Vol. Center Ray Graves found the right angle to obliterate two Tide defenders with one ferocious block.

The Vols had now won 27 straight games in regular-season play, and three of these came at the expense of Coach Frank Thomas's Crimson Tide. Excluding the Rose Bowl loss of the previous year, the Alabama touchdowns accounted for the first scoring against the Vols since the LSU game in October 1938.

The reason Butler saw so much action against Alabama was that Bob Foxx, who had been the tailback for most of the early season, suffered an injury that side-lined him for much of the game. A crowd of 25,000 filled every seat in the venerated Birmingham stadium.

A large delegation of UT supporters was at the Southern Railway Station in

Knoxville when the football team returned Sunday morning at seven o'clock. The still-sleepy players exited their Pullman cars to the cheers of hundreds of their fondest admirers.

Tennessee	0	14	0	13	27
Alabama	0	6	6	0	12

UA	Nelson, run 14 (kick blocked)
UT	Hust, pass from Butler 10 (Newman kick)
UT	Butler, punt return 48 (Newman, kick)
UA	Brown, punt return 58 (kick failed)
UT	Balitsaris, pass from Warren 7 (Newman kick)
UT	Balitsaris, pass from Warren 23 (kick failed)

Ray Graves Remembers

"Butler's 68-yard run got me to thinking about his great run in 1939 against Alabama. That Butler was something. Even back in high school, when I was at Central and he was at Knoxville, you never knew which way Butler was going to run. He would change directions two or three times.

"He gave everybody an incentive to make their block at the line of scrimmage and then get up and try to make another one. He'd say, I might see you again. In the huddle, he'd encourage you that way. I was credited with one of the blocks on his 1939 run.

"Neyland knew how to get the most out of his quarterbacks. He would install special plays for the use of whichever quarterback he felt could do something special. Neyland would open the season with an easy game, then play a little tougher one and have three really tough games all season.

"My job on campus was as a janitor in the Athletic Department. I got there early in the morning and checked things out. I knew more about Neyland than he would have thought possible. He kept a diary, and I knew who was lining up where and what was going on about everything.

"After the Sugar Bowl, when we lost to Boston College, he said in his notebook that we might have left the game on Shields-Watkins Field back in Knoxville. I was on a work scholarship. Everybody had a little something to do—everybody but Suffridge.

"I got to where I would tell the other players what the notebook had to say about them. I got pretty popular about that time.

"Alabama was a game we always pointed for, from spring practice on. Jimmy Nelson was the Alabama tailback. He was tough. If you were going to have a good season, you had to beat Alabama. It was a rivalry, and it still is. We came back on the train from Birmingham late that night. There was a big crowd waiting for us, but the time didn't matter. They would have shown up no matter what time the train pulled in."

> *"Alabama was a game we always pointed for, from spring practice on. . . . If you were going to have a good season, you had to beat Alabama."*
>
> —Ray Graves

Vols 14, Florida 0

A couple of products of the Sunshine State, Bill Nowling and Buist Warren, were the principal authors of a 14–0 Tennessee victory over the team from the two players' home-state university, the Florida Gators.

Fresh from their emotional triumph a week earlier over Alabama, the Vols were in position to have their apple cart overturned by the Gators. According to one writer, the Tennessee squad took a lackadaisical approach to Florida's invasion. "Seldom has a team displayed less fire and ambition," said the account in the *Knoxville Journal,* the city's morning newspaper at the time.

Nowling and Warren, on the other hand, were taking no chances that they might be ridiculed on their next trip home. They didn't want to risk the embarrassment of explaining away a loss to the Gators, a team that in those days typically was less of a powerhouse than their modern counterparts. In fact, the 1940 Florida team did well to fashion a 5–5 mark.

Nowling posted the first touchdown, which covered 48 yards. He traveled the distance virtually untouched, thanks to a Gator defense that was packed in close. Once he passed the line of scrimmage and veered right, he was home free. UT later retired Nowling's jersey number, 32. He was one of four Vols who died for their country in World War II.

Warren clinched the victory over Florida coach Tom Lieb's ball club. With blocks from Nick Weber and Lloyd Broome springing him past the line, Buist ran 49 yards to pay dirt in the fourth quarter. Ike Peel and Fred Newman added extra points after each of the two scores.

The Gators attempted some razzle-dazzle offense in the hope of being competitive, but their quarterbacks spent so much time brushing off their grass-stained pants after being tossed for losses that their attack never posed a real threat.

Bob Suffridge, in the final season of a three-time All-America career, was the UT lineman most credited with

The undefeated teams of 1938, 1939, and 1940 gave UT cheerleaders ample opportunity to fire up the student body.

tackling the Florida field generals behind the line of scrimmage. A positive note for the Gators was that they managed to complete half of their 22 passes. On the negative side, even those successful throws inflicted little damage.

Florida	0	0	0	0	0
Tennessee	0	0	7	7	14

UT   Nowling, run 48 (Peel kick)

UT   Warren, run 49 (Newman kick)

Ray Graves Remembers

"Florida had a few players back then, but they weren't that good. We always felt like they were the beach boys. We kidded Nowling and Warren, who were from Florida, about being beach boys.

"Coming after the Alabama game, there was a natural letdown for Tennessee. Like the newspaper said, 'Seldom has a team displayed less fire and ambition.' Florida just didn't have enough good players.

"Florida played us a pretty good game, considering everything. Nowling and Warren tried to get us ready for them.

"Suffridge was probably the best defensive lineman I ever saw in high school, college or pro football. He was football-smart; I can tell you that. When he played for the Eagles, he blocked three consecutive extra points Sammy Baugh was trying to kick.

"I remember back in high school, at Knoxville Central, we were getting ready to play Johnson City. It was raining and they almost called the game off. But then they decided to play. I remember Suffridge told us he was going to block three punts that day. That's exactly what he did.

"He certainly was a great one. No one blocker could handle him. He was so fast and so strong in the shoulders.

"Another anecdote about Suffridge: He wasn't always as smart as he thought he was. There were four of us who were going to go play a basketball game over at Maryville and pick up a little extra money. I ran into Suffridge at the barber shop and asked him to join us. I told him we'd divide the pot five ways.

"He told me, no, that those people would be coming to see him, not us, and he deserved a bigger share of the gate. So I told Suff, 'Okay, we'll give you 20 percent, and the other four of us will divide the rest.' He said that would be all right.

"General Neyland always wanted to attack a team at their strength. He felt if you could beat them at their strong point, you were going to win the game. He had the philosophy of a general. He didn't try to make a lot of friends as a coach, and he didn't want any.

"Butler and Warren were our tailbacks, Butler the better runner, Warren the better passer."

Vols 28, LSU 0

Since LSU under Bernie Moore was no slouch, Tennessee's 28–0 shellacking of the Tigers in 1940 stamped the Vols unmistakably as one of the nation's premier squads.

"As close to perfect as it is possible for any team to approach" was the way one newspaperman described the team's performance. Neyland's troops scored a touchdown on their first possession, added two in the second quarter, and ended the scoring with a touchdown in the third.

Although Neyland usually avoided bragging on his team, he broke from his normal conservative mold to proclaim the work of the first unit the best he had seen by the Vols since he became head coach in 1926.

The Vols' first possession yielded a touchdown, providing enough points, it turned out, to send the Tigers back to

Baton Rouge with their plans for an upset in tatters. Some deadly blocking aided the 68-yard drive that Van Thompson, making his first start at tailback, engineered.

Norbert Ackermann's interception led to the second touchdown, which came when Lloyd Broome bulled across from the 1.

The Tigers committed the common—and ill-considered—blunder of punting the ball to Johnny Butler one time too many. The Knoxville product, who decades later would be inducted posthumously into the Tennessee Sports Hall of Fame, sprinted down the sidelines, reaching the 3-yard line before being bumped out of bounds. Two plays later, Butler plowed across for the score. A 35-yard pass from Bob Foxx to Jimmy Coleman produced the final touchdown.

Tennessee's defense made mincemeat of LSU's widely ballyhooed offense, with Bob Suffridge and some of his up-front teammates rendering the Tigers' stars harmless any time they came within smelling distance of the goal.

Captain Norbert Ackermann provided leadership for the 1940 squad.

LSU	0	0	0	0	0
Tennessee	7	14	7	0	28

UT   Foxx, run 5 (Foxx kick)

UT   Broome, run 1 (Newman kick)

UT   Butler, run 2 (Newman kick)

UT   Coleman, pass from Foxx 35 (Foxx kick)

Ed Cifers Remembers

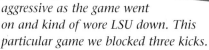

"LSU was a very good team, which gave us a knock-down, drag-out fight. We got more aggressive as the game went on and kind of wore LSU down. This particular game we blocked three kicks.

"I felt any time we were about equal with an opponent we should win because we had a better coach. That was quite a compliment by Neyland that this was the best performance by a first team. He wasn't one to brag much about a team. Coming from him, it was most unexpected. Neyland expected you to play well.

"Van Thompson was one of several tailbacks—Van Thompson, Johnny Butler, Buist Warren, Bunzy O'Neill, and Red Bailes from out at Central. There wasn't a great one among them. They were all about equal.

"Van was the best passer, followed closely by Buist. Why Van got the start I don't know. Buist and Butler were also available and played a lot. Butler wasn't big. He was hard to tackle. Van was the biggest of the group, which gave him an advantage in running the 10 play.

"As far as keeping everybody happy, Neyland didn't worry about that. He would play you if he thought you deserved it, and he wouldn't if he thought you didn't deserve it. They were good players, but there weren't any Cafegos among them.

"Norbert Ackermann, who was our center, had an interception against LSU. Of course, at that time we had single-platoon football. Under Tennessee's defensive

36 alignment, the center and fullback both played linebacker. The blocking back and wingback were halfbacks on defense, and the tailback played safety.

"All Johnny Butler needed to have a great punt return was one good block. He didn't have exceptional speed, but he had a knack for following his blockers. The year before, against Alabama, Butler had one of the best punt returns ever when everybody on the Alabama team had a crack at him. Johnny was quite a guy. He had a way of making people miss him."

Vols 40, Southwestern 0

With pressure lessened after the one-sided victory over LSU, the Vols went to Memphis to enjoy a 40–0 romp over little Southwestern (now known as Rhodes College). Playing on a drenched field, they proved that they were as competent in the mud as they were on dry turf.

The heavy rains had reduced the size of the crowd to an estimated 8,000—most of whom wisely departed the premises after the Knoxville visitors surged to a 27–0 lead before halftime. The Vols sent so many players into combat, limiting the amount of time each was allowed to stay in the game, that there were no big heroes among the orange-shirted athletes.

Headlines, such as they were, concentrated on the fact that Abe Shires gave a performance at the line that came closer than most to demonstrating his nearly boundless potential. Sportswriters called it the veteran West Virginian's finest game.

About the only other matter of note was an impressive kickoff by Ray Graves that traveled through the end zone and splattered the face of a spectator who wasn't paying enough attention to get out of the way.

Southwestern	0	0	0	0	0
Tennessee	6	21	7	6	40

UT	Thompson, run 37 (pass failed)
UT	Butler, run 32 (Newman kick)
UT	Newman, run 2 (Newman kick)
UT	Mulloy, pass from Warren 21 (Aurelia kick)
UT	Nowling, run 34 (Foxx, kick)
UT	Thompson, run 1 (pass failed)

Ed Cifers Remembers

"It was an overcast day. There had been a lot of rain. I remember that. On the opening kickoff a Southwestern player made a good run. I met him head-on. It was probably the roughest collision I had ever experienced.

"Southwestern was a notch below Chattanooga. We had to play a game in Memphis every year. I'm sure Ed Crump, the political boss in Memphis, was the reason. Southwestern was a small school.

"Against a team like that Neyland would play his first team the whole opening quarter. Then he would use second and third teams in the second quarter. The first team would play about seven minutes of the third quarter, and from that point it would be substitutes playing the rest of the way.

"He substituted whole teams—all 11 players going in or coming out. I don't ever remember Neyland trying to run the score up on anybody. He just didn't do it. When he had the third team in there, he couldn't tell them not to score. But as for running up the score, no.

> "I don't ever remember Neyland trying to run the score up on anybody. He just didn't do it."
>
> —Ed Cifers

"They didn't have the offenses back then they have now. So if Neyland got 13 points up on somebody, he would sit on his lead. Abe Shires was a character, the nicest fellow you'd ever want to know, and a good football player. He was fast, and he was big. He had no interest in playing professional ball.

"Some of the sportswriters criticized Tennessee for playing teams like Southwestern."

Vols 41, Virginia 14

Sportsmanship as old-timers fondly recall it may have been at its apex in the Virginia game, an epic at Shields-Watkins Field that the Vols captured, 41–14. It was their 30th straight regular-season victory.

Newspaper accounts, though crediting the Vols and tailback Van Thompson in particular, asserted that the most prolonged applause of the afternoon occurred when Virginia hero Bill Dudley limped from the field late in the game.

The courageous Virginia back, who had dazzled the crowd with his running, passing, and kicking, received a standing ovation "such as has seldom been seen and heard" at the old field on 15th Street. The 8,000 partisans stayed on their feet several minutes in appreciation of one of the most heroic individual performances ever witnessed locally.

Dudley, though representing the lesser team, had played brilliantly. Aside from his offensive accomplishments, he had been Virginia's primary defensive force. Furthermore, his 87-yard kickoff return accounted for Virginia's second score. That tally came a short time after a Dudley touchdown pass had accounted for the Cavaliers' initial appearance on the scoreboard in the third period.

Tennessee opened the scoring in the first five minutes and added to its margin through most of the game. Thompson returned a punt 25 yards to his 38. A pass from Thompson to Bob Foxx was instrumental in working the ball down to the Cavaliers' 2-yard line, from which point Bill Nowling carried it across.

With every man who was dressed out entering the fray at one point or another, Tennessee scored in every period. The Vols tallied two touchdowns in the first, one in the second, two in the third, and one in the closing minutes. Coach Neyland employed his starters for only 12 minutes.

In the days leading up to the game, there was much fear that all-time All-America guard Bob Suffridge's ankle, injured in the Southwestern game, might not respond to treatment, thus limiting the star lineman's participation for the rest of the season. But trainer Mickey O'Brien had the Knoxville native in playing shape well before game time, allowing chronic UT worriers to breathe easily.

Romping through their workout, the 1940 Vols backfield included, from left, Bob Foxx, Bill Nowling, Van Thompson, and Ike Peel.

Virginia	0	0	7	7	14
Tennessee	14	7	13	7	41

UT	Nowling, run 2 (Foxx kick)	
UT	Thompson, run 6 (Foxx kick)	
UT	Newman, run 2 (Newman kick)	
UT	Newman, run 3 (Newman kick)	
UT	Swartzinger, run 5 (pass failed)	
UV	Gianakos, pass from Dudley 9 (Schlesinger kick)	
UT	Broome, run 3 (Meek kick)	
UV	Dudley, kickoff return 87 (Dudley kick)	

Ike Peel Remembers

"They were trying to build up Bill Dudley, Virginia was, and he was a fine football player—later won the Heisman Trophy. But we were a cocky bunch of guys, and we finally wore him down in the fourth quarter. He had been beaten up pretty bad, and our fans gave him a standing ovation when he left the game.

"He did his best playing against our first team. How were you going to get Bob Suffridge and Abe Shires up for a game unless it was against Alabama?

"Speaking of Suff, he was the best lineman I ever saw. He was quick and strong, the best player at his position anywhere. He would get in the opponent's backfield and get to the tailback as soon as the ball got there. There was no single-wing center who could block him.

"Suffridge was supposed to be hurt coming into this game, but you never knew about him. He'd limp around and try to come out of a game if he could get by with it. I remember one time he called time out. We asked him why. You know what he told us? They're announcing scores, and he wanted to check his parlay sheet.

"They say the crowd was only 8,000, but stuff like that didn't matter to us. We didn't care if there wasn't but four people out there.

"Virginia ran the single wing, and Bill Dudley moved around. I guarantee you Suffridge and Ed Molinski weren't going to chase him, and neither was Shires.

"Bob Foxx was a great athlete who could play anything. He was a better wingback than tailback because he hadn't played a lot of tailback, and he would get a little jittery back there. If he had played it a lot, he would have been okay.

"I don't know how much you've got about Leonard Coffman in your book, but it should be quite a bit. He was a great football player. Neyland liked him because he was tough. He was one tough football player. He was good on defense. Not a great runner, but adequate.

"Our running at fullback wasn't real good. Joe Wallen was slow. Ox Newman played some, but got hurt, and we didn't hear any more about him."

Vols 33, Kentucky 0

While it was generally considered a lead-pipe cinch that Tennessee would beat Kentucky, there was fear at halftime that the Wildcats might sabotage the Volunteers' bowl dreams as previous Big Blue teams had done on other occasions. As intermission arrived, the Vols nursed a slender 7–0 lead, owing to a blocked kick that gave Tennessee its first scoring opportunity.

One quality perhaps typified Tennessee teams of the era more than any other: a resourcefulness that enabled a substitute to step up and do what was needed if somebody playing ahead of him couldn't quite cut it on a particular day. Buist Warren was the hero of the 33–0 shellacking the Vols pinned on Kentucky.

Warren got the Vols out of a hole in the first quarter by returning a punt 47 yards. Then in the third period he brought back another Wildcats punt, this one for 40 yards, putting the ball at the 20. He threw to Jimmy Coleman for the score.

Newspapers gushed about Warren's 40-yard return. One reporter wrote that "time and time again he seemed certain to be flattened, but by some pedal legerdemain he managed to remain upright and continue goalward."

With the fourth-quarter countdown under way, the Shields-Watkins public address announcer called out the names of the seniors making their last appearance before the home crowd. And an impressive list it was, including such legendary Vols as Bob Foxx, Bob Suffridge, Abe Shires, Ed Molinski, Ed Cifers, and Captain Norbert Ackermann.

Mike Balitsaris accounted for two Tennessee touchdowns. The others, one apiece, came from Jimmy Coleman, Bob Andridge, and Fred Newman. Kentucky remained scrappy throughout, providing the tough competition that could be expected every time the Wildcats renewed the border-state rivalry.

Kentucky	0	0	0	0	0
Tennessee	0	7	7	19	33

UT	Balitsaris, pass from Butler 9 (Newman kick)
UT	Coleman, pass from Warren 7 (Foxx kick)
UT	Andridge, run 1 (pass failed)
UT	Balitsaris, pass from Butler 27 (Newman kick)
UT	Newman, interception return 37 (run failed)

Bob (Breezer) Andridge had the speed and sure hands that made him a dependable pass receiver for the 1940 Vols.

Van Thompson Remembers

"Kentucky gave Tennessee a tough game most years because they were usually near the bottom of the league and they thought if they beat Tennessee or put up a good fight that meant they had had a good season. Tennessee was on top, and it was tough to get ready for Kentucky.

"This was another game where I didn't play much. I started, but got kneed in the first period and went to the locker room. I had just made a cut when it happened. I think it was a linebacker who did it.

"Buist Warren was the best passer on the squad, and he did a good job the rest of the way. Buist was listed as

FOXX
LHB

PEEL
QB

NOWLING
FB

THOMPSON
RHB

TENNESSEE VOLUNTEERS
1940

COLEMAN
LE

SHIRES
LT

MOLINSKI
LG

CAPT
ACKERMAN
C

SUFFRIDGE
RG

LUTTRELL
RT

CIFERS
RE

Newspapers created a headshot montage to celebrate the achievements of the 1940 national champions. Clockwise, from top left, are Bob Foxx, Ike Peel, Bill Nowling, Van Thompson, Ed Cifers, Bill Luttrell, Bob Suffridge, Norbert Ackermann, Ed Molinski, Abe Shires, and Jimmy Coleman.

1940

third-team tailback, but Neyland impressed on him that he needed to be ready if Johnny Butler or I got hurt. So Buist received as much attention in practice as Butler and I did. Buist was ready to go when I got hurt.

"I don't think there has been a better bunch of football players than the seniors of 1940. Suffridge was the best guard I ever saw. I'm convinced he could play today despite his size.

"Abe Shires was mean, real mean. Oh, man, was he mean! Ackermann, Cifers, Foxx, all of them were great players. It seems today that coaches complain that they don't have a fullback, or don't have a center, or don't have an end. They don't seem to have enough players even though they've got a hundred or so out there.

"I haven't been to a game since Reggie Cobb played tailback, about 1988. But you never get that orange blood out of your system."

Vols 20, Vanderbilt 0

Another perfect regular-season campaign, the third in a row, came to a close in Nashville, where the Vols trampled Vanderbilt, 20–0.

Although drums were beaten fervently in the Knoxville area on behalf of a second straight trip to the Rose Bowl, it was less than 30 minutes after the game ended in Nashville that an announcement came from New Orleans. Tennessee and Boston College would hook up in the January 1 Sugar Bowl. This made the Louisiana classic the one bowl extravaganza graced by two undefeated teams.

Conditions for the Tennessee–Vanderbilt season-ender were far from ideal. It was cold, and it was wet. But one man who didn't let the abominable weather bother him was Johnny Butler, UT's brilliant tailback.

The clinching touchdown for the Vols came in the final period and had Butler's footprints all over it. After returning

a punt to the Vanderbilt 47, Butler took off over right tackle, advancing to the 23. After one play gained 4 yards, another lost 2, and a third gained 8, Butler decided it was time to fish or cut bait.

The decisive play from the 13 was a double lateral in which Fred Newman pitched to Nick Weber, who in turn tossed to Butler. Johnny skirted left end and negotiated his way past the goal line, after which Newman's extra-point kick made the score 20–0.

If Vanderbilt had plans to mount a comeback at any stage of the game by taking to the air, the sloppy weather disabused them of the notion. Everyone was afraid of tossing the ball around any more than necessary.

Tennessee	0	7	6	7	20
Vanderbilt	0	0	0	0	0

UT   Foxx, run 7 (Foxx kick)
UT   Warren, run 35 (kick failed)
UT   Butler, run 13 (Newman kick)

Ike Peel Remembers

"It was cold and rainy in Nashville when we played Vanderbilt. We had switched to the Tennessee Central out of Harriman after getting on board the L&N in Knoxville.

"The fans were very excited about the third straight unbeaten season. The players were conscious of it, but not as excited as the fans. We had a good solid team, but we were hacked off that we went to the Sugar Bowl rather than the Rose Bowl.

"On Butler's run for the third touchdown, it was supposed to be a pass, but Butler saw the opening and took

off. There was no catching Johnny Butler when he got into the clear. He was a great running back, the best open-field running tailback I had seen. He had the ability to turn it on and to cut—a great cutback runner.

"I roomed with Butler for about a year, but I couldn't take that. He was a wild man—a good guy, but wild.

"That was a good team, the 1940 Vols, but if they hadn't thought they were so good, they would have been better. One reason we lost the Sugar Bowl was that nobody wanted to go. Except me, that is. I would have gone across the street for a chance to play another game. But I was younger than the others.

"After the game, down in New Orleans, we had a hell of a time. We practiced in Biloxi, about 100 miles away, but the night of the game we had a big time."

Boston College 19, Vols 13 (Sugar Bowl)

In a defeat that reportedly galled Bob Neyland like no other, hanging in his craw for the great coach's remaining years, the Vols succumbed to Frank Leahy's Boston College Eagles, 19–13, in the Sugar Bowl at New Orleans.

Whether it was the presence of Leahy, a coach on the rise who would later accomplish great things at Notre Dame, that motivated Neyland, he never got over the loss. Or maybe it was the way little Charlie O'Rourke drove the Eagles to their winning touchdown with four minutes left and the score tied at 13.

One newspaperman described the BC tailback this way: "A wisp of straw among massive oaks." He was scrawny and deadpanned. The winning drive was for 80 yards, included a combination of passing and running and reached a climax when O'Rourke faked a pass and then raced through the Tennessee defense for the final 24 yards.

From the standpoint of 75,000 fans attending the Sugar Bowl, a tie would probably have been appropriate. The

bowl sponsors succeeded in attaining their goal of evenly matching two great teams, with even the game statistics testifying to a virtual standoff.

Van Thompson and Buist Warren accounted for Tennessee touchdowns, but it was an errant pass that sealed the Vols' doom after O'Rourke's spectacular touchdown put the Eagles on top. And who intercepted Tennessee's last desperate throw? It was the ever-present Mr. O'Rourke.

The Vols went into intermission nursing a 7–0 lead, but the talented New Englanders bounced back to tie the game twice before mounting their decisive 80-yard march.

The defeat was especially tough for UT to swallow, inasmuch as the 1939 Vols, who had also outplayed everyone on their regular-season schedule, had come up short on their trip to Pasadena and the Rose Bowl.

Boston College	0	0	13	6	19
Tennessee	7	0	6	0	13

UT	Thompson, run 4 (Foxx kick)
BC	Connolly, run 12 (Maznicki kick)
UT	Warren, run 2 (run failed)
BC	Holovak, run 1 (run failed)
BC	O'Rourke, run 24 (kick failed)

Norbert Ackermann Remembers

"Neyland, as everybody knows, was a strict disciplinarian coach, both for himself and his team. But in the third quarter, I think he was starting to think about the 1941 season and mixed up his lineup quite a bit to

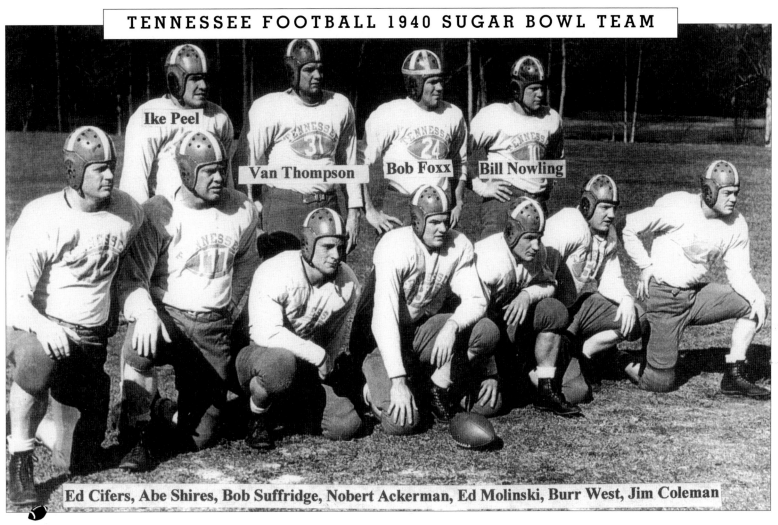

TENNESSEE FOOTBALL 1940 SUGAR BOWL TEAM

Ike Peel

Van Thompson   Bob Foxx   Bill Nowling

Ed Cifers, Abe Shires, Bob Suffridge, Nobert Ackerman, Ed Molinski, Burr West, Jim Coleman

The 1940 Vols, with the starters seen here, were rudely surprised by Boston College in the Sugar Bowl.

1940

T

44

give experience to some of his younger players. I think that's part of the reason Tennessee lost to Boston College.

"I may be wrong about that. My memory might be playing a trick on me, but it seems that was the situation. Eventually, it seems that he got the regulars back in there.

"Charlie O'Rourke was a great player who stood out on both offense and defense. O'Rourke even got the interception that ended Tennessee's bid to pull it out at the end. That was a tough ball game, and we knew going in Boston College was a fine team.

"And Frank Leahy was a young coach on the rise, who next went to Notre Dame. Neyland tried his best to schedule Notre Dame, hoping to get another crack at Leahy, but it never worked out.

"It was a well-played game that could have ended in a tie, and it would have been fair to both teams. But Boston College won, and that's the way it goes sometimes."

1940 National Review

Few teams have dominated an era as resoundingly as the Minnesota squads of the 1930s. The Golden Gophers won national championships in 1934, 1935, and 1936.

The Gophers, under Hall of Fame coach Bernie Bierman, were respectable in 1937 and 1938, dropped off to an unacceptable 3–4–1 in 1939, and bounced back to 8–0 in 1940, sharing national-title honors with Tennessee and Stanford.

The following year's Minnesota team was considered even stronger by most experts than the 1940 team and captured the school's fifth national crown in eight seasons.

But the 1940 Gophers' claim to recognition as the best in the land was validated on a cold, dreary day in November when they stopped All-America Tom Harmon in the mud en route to a 7–6 victory over the visiting Michigan Wolverines.

Long after all three had left campus, Abe Shires, left, and Ed Cifers, right, renewed their acquaintance with the legendary sportscaster Lindsey Nelson.

Harmon, who ran wild against everybody else on his way to winning the Heisman Trophy, was overshadowed by Minnesota's Bruce Smith, who ran for 116 yards and scored the winning touchdown. Michigan's missed extra point after its touchdown doomed the Wolverines.

Stanford, which finished second in the AP poll, relied on an explosive T-formation attack under innovative coach Clark Shaugnessy. Quarterback Frankie Albert sparked the razzle-dazzle Indians (as they were known as in those days) to a 21–13 win over Nebraska in the Rose Bowl to climax the perfect season.

The loss to Minnesota was Michigan's lone setback, but it cost the powerful Wolverines both the national title and the Big Nine championship. Boston College, Texas A&M, Nebraska, and Mississippi State were other schools that figured in national-title conjecture in 1940.

The most unforgettable event in 1940 came in the Dartmouth–Cornell Ivy League tilt. Unbeaten Cornell's "winning" points came on a fifth down mistakenly awarded by the referee. Cornell immediately forfeited the victory to Dartmouth, setting an example of sportsmanship that hasn't been duplicated too many times since.

The 1950 Vols

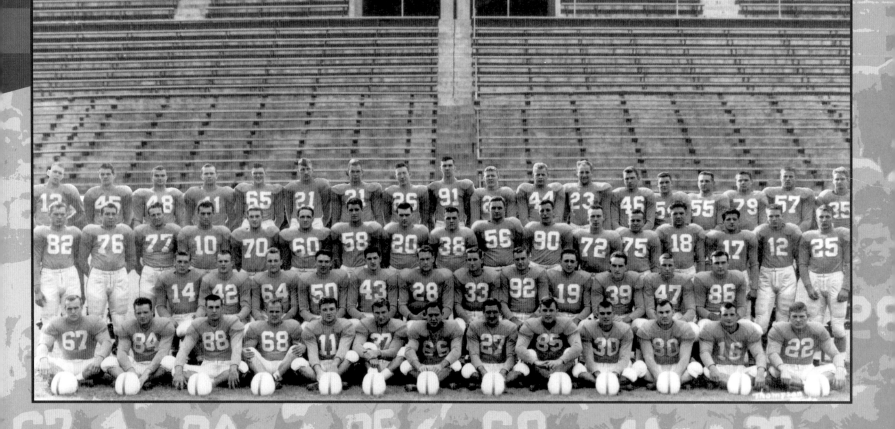

Chapter 3

1950

The immediate postwar years were unusually difficult for Robert R. Neyland. When the General failed to find immediate success on his return from Army duty in World War II, the inevitable rumors emerged around Knoxville.

Football had passed Neyland by during the years he was serving in the Asian theatre of operations. The single-wing formation was hopelessly out-of-date. The crusty Neyland wasn't the man to implement the new slick offense, the T formation. Two-platoon football had arrived, over Neyland's protests, and everybody knew he wouldn't be able to adjust to a system he detested.

Not many people underestimated Neyland, a man of massive intellect, but a few did at this particular time. The UT coach, fed up with the losses his teams sustained in the immediate postwar years, developed two-platoon teams that were better and more versatile than any of his contemporaries put together.

The 1950 and 1951 Tennessee teams, coming in the twilight of his career, were two of the most capable Neyland ever fielded.

The 1950 coaching staff. Seated, from left, are Al Hust, L. B. (Farmer) Johnson, Head Coach Bob Neyland, Harvey Robinson, and Ike Peel. Standing, from left, are Ralph Chancey, Billy Hilderbrand, Mickey O'Brien, Hodges (Burr) West, Chan Caldwell, and Emmett Lowery.

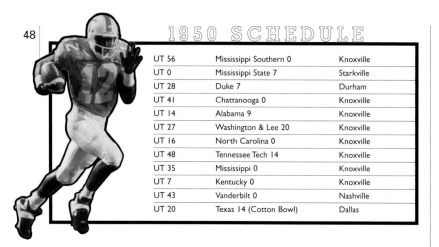

UT 56	Mississippi Southern 0	Knoxville
UT 0	Mississippi State 7	Starkville
UT 28	Duke 7	Durham
UT 41	Chattanooga 0	Knoxville
UT 14	Alabama 9	Knoxville
UT 27	Washington & Lee 20	Knoxville
UT 16	North Carolina 0	Knoxville
UT 48	Tennessee Tech 14	Knoxville
UT 35	Mississippi 0	Knoxville
UT 7	Kentucky 0	Knoxville
UT 43	Vanderbilt 0	Nashville
UT 20	Texas 14 (Cotton Bowl)	Dallas

Vols 56, Mississippi Southern 0

The widely ballyhooed freshmen of 1948 were ready to make their mark by 1950, proving again that Coach Neyland could not only adjust to the times but could stay a step above his contemporaries on the coaching tower.

The team from Mississippi Southern (now the University of Southern Mississippi) absorbed the first shock of the re-built single-wing machine. As would happen so often over the next couple of years of national dominance, the names that would resound when Tennessee football was played included Kozar, Lauricella, Rechichar, Daffer, and Polofsky.

UT's overwhelming numbers wore out the Southerners (as the school's teams were nicknamed before they became the Golden Eagles) with a well-balanced attack. The Vols scored a single touchdown in the first period, three in the second, one in the third, and three more in the fourth. Tail-back Hank Lauricella and fullback Andy Kozar accounted for two each. Tailback Herky Payne, fullback Dick Ernsberger, wingback Bert Rechichar, and end Francis Stupar scored a touchdown apiece.

Rechichar, a two-way player in an era of one-way specialists, showed his toughness when he made his debut as a safety. The rawboned junior from Belle Vernon, Pennsylvania, had earlier made his mark at wingback. But as a safety he roared through the Southerners for a 72-yard punt return that delighted the crowd of 23,000 at the newly enlarged Shields-Watkins Field.

Pat Shires, one of five tailbacks Neyland employed in the rout, divided his contributions between directing the offense and kicking extra points, a total of seven of them against the Southerners. The brother of Abe Shires, a previous All-America tackle, directed an 87-yard scoring drive.

Mississippi Southern was plainly outmanned as the final score indicates. Nonetheless, a good time was presumably had by all at the most colorful presentation in the long history of UT football. A total of 22 high school bands serenaded the crowd, part of the celebration observing Neyland's 25th season as head coach.

The Vols' offensive display thrilled their fans. It was clear that there was nothing antiquated about the reverses, fakes, buck laterals, pitchouts, and other modes of trickery most people wouldn't have associated with the old-time single wing. UT football was destined to be exciting and different in 1950 even though a major disappointment lay just ahead.

Mississippi Southern	0	0	0	0	0
Tennessee	7	21	7	21	56

UT	Ernsberger, run 3 (Shires kick)
UT	Polofsky, run 5 (Shires kick)
UT	Payne, run 16 (Shires kick)
UT	Kozar, run 2 (Shires kick)
UT	Lauricella, run 9 (Shires kick)
UT	Rechichar, punt return 72 (Shires kick)
UT	Kozar, run 8 (Shires kick)
UT	Stupar, recovery of blocked punt in end zone (Kyker, kick)

Gene Felty Remembers

"*Going into the 1950 season, people had been saying the single wing was over the hill and that Tennessee needed to be using the T formation. That worked out well for General Neyland because it was difficult for teams to get ready for the single wing since they had been working defensively against the T.*

"*Fans said not only was the single wing over the hill, but so was General Neyland. They still respected what he stood for and what he had accomplished, but they thought his coaching methods were things of the past. One of the few schools still using the single-wing formation was Princeton. On a smaller scale, Emory & Henry College under Conley Snidow was using the single wing with outstanding success.*

"*General Neyland put in the buck lateral series in the 1949 season, which allowed us to do the things the T formation did, with lots of deception. The center got the ball on a direct snap to the tailback or fullback. The fullback could keep, or he handed off the ball to the quarterback. Sometimes the quarterback would pitch the ball to the tailback.*

"*Harvey Robinson was the assistant coach who put all that stuff in. We knew we were going to get better because we had about 30 players who could have been standouts anywhere they were. In 1950, of course, Lauricella and Payne were the boys at tailback. Lauricella had played safety a lot his sophomore year but was the tailback after Hal Littleford graduated.*

"*Bert Rechichar was a great player, but he was always homesick and wanted to go home. They caught him at the bus station pretty often, getting ready to go home, but they always managed to bring him back. He was just homesick.*

"*Pat Shires was another single-wing tailback. But he got hurt and was mainly a placekicker from that point.*

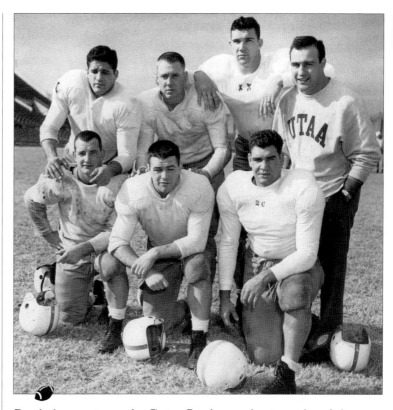

Ready for practice at the Cotton Bowl were, front row, from left, Whig Campbell, John Michels, and Francis Holohan; and, back row, from left, Joe Maiure, Pat Shires, Doug Atkins, and Andy Kozar.

"*We pretty much scored at will against Mississippi Southern. They weren't nearly as good as they are now. I think the ease with which we got past Mississippi Southern may have contributed to the loss against Mississippi State because we were probably overconfident.*

"*Neyland was not only a great coach, but he had the ability to know what was going to happen before it actually happened. That was an amazing talent. I have never heard of anybody doing that since that time the way General Neyland could.*"

Mississippi State 7, Vols 0

Talk about revolting developments. Tennessee's showdown with Mississippi State turned out to be exactly that as the troops from Starkville ground out a 7–0 victory over the highly regarded—but in many ways, still unproven—Vols.

There was nothing fancy about the single touchdown that decided the fray. The Bulldogs took the opening kick-off, returned it to their own 45 and then proceeded to ram the ball down the Big Orange's throat with 14 straight running plays. The final thrust came from 9 yards out.

Tom Rushing, a powerful running back who overshadowed a later Mississippi State great, Joe Fortunato, at that stage of his career, stuck the dagger in UT's heart when he took the ball, headed for a tackle slot, and then raced outside for the necessary scoring yardage.

Tennessee made only one serious scoring threat, a do-or-die drive in the final four minutes that fizzled out deep in Mississippi State territory. Inside the State 10, Herky Payne launched a pass across the goal to Bert Rechichar. The usually dependable Rechichar appeared to have the ball in his grasp, only to drop it at the last instant.

A fourth-down run failed to dent the Bulldogs line, and Mississippi State took over at the 7-yard line. That was the last opportunity for the Vols, who perhaps should have been prepared for a tough afternoon in light of Mississippi State's 68–0 victory a week earlier against Arkansas State.

Tennessee, which always delighted in using its speed to overcome an opponent's bulk, was probably a bit more crestfallen than usual, because the Mississippi State victory was led by a back who certainly qualified as a lightweight in the literal sense.

Frankie Branch, whose soaking-wet weight was 130 pounds, received credit for outplaying the Vols' more heralded backfield, which included Rechichar, tailback Hank Lauricella, fullback Andy Kozar, and blocking back Jimmy Hahn.

The Bulldogs could claim a statistical advantage as well as a scoreboard edge, chalking up 15 first downs to seven for Tennessee. There were heroes aplenty for the State defense, which played the dominant role in giving coach Arthur (Slick) Morton one of his most memorable victories.

Tennessee	0	0	0	0	0
Mississippi State	7	0	0	0	7

MSU   Rushing, run 9 (Stainbrook kick)

Jimmy Hill Remembers

"Ralph Chancey was the coach who worked with the defensive backfield, at least that part of practice in which we split into individual position groups. General Neyland undoubtedly got with Ralph and went over the information and practice routine he wanted emphasized each day.

"Farmer Johnson, the defensive-line coach, headed up the defense, but they didn't use the term coordinator back then.

"Then, of course, we had the scouting reports from whoever was assigned scouting duties. The basketball coach, Emmett Lowery, scouted Kentucky. Hugh Faust had two important games, Alabama and Vanderbilt. It may have been Sheriff Maples who scouted Mississippi State in 1950. I'm just not sure.

"The reports weren't nearly as complete and far-reaching as they are today when we have computers and so forth, but it was as much information as we could handle in getting ready for a game.

"J. W. Sherrill and I had enough interceptions over our careers that I don't think anybody enjoyed throwing the ball against either one of us. I believe this is right. Except for the Cotton Bowl, where Texas had one, nobody completed a touchdown pass against us.

We played against some good quarterbacks—the cream of the crop.

"In the Mississippi State game, State did not have a single yard passing, and we only had 10 yards. The only thing I can put my finger on to explain our loss is that they had the football most of the afternoon. My memory is that Mississippi State scored and then we spent the rest of the day making sure they didn't do it again.

"That game helped us because it made us grow up. We realized somebody could pin our ears back. We didn't make many mistakes after that game. The Alabama game that season was the springboard, helping us realize we had a pretty good group of football players and that we were going to be a winning team.

"General Neyland took it like he did most losses. He told us, 'Look around, guys, your teammates are your only friends, the only ones that understand that you could have lost this game.' We knew that Mississippi State had put it to us, and that was the way it was.

"Slick Morton, the Mississippi State coach, had his team ready to play. Somebody said this was considered the biggest victory in his career. Frankie Branch, their quarterback, wasn't big enough to play college ball, but he did.

"Although Bert Rechichar was best known as a wingback, he played both ways and was a great safety. He was very fast, although most people thought he wasn't. He looked heavy-footed. John Michels and Francis Holohan, like Rechichar, were very tough guys, who I was happy to have on defense."

Hitting on all cylinders a week later, the Vols took their frustration out on the Duke Blue Devils, who were considered a pretty potent team in their own right after victories over South Carolina and Pittsburgh.

Perfectly executed blocking, the characteristic that most typically characterized Neyland teams, was in full view on two plays that were critical in Tennessee's 28–7 victory over the Blue Devils at Durham.

Also, in keeping with Neyland's maxims, the Vols took care of important business first by shutting down the justly famed Billy Cox and Company, otherwise known as the Duke offense. The 30,000 fans who watched the game under cloudy skies had to wait until the final period to see their home heroes dent the Tennessee goal line.

Tom Jumper, a sophomore guard from Chattanooga, was credited with the most devastating downfield block on a 62-yard touchdown run by Hank Lauricella that broke up a scoreless tie early in the second period. It's a safe bet that each UT blocker did his job thoroughly as Lauricella scurried outside and then threaded the sideline for the go-ahead score.

Lauricella's complementary backfield mate, Andy Kozar, bulled ahead 41 yards to set up the Vols' second touchdown a few minutes after the initial score. Andy tore over right guard to the 5-yard line, from which point Lauricella found Vince Kaseta in the end zone.

Interceptions by W. C. Cooper and Jimmy Hill paved the way for the third and fourth touchdowns and typified the way Tennessee countered Duke's famed passing game. The Vols allowed only 12 completions out of 28 attempts in the face of an all-out attack by the triple-threat Cox.

As capably as Lauricella ran the Tennessee offense, the New Orleans junior perhaps made his most significant contribution as a punter. His 43-yard average on nine kicks obscured the fact that he could have increased that average if he had not chosen to punt out of bounds several times. A favorite Neyland maneuver, the quick kick, yielded one Lauricella effort of 78 yards..

With Tennessee scoring twice in the second period and once each in the third and fourth, the visiting Vols had a 28–0 edge before Duke crossed the goal for its only touchdown. Cox made the lone score from the 2 to climax a 60-yard drive.

The loss was a bitter pill for Wallace Wade's fine Duke team, which found the combination of Lauricella's punting and four Tennessee interceptions too much to overcome.

Tennessee	0	14	7	7	28
Duke	0	0	0	7	7

UT	Lauricella, run 62 (Shires kick)
UT	Kaseta, pass from Lauricella 5 (Shires kick)
UT	Kozar, run 1 (Shires kick)
UT	Shires, interception return 69 (Shires kick)
Duke	Cox, run 2 (Souchak kick).

John Gruble Remembers

"Billy Cox and I were on the same high school team at Mt. Airy, North Carolina. We both played in the Shrine all-star game, North Carolina versus South Carolina, at Charlotte after our senior year. Cox was Duke all the way. It was automatic. I was choosing between Tennessee and North Carolina.

"When North Carolina told me I might be a regular by my senior year, I decided to go to Tennessee, where I had been recruited by Harvey Robinson, a super guy. Coach

From left, Pat Shires, Roy (Looney) Smith, Bert Rechichar, and Hank Lauricella look forward to the Cotton Bowl.

Robinson told me it was wide open at UT. By the midway point of my freshman season, I was starting. Freshmen could start that season.

"Billy Cox was Mount Airy's gift to Duke, and I was Mount Airy's gift to Tennessee. That's what the local newspaper said when we headed out to college. He was a fine all-around tailback, runner and passer.

"The blocking for Lauricella was excellent. We ran right 10 or right 9. Both guards would pull. The right tackle and end would double-team the tackle or end. The fullback and blocking back would take the tackle. The left tackle and I would go across and make a block downfield.

"I didn't get much opportunity to catch the ball, but I did get a big one for a touchdown in the Cotton Bowl.

"That was the key play of the whole game. Lauricella made his great run for 75 yards, ending with the ball on the 5. Then General Neyland put Payne in for Lauricella because that was where Payne was dangerous, down near the goal line.

"Three running plays didn't gain an inch. They called a sweep left pass or run. I made a temporary block, like it was a running play, and the defensive player went for Payne, so I slipped right in behind him. Payne was right on the money with the pass, right at the letters. I did hear Herky call my name. He was trying to get my attention.

"In the Duke game, it was two great coaches who had a lot in common going against each other. They were both defensive-minded coaches.

"Lauricella was a tremendous kicker, who sailed them high and deep. He was a great triple-threat football player.

"I've got one story on Doug Atkins. In practice, as a freshman, it was Doug's turn to be playing defensive end. So they came after him from the offense, two-on-one blocking. They picked him up and carried him back to where General Neyland was and just dropped him. Doug knew Neyland saw him.

"Next time around, they tried it again. He came in low, but with both arms up. He split them and made the tackle. They didn't yell again. And Doug Atkins was born."

This famous photo shows the blocking for Hank Lauricella on his 75-yard run against Texas.

LAURICELLA 3 YDS PAST LINE OF SCRIMMAGE ON 75 YD RUN AGAINST TEXAS IN COTTON BOWL JANUARY 1st 1951

HAHN HITS MENASCO

KOZAR TAKES OUT GEORGES

LYONS DELAYS McFADIN

MICHELS HEADS FOR DILLON

RECHICHAR AND KASETA FLATTEN DAVIS

CUNNINGHAM AVOIDS STROUD, FINALLY MAKES TACKLE 70 YARDS DOWN FIELD

GRUBLE LUNGES TOWARD OCHOA

Vols 41, Chattanooga 0

With their thoughts directed toward the following week's engagement with Alabama, the Vols drubbed little Chattanooga, 41–0, before a crowd that numbered only 13,000. The slim turnout was probably a result of the fans' anticipating the showdown with the Crimson Tide. Many of them obviously weren't that interested in seeing the Moccasins shoved around.

But one interested spectator at the massacre was Harold (Red) Drew, the head coach of Alabama, who had brought with him on this scouting mission two of his most trusted assistants, one of whom was fabled line coach Hank Crisp. The trio probably returned to Tuscaloosa with clean notebooks as the Vols dispatched the Moccasins in humdrum fashion without resorting to new-fangled maneuvers.

Sticking to the basics, Tennessee scored two touchdowns in both the first and third periods, along with one each in the second and fourth. Neyland strayed from his regular contributors to the offense by employing such reserves as W. C. Cooper and Pat Shires. Even the longtime holder for placements, Harold Johnson, served in a different capacity: He was allowed to kick the extra point after the final touchdown. His effort split the uprights.

The most spectacular of the Vols' afternoon delights was a 38-yard touchdown strike in which Cooper faded back and threw one toward the goal. Wingback Bert Rechichar, stretching for all his worth, caught it at the 11 and ran across the goal line untouched.

Shires uncorked a play in the fourth period that created a buzz in the small audience. The tailback brother of former UT line great Abe Shires faked a pass to his left, then took off down the right side 42 yards for a score. Earl Campbell's block helped clear the path by obliterating the Moccasin with the best chance of foiling the play.

Coach A. C. (Scrappy) Moore's ball club was badly out-manned. The visitors managed to net only 14 yards' rushing for their afternoon's work. Tennessee stuck to the ground in scoring its first three touchdowns, two of which were scored by fullback Dick Ernsberger and the third by fullback Andy Kozar.

Hal Ledyard, Chattanooga's truly outstanding quarterback, enjoyed a fruitful afternoon early in a career that would pay big dividends in later seasons. Ledyard, a sophomore substituting for the injured Rufus Evans, found a favorite passing target in Joe Elizer.

Chattanooga	0	0	0	0	0
Tennessee	14	7	13	7	41

UT	Ernsberger, run 2 (Shires kick)
UT	Ernsberger, run 5 (Shires kick)
UT	Kozar, run 2 (Shires kick)
UT	Carter, pass from Lauricella 15 (kick failed)
UT	Rechichar, pass from Cooper 31 (Kyker kick)
UT	Shires, run 43 (Johnson kick)

Ted Daffer Remembers

"I don't know why the crowd wasn't any larger. You've got to remember, of course, that the stadium only seated about 35,000 during that era. Back then not many women attended the games. But now they get into it, big time. And I think that helps explain why the crowds now are so large, comparatively speaking.

"We used the Chattanooga game to get ready for Alabama. The starters only played about half of the game.

Neyland didn't want to beat anybody like Chattanooga or Tennessee Tech too bad because they might not come back and play us anymore.

"Chattanooga and TPI [Tennessee Tech] were our favorite pushovers back then, but Chattanooga sort of got even when they beat us in 1958. I was sitting in the stadium for that game.

"The two games that drew best were Alabama and Kentucky. That was when Kentucky had Bear Bryant as coach and Babe Parilli at quarterback.

"We were just getting started on the two-platoon era about that time. People probably don't realize it, but we [the defense] worked some on offense in spring practice because the General felt that was the best way to learn what the defense should be expecting. So I spent most of my time in spring practice running plays with the offense.

"I'm talking about learning to do things methodically. So when we ran an offensive play, it would require us to do things like count 12 steps and then half a step. It was all done in a very well-organized manner.

"A player I worked with all the time was Francis Holohan, the other defensive guard. He was one very tough football player. We would work together on one of us staying put and the other one rushing the passer. I was maybe faster so I usually rushed. But Holohan was tremendously tough. I always felt he deserved more credit than he received.

"Farmer Johnson was my coach. He didn't try to change anything I did. He was a real good coach.

"I want to tell a little story about Doug Atkins, who I still look on as one of my best friends. Not many people other than the guys on the football team realize that one day I wrestled Doug and pinned him down on the ground.

"It was the funniest thing in my life. Doug used to hammer on me all the time. He never hurt me, but he wanted to let me know who was strongest. Well, one time I got even with him. I had a friend who was a professional wrestler. I asked him if there was any way I could take care of Atkins.

"He said, 'Yes, here are the things you have to do.' So he came up with this hold that would get Doug down so that he would worry I would break his neck. This happened after practice one day. He had never done any wrestling, and this friend showed me how to do it.

"I got Doug down, and he couldn't get up. He said he gave up and let him back up. 'No,' I said, 'you've got to apologize.' He said he never would. So I snapped his neck, like to have broken it. So he apologized, but I wouldn't let go until he said, 'Pretty please.' What made it so great was that it happened with the entire football team looking on.

"Doug was a real character. But when he got up, I started running and I made a point of staying away from him for a week. He might have killed me. That was sometime during the 1950 season."

Vols 14, Alabama 9

Ed Morgan, a sophomore wingback from Hendersonville, North Carolina, assumed the hero's mantle with a little old-fashioned trickery as the Vols defeated Alabama, 14–9, at Shields-Watkins Field in a renewal of the South's top gridiron classic.

Under Neyland, Tennessee stuck to the script without much chicanery in the normal course of events. But times weren't normal in the fourth period. Tennessee had its back to the wall, trailing 9–7, with only a few minutes left on the clock. Neyland decided it was time to try something different.

Reaching into his bag of tricks, he sent tailback Hank Lauricella off guard. Suddenly Lauricella flipped the ball back to Morgan, who ran 23 yards into Alabama territory. A goal-line stand thwarted the effort, but a short time later Tennessee had another chance.

This time, on virtually the same call, Morgan went 28 yards, again befuddling the Crimson Tide defense. The drive

56 carried to the Alabama 5-yard line, at which point Andy Kozar went across the goal line for his second touchdown of the game, giving the Vols their winning margin.

A crowd of 52,000, the largest gathering at a sports event in the state's history, watched this spectacular finish. The game was a sellout, but there were still 8,000 unsold tickets the day before.

Play after play, it was the bruising Kozar who made the UT offense productive enough to overpower the Tide. The battering ram from St. Michael, Pennsylvania, had 68 yards on 13 carries, not in themselves overpowering statistics. But his timing was perfect.

On the first touchdown drive, Kozar carried twice for 21 yards and then added the final 2 yards for the score. Tennessee power football was at its relentless best for the winning touchdown, which came with only a minute left.

With a first down at the Alabama 5, Kozar powered for 1 yard, Herky Payne picked up 3 more on a pair of runs, and then Kozar gained the final yard that produced the score. Tennessee's defense, facing a talented stable of backs performing for Coach Red Drew, had its hands full against such splendid Alabama players as Ed Salem and Bobby Marlow. But the defense made a statement on some devastating plays, including Tommy Jumper's crushing tackle of Salem on a punt return.

Alabama	3	0	6	0	9
Tennessee	0	7	0	7	14

UA   Lutz, field goal 9

UT   Kozar, run 2 (Shires kick)

UA   Marlow, run 43 (kick failed)

UT   Kozar, run 1 (Shires kick)

Ed Morgan Remembers

"I was a sophomore that year, playing behind Bert Rechichar. When you're a sophomore on a team with that much talent and you get to even play at all, you're lucky. The reverse was something we didn't do very often. I think we took Alabama by surprise.

"I was in there because I had good speed. I didn't know they were going to call the play until I got in there. Harvey Robinson was the coach who set up the call. The first time we ran it was a deep reverse. The tailback goes to the right, and the wingback comes by, takes the ball, and runs left.

Ed Morgan, extreme left, made key plays in 1950 as backup to Bert Rechichar at wingback.

"Herky Payne was the tailback, and Alabama players went after him, leaving me a pretty wide-open field. The second play was a close-in reverse, and I got some good blocking. The second-team backfield was in, but we had the first-team line. John Michels was in there, and so was Kaseta, who was an excellent blocker. Jim Haslam was in there at the time.

"We had come a long way from the Mississippi State game. We fell behind but didn't get down on ourselves. We felt we could come back and win. Hugh Faust, a good offensive coach, had scouted Alabama. He came up with a good plan. He put together plays just like Alabama would run them.

"Alabama was our biggest opponent, followed by Kentucky. Kentucky didn't have the tradition of Alabama. Andy Kozar was a good runner, who ran the plays exactly the way they were drawn up. We had a great pair of fullbacks, Kozar the better runner and Ernsberger the better blocker. Andy was a little stronger as a runner.

"I remember he was a great diver at the goal line. They worked on that hard in practice, diving into a sawdust pit, the tailbacks and fullbacks.

"I was glad I helped win the Alabama game because I had dropped a pass that would have tied the Mississippi State game that year. It was tipped by a defensive player, but I should have had it.

"After the game, General Neyland asked me if it had been tipped. I told him, 'Yes, but I should have had it.' He said, yeah, I should have, and that's all he ever said. It was catchable. That was the last game we lost for a long time.

"I came to UT from Hendersonville because I liked the mountain area. Knoxville was a lot like home. Those were happy years. It was great to play on such a talented team. After I graduated and went to the service, I came back and got another degree, in engineering. After a short stay at Champion Paper Company in North Carolina, I went to work for the space program down in Florida."

Vols 27, Washington & Lee 20

Coach Neyland used the word "goofy" to describe odds-makers who favored Tennessee by three touchdowns over Washington and Lee. The characterization proved prophetic when the Vols eked out a 27–20 victory over the visiting Generals.

The strength of Washington & Lee was borne out by game statistics that showed a whopping 19–8 first-down advantage for the Generals, who were led by a fleet of talented backs headed by quarterback Gil Bocetti. But it wasn't at all unusual for Tennessee to lose the statistics battle and win the war, which is what happened that October 26 afternoon.

Fortunately for the Vols, the game wasn't fought so much in the trenches as in the open field. The talents of Bert Rechichar and Jimmy Hahn, the less heralded of starting backs, were instrumental in allowing Tennessee to slip past W&L.

With 20,000 fans in attendance, the Vols scored their first touchdown as the gentlemen among spectators in the west stands were removing their fedoras just after the game started. Rechichar, playing safety and standing at his goal awaiting a punt, proceeded to knife his way through the entire Washington and Lee team for the game's first score.

Hahn, the blocking back, went 83 yards on a kickoff return, and Rechichar brought an interception back 50 yards for another touchdown. A more conventional tally came when Herky Payne darted into the end zone from the 5-yard line after taking a lateral from Bernie Sizemore.

Down 27–6, the Generals fought gamely, posting scores mostly in the final period behind the work of the talented Bocetti, who experienced some success against the Tennessee secondary. The Volunteers moved exclusively on the ground, throwing nothing but incompletions in three tries.

Newspaper accounts credited junior lineman Ted Daffer with playing the best game for Tennessee, decorating his dossier with two blocked punts. It was no wonder he garnered All-America honors as the season moved along. Neyland issued a five-word statement after the game: "I claim we were lucky."

Washington & Lee	0	6	0	14	20
Tennessee	7	20	0	0	27

UT	Rechichar, punt return 100 (Shires kick)
W&L	Michaels run 2 (kick failed)
UT	Hahn, kickoff return 83 (Shires kick)
UT	Payne, run 5 (Shires kick)
UT	Rechichar, interception return 50 (kick failed)
W&L	Leister, fumble recovery in end zone (Michaels kick)
W&L	Michaels, run 1 (Michaels kick)

Jim Haslam Remembers

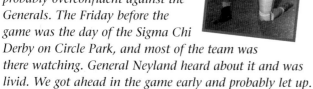

"Going into the Washington & Lee game, I remember we had beaten Alabama the week before and were probably overconfident against the Generals. The Friday before the game was the day of the Sigma Chi Derby on Circle Park, and most of the team was there watching. General Neyland heard about it and was livid. We got ahead in the game early and probably let up.

"We lost the statistics battle, but that was Tennessee football at its best: Play for and make the breaks. When one comes your way, score. Press the kicking game. It is here the breaks are made.

"As I remember it, one touchdown came on a kickoff return, and another on a punt return, and a third on an interception return.

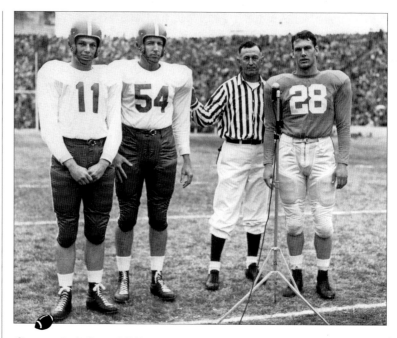

Captain Jack Stroud (28) represented the Vols at the coin toss setting the stage for the 1951 Cotton Bowl game.

"Gil Bocetti was a very good quarterback. It was the first time we ever saw a split T–option quarterback. They gave us a whole lot of trouble, and if you remember, Jack Scarbath of Maryland did the same thing to us in the Sugar Bowl. Bocetti was very adept at running the option, especially faking the pitchout and keeping the ball. He went up and down the field in the last quarter and enabled them to score twice and make a ball game of it.

"We did a little two-platooning in 1949, but in 1950 they changed the rule to allow unlimited substitutions, and General Neyland quickly went to the two-platoon system. There were a couple of people who played both ways, notably Jack Stroud at both offensive and defensive tackle, and Bert Rechichar at wingback and safety, but everyone else played either offense or defense.

"Harvey Robinson was the offensive coach, and Farmer Johnson was defensive coach. Some players liked two-platooning, and some didn't. Mainly, the backs and ends at the so-called skill positions would rather be carrying the ball and catching passes than making tackles. For the most part, it was popular with the team.

"We were really a close-knit bunch. We lived together in the stadium, and everyone liked everybody else. We didn't have cars, so we couldn't go anyplace. We were always together."

Vols 16, North Carolina 0

If you disregard a couple of short bursts for touchdowns by the ever-dependable Herky Payne, it was a pair of defensive gems that created lasting memories in UT's 16–0 victory over North Carolina.

A homecoming crowd of 38,000 withstood the cold November weather and watched Tennessee foil the revenge mapped out by Carl Snavely's Tar Heels for a loss suffered at the hands of the Vols the previous year in Chapel Hill.

Payne scored both UT touchdowns in the first half; each covered a yard and was set up by a fumble. A 33-yard drive in the first period provided the initial tally, highlighted by a pass from Hank Lauricella to John Gruble, a North Carolina native who had migrated to Tennessee.

The second score consumed a mere 7 yards, with Bud Sherrod's pounce on a Tar Heel bobble in the second quarter providing the opportunity. Three plays later, Payne bulled across.

One of the two aforementioned defensive gems in the third period set up the remainder of Tennessee's scoring. Bill (Pug) Pearman, another North Carolinian striving to make life miserable for his home state's bellwether university, was a general nuisance throughout the game. He reached his peak of annoyance when he knifed through the Tar Heel line and threw fullback Dick Weiss for a safety.

Hank Lauricella, who yielded offensive honors to Payne (two touchdowns) and Andy Kozar (138 yards' rushing), bailed out his fullback buddy Kozar with a masterful defensive play that saved a touchdown. As Kozar headed toward the goal, reaching the Carolina 8-yard line, the ball inexplicably popped from his grasp and into the hands of North Carolina's Dick Bunting.

With two blockers ahead of Bunting and only Lauricella in his path, a Tar Heel touchdown looked inevitable. But using both his brains and his instincts, Lauricella maneuvered himself into position for the tackle. By retreating a little at a time, he gave up some yardage but avoided a fatal step that would have allowed Bunting to get past him.

Snavely was more than willing to extol the Vols after the game. "That's a football team Tennessee had out there today," the self-effacing coach commented to the gathered reporters outside his dressing room. "Bob Neyland's boys hit like I like to see a team hit. Why, man, that's the best team we've played this year."

North Carolina	0	0	0	0	0
Tennessee	7	7	0	2	16

UT   Payne, run 1 (Shires kick)
UT   Payne, run 1 (Shires kick)
UT   Safety, Weiss tackled in end zone by Pearman

Gene Moeller Remembers

"I had a broken leg and missed the North Carolina game. They thought at first it was a bruise, but X-rays later showed it was a break. I remember a lot about the game, however, including

the big defensive play by Lauricella. He was smart, so instead of busting in on Bunting, he used his feet and his mind to make the touchdown-saving tackle.

"He had played some safety in 1949 and knew what to do. That season, people played both ways. There was a limit on how many substitutes you could make at a time. But by 1950, we had unlimited substitution, so Lauricella played only tailback.

"Carl Snavely was the coach at North Carolina, one of the most respected in the nation. His philosophy was very similar to Neyland's. He stressed fundamentals, much the way General Neyland did. He was one of the gentleman coaches of that era.

"Lauricella and Herky Payne shared the tailback duties in a very sensible way. Hank was often the tailback who had the responsibility of getting the ball from our 25 to the opponent's 15 or 20. Then Payne would often take over as the power runner. Herky also had a good arm and was sort of a side-arm passer.

"Herky was always a cutup, a guy with a great sense of humor. He liked to kid around. We had a similar situation at fullback, where Dick Ernsberger and Andy Kozar alternated. Andy was the straight-ahead power runner, and Ernsberger was maybe a little more nifty on his feet.

"We linebackers rotated with Gordon Polofsky, Bill Jasper, and me playing most of the time. Moose Barbish wasn't with us until the following season. They tried to keep somebody fresh in there as much as they could. The General's philosophy on linebacker play was to stay a couple of steps behind the runner as we ran parallel with the line of scrimmage. That way, if he made a cut, you were right there with him. Or, you could catch up with him if he turned upfield.

"Polofsky was a terrific guy. He was like me and most guys back then in that they didn't come from an affluent background. So we appreciated everything about getting a chance to come to the University of Tennessee. Gordon was a little older than I was, and he tried to help me all he could.

He would praise you when you did the right thing, and he would try to help you out every way he could.

"Jasper was another fantastic guy. He passed away a few years ago. He came back from mowing the lawn, sat down, and was gone, just like that.

"Our guys did everything together and built lasting friendships. It was all a team effort. We ate together, we prayed together in the dining hall, and we went to church together. We'd go over to Ellis and Ernest Drugstore, then we'd hitch a ride downtown to see a show and hitchhike back. There was nothing like the comradeship we had. I spent 22 years in the military and four-and-a-half years here, and the comradeship was more memorable here than it was in the Army.

"By the way, you didn't ask me about him, but Francis Holohan was a guy who didn't get as much credit as he deserved. Ted Daffer made All-America and was a great player, but Holohan at the other defensive guard spot took up the blockers, and that allowed Daffer to use his speed and quickness to go get the runner.

"The guys on the 1951 team were instrumental in building the Lettermen's Wall of Fame honoring all letter-winners, women and men, at UT. I remember being impressed by the Vietnam Memorial and thinking this would be a great thing to have at UT to honor all our letter-winners.

"After it was approved by UT, Gordon Polofsky and Pat Shires put in countless hours making it a reality. They spent months looking up addresses, calling people, and in general turning wherever they could to raise money. Bob Davis also helped tremendously. We are all very proud of the Wall, especially when somebody comes back to campus with their family and finds a name up there on the Wall. We especially wanted to honor those who came before us."

> "Our guys did everything together and built lasting friendships. . . . There was nothing like the comradeship we had."
>
> —Gene Moeller

Vols 48, Tennessee Tech 14

With three Southeastern Conference foes lying ahead, Tennessee used its game with Tennessee Tech to highlight some players who would help the Vols in the home stretch of the 1950 season. Clearing the bench, Coach Bob Neyland exhorted his troops to a 48–14 rout of the Golden Eagles.

Considering that the Vols tallied four first-quarter touchdowns, there wasn't much suspense in the match-up of the two Volunteer State universities. Before they returned to Cookeville, however, the Eagles treated the 10,000 spectators at Shields-Watkins Field to a host of "hocus-pocus" tricks, as a Knoxville newspaper referred to their wide-open brand of football.

After one period, it looked like the visitors might suffer a record-setting setback. The first indication of a blowout occurred only two minutes into the game when Hank Lauricella raced off right tackle 81 yards to put the Vols on top. By the time the second quarter got underway, Tennessee had rolled to a 27–0 advantage.

But here came Tech pounding back, a little too late to threaten the Vols, but nonetheless pleasing to the fans who had come to Knoxville from Putnam County to watch their team in action.

Phillip Webb was a gritty quarterback for the purple-clad players from Tennessee Tech (known then as Tennessee Poly or TPI). Twice he found Flavious Smith open in the end zone for touchdown passes, with both scores coming in the second period.

The UT lead was only 27–14 at halftime, but the Vols sealed the victory with two more touchdowns in the third period and one more in the fourth.

Neyland met his goal of giving his reserves some game-time experience, employing a total of 47 players by halftime.

Harold Johnson, the ball-holding part of the Pat Shires–Johnson placement combo, traded places with his favorite kicker and booted two of Tennessee's extra points in the mismatch. Ole Miss, Kentucky, and Vanderbilt lay ahead, three dangerous opponents for the vaunted Vols.

Tennessee Tech	0	14	0	0	14
Tennessee	27	0	14	7	48

UT   Lauricella, run 81 (kick failed)
UT   Kozar, run 3 (Shires kick)
UT   Carter, pass from Payne 23 (Shires kick)
UT   Carter, pass from Payne 45 (Johnson kick)
Tech Smith, pass from Webb 5 (Potter kick)
Tech Smith, pass from Webb 6 (Potter kick)
UT   Sherrod, return of blocked punt 30 (Shires kick)
UT   Kaseta, pass from Lauricella 32 (Shires kick)
UT   Shires, run 3 (Johnson kick)

Harold Johnson Remembers

"General Neyland for a game like Tennessee Tech allowed the regulars to play only long enough to make sure we were going to win. One of my favorite stories about him was that in a game like this one he told the team, 'If you don't go out there and assert your superiority, the SOBs will begin to think they are as good as you are.' I am not sure whether that was said before a ballgame or in the coaches' dressing room, but I remember it distinctly. What he meant was to get out there and kick hell out of them early. Let them know who they were playing and get it over with.

"He used games like Chattanooga and Tennessee Tech to get ready for other opponents, rather than to build up depth. The story is—fact or fiction—that when Alabama

The Vols arrive at their hotel following the flight from Knoxville to Dallas for the Cotton Bowl.

switched to the split-T formation, he called Chattanooga coach Scrappy Moore and told him he has a new offense. We didn't have these games to create depth because spring practice went from February to May, which gave the General plenty of time to find out who could play.

"Up until I came along, the kick holders and even the kickers were people who played other positions. They weren't specialists. But after my knee injury, General Neyland told me that I had been hurt playing for Tennessee, and my scholarship was as valid as anybody else's. So he let me help coach the freshmen one year, and he allowed me to hold for placements.

"General Neyland built up our opponents in the press, but I don't remember him doing that to us. He was always very realistic. I don't remember the General ever misleading his coaches or the team about what was to be expected. The lack of great emotion on game day was what I remember vividly. The General would just go over the game maxims while we lay there on those old mattresses, and then we would go out there and just do our jobs.

"But we were disciplined. I saw a picture of us sitting on the bench at the Cotton Bowl, all of us just sitting there with our helmets on. Somebody asked how we managed to sit there quietly instead of being up and shouting and carrying on. I told him it was simple: 'The General just told us to sit there.'

"I honestly felt that in 1950 and 1951 he thought Kentucky had better personnel than we did. But he felt we were going to win because we did a better job with the personnel we had."

Vols 35, Mississippi 0

Fearful of an Ole Miss running game that featured two of the nation's most explosive backs, Tennessee wouldn't be outdone when it came to advancing the ball on the ground, romping to a 35–0 victory.

Ole Miss's fabled combine of John (Kayo) Dottley and Showboat Boykin received an advanced education from such Vols as Hank Lauricella, Andy Kozar, Herky Payne, and Dick Ernsberger, whose combined running allowed the Vols to all but abandon their heralded passing attack.

The Rebels on defense were looking for the pass, installing an eight-man line designed to harass Lauricella into throwing interceptions. But the Vols moved smoothly overland, including contributions of 39 yards by Lauricella, 82 by Kozar, 24 by Payne, and 56 by Ernsberger. Payne and Kozar scored two touchdowns each, while Ernsberger chalked up the fifth.

Lined up like soldiers, the Vols await battle in the Cotton Bowl.

The 25,000 fans, mostly UT partisans, gave a respectful ovation to Dottley late in the game. They recognized him as one of the most courageous opponents ever to play on the Shields-Watkins turf, taking everything offered by Doug Atkins, Bill Pearman, Ted Daffer, Gordon Polofsky, and other members of the unyielding Tennessee defense.

Dottley carried 22 times for 79 yards, but it was a frustrating afternoon for the great Rebel battering ram, not only because his team lost but because he and Boykin were turned back when they had four downs to get the ball across from inside the Vols 5-yard line. That was as close as Ole Miss came to the goal line, despite its formidable offense.

Tennessee's third-quarter defensive stand was followed shortly by a 55-yard touchdown burst by Kozar, at which point, Neyland later told the press, he felt "rather secure."

The shutout validated the strength and resourcefulness of the UT defenders. Gordon Polofsky, junior linebacker, was credited with one Tennessee tackle that resounded so loudly it reverberated throughout the stadium.

According to one newspaper account, "Polofsky hit Dottley on the first play of the second quarter harder than the SEC's leading ground-gainer had been swatted all season. Dottley was slamming through guard and apparently headed for daylight. All at once Polofsky came after him like a hungry tiger after his prey. The crash made the crowd suck in its breath in awe."

Back in those days, you could hear the popping of leather all over the stadium. Acoustics weren't quite the problem later encountered when attendance figures reached 107,000.

Mississippi	0	0	0	0	0
Tennessee	14	0	7	14	35

UT   Payne run 2 (Shires kick)

UT   Kozar, run 4 (Shires kick)

UT   Kozar, run 55 (Shires kick)

UT   Morgan, pass from Payne 9 (Shires kick)

UT   Ernsberger, run 3 (Shires kick)

Andy Kozar Remembers

"John Dottley was such a tremendous athlete that General Neyland actually named some plays after him for scrimmage purposes by the defense. I'm not talking about the Mississippi game specifically. Certain kinds of runs other opponents used were called Dottley plays because Dottley was so dangerous.

"What a lot of people didn't realize was that Dottley played on defense as well as offense. He played almost the entire game. General Neyland went into this game fearful that it might be like the Mississippi State game we lost earlier in the season.

"He was afraid we wouldn't be ready because we had enjoyed some success leading up to it, but more important, he was afraid our minds would be on the Kentucky game coming up a week later. That's all the fans were talking about, the Kentucky game. What a match-up! And we hadn't even played Ole Miss yet.

"He was so worried about it that on Friday afternoon he had a practice session, the freshmen against the defensive unit. Normally our Friday practices were just walk-throughs, but not this time. He insisted on having one more practice because he was fearful of another Mississippi State.

"The goal-line stand was a matter of pride more than anything else. My run after that was just a matter of adding an insurance touchdown, which Neyland realized would give us a lead that would be very hard to overcome. He later apologized to Johnny Vaught, the Ole Miss coach, for the final score because he absolutely did not believe in running up the score.

"An unusual thing happened after that touchdown. I was sick that day and had taken Kaopectate, but my stomach was still a little upset. When I reached the end zone, I jumped over the fence and continued running right into our dressing room bathroom.

"When people say General Neyland practiced a play 500 times before he would use it in a game, they are talking about spring practice and fall practice for total number. We would take a play and run it and run it and run it. That wasn't for all plays, understand. But it was done for key plays, like the 10 play—the plays that required the most precision.

"This game was a shutout, but Neyland never made a great point of shutting anybody out. Statistics to him were immaterial. He knew you could use statistics and lie until you were blue in the face. Any of us could have run for 1,000 yards a season if it had mattered. But Neyland always had two or three backfields, and he didn't care as long as we won the game.

"We had Lauricella and Payne at tailback, Dick Ernsberger and me at fullback, Bert Rechichar and Ed Morgan at wingback, and Jimmy Hahn and Bernie Sizemore at blocking back. Neyland just kept moving people in and out of the game. His only goal was to win games. To him, starting meant nothing.

"The exceptions were some line positions. For instance, Bob Davis at center. He was unbelievable. And he had so

many different snaps to make in the single wing. He would put it exactly where you wanted it. Either in 1950 or 1951, Movietone News or one of the other newsreels named Bob as the All-America center. Bob was one of the greatest.

"One thing Neyland was really bothered by was people betting on games. Fans, I mean. He did everything in his power to keep the score from making the so-called line. He didn't want people betting on the Vols. I've seen times when he kicked the ball, and I am sure it was to keep people from winning their bets. Finally, people said, 'Don't ever bet on Tennessee.'

"Like in the Ole Miss game, if he could score a couple of touchdowns and then stop the opponent, he was happy with the score.

"Another thing: Neyland didn't really like the forward pass. He wanted to run the ball, partly because he thought passing carried too many risks. One of our ends, Tex Davis, said before he came to Tennessee, he asked one of the coaches how often Neyland passed. The coach told him about 30 or 40 times. Davis said he thought that meant 30 or 40 times a game, but what the coach really meant was 30 or 40 times a season.

"What I'll remember most about Neyland was that he taught us how to live. He was always a sea of calm. We would be nervous about how a game was going, or about anything else, and he was always the same. People who knew him say he could have been anything he wanted to be in the way of a career, and he chose coaching.

"That was the University of Tennessee's great good luck."

Vols 7, Kentucky 0

The national media descended in droves on Knoxville for the long-awaited Tennessee–Kentucky game. They departed Saturday night and Sunday suitably impressed with both squads after the Vols managed to pin a 7–0 defeat on the previously unbeaten Wildcats.

A clash of epic proportions—pitting coaching giants Bob Neyland and Bear Bryant as well as backfield stars Hank Lauricella and Babe Parilli—the game shared center stage with a snowstorm that racked the city Thanksgiving night. A sellout long before kickoff, the contest was played before 45,000 fans, with another 7,000 ticket holders unable to reach the stadium because of weather conditions that made driving hazardous throughout East Tennessee and Eastern Kentucky.

It took 100 workers, many of them UT student volunteers, to remove the snow from the tarpaulin, which had been put in place shortly before the first flakes began falling. The field was in perfect playing condition, but spectators had a tough time finding their seats in the snow-blanketed stadium.

Temperatures recorded at around 10 degrees took their toll, playing a huge role as both sides coughed up the ball in uncharacteristically large numbers. Kentucky had nine fumbles, almost equaled by the eight charged to Tennessee. Neyland couldn't believe the statistics.

"I can't remember a Tennessee team fumbling that much," he declared. "I'll tell you this much. It was one of the most vicious football games I ever saw. Brother, those boys were really crackin' out there, and I mean both teams. You don't see a game like that very often."

Tennessee's defense was stupendous, forcing Parilli to run for dear life and holding the Kentucky running game to 36 yards. Ted Daffer, Roy Smith, Bill Pearman, Doug Atkins, and Bud Sherrod were all credited with contributing to UT's stifling defense.

From a scoring standpoint, one play in the second quarter decided the outcome. Hank Lauricella threaded a 28-yard completion to Bert Rechichar in the north end zone for the game's only touchdown, followed by Pat Shires's

The 1950 Kentucky game was a classic, which the Vols won, 7–0, in bitter cold.

1950

T

extra-point kick. That was all it took as the Tennessee defense carried the day for the final two quarters.

The classic meeting of the two top teams from the Southeastern Conference created a crisis situation for the bowl sponsors, all of whom wanted to sign up the Vols and Wildcats. The Vols had already picked the Cotton Bowl to meet Texas. Shortly after the Tennessee game, the Sugar Bowl selected Kentucky as the opponent for Oklahoma.

Kentucky	0	0	0	0	0
Tennessee	0	7	0	0	7

UT   Rechichar, pass from Lauricella 28 (Shires kick)

Bert Rechichar Remembers

"I'll tell you what. Babe Parilli wasn't a bad quarterback. He had potential to be a great quarterback, but he had a little handicap in his speech, and he couldn't check off like he needed to. But he was a nice guy, and I respect him. The only thing about him, he never scored against Tennessee in three years.

"He was a great quarterback. He played for Green Bay mainly. We had Kentucky's ticket when Bear Bryant was there. Bryant already had a good reputation. The General wouldn't trust him one iota. He'd have somebody stationed down at the river field looking around to see if he had somebody scouting on us.

"He sent Gus Manning up there on the boondocks up on the hill with his spy glass to make sure Bryant wasn't scouting us. They didn't have anybody spying on us. I told the General one day you're wasting your time looking for spies. We'll take care of Kentucky and Bear Bryant.

"The touchdown was in the second quarter. It was cold that day. Lauricella threw out of that 71 pattern we had. John Gruble was in front of me, and I thought he was going to catch it. But I looked up at the ball coming our way, and I said, 'I'll take that, John.'

"I think it was intended for Gruble. I was about 7 yards behind John. He reached up to catch it, but I let him know I had it. I'd like to take a look at it on film someday.

"It was about seven degrees that day. Your fingers froze in the pregame warm-ups. We looked like the pros coming out there. Neyland had us wearing those black stockings. You had some stick-em you place on your hands, but we didn't wear gloves. It was cold.

"My mother and brothers came down for the game from Pennsylvania. A man came along and heated up some bricks that he took up to my mother to help keep her feet warm. They got here before the snow, but it took them 24 hours to get home. There was about four feet of snow in Pennsylvania.

"We felt we could win the game, but it was a matter of getting in there and scoring. There were a whole bunch of fumbles that day.

"Kentucky had a damn good team. They had Dopey Phelps as a runner. And Parilli. And Bob Gain. There was nothing short about Kentucky. That was a big game for us. I had the opportunity to play wingback and safety. I played 60 minutes that day. But I didn't mind. I enjoyed it.

"We had a great game plan that was unaffected by the weather. Everything went smooth, but the worry was when we were going to score. Lauricella was a fine player. It was a good game, a classic, and everybody in Tennessee was happy."

Vols 43, Vanderbilt 0

With a Cotton Bowl invitation crammed in their pockets, the Volunteers traveled to Nashville and stormed past Vanderbilt, 43–0, a whitewashing that seemed unimaginable in

Jimmy Hill, seen here fending off a tackler, joined J. W. Sherill as a ball-hawking defensive back in 1950.

light of the Commodores' much-hyped passing combine of Bill Wade–to–Bucky Curtis.

Rather than allow the Vanderbilt aerial team to nibble away at their defenses, the Vols boldly chose to shun the soft approach and go pell-mell for interceptions. Altogether, four of Wade's passes landed in the hands of UT defenders, a fortuitous situation that rendered the Wade-Curtis tandem ineffective.

Even if the Vanderbilt passing game had clicked, there wasn't any way the home team could have offset the Vols' ferocious offense, most of which happened on the ground.

Herky Payne, Hank Lauricella, Andy Kozar, and Dick Ernsberger zipped through holes created by a powerful line that destroyed the Commodores' defense.

In fairness, however, it was the third period before Tennessee could work its will on a consistent basis against the Vandy front. UT's halftime advantage was a mere 10–0, the result of a touchdown pass by Lauricella to Vince Kaseta for 27 yards and a field goal by Shires.

Increasing the lead were Payne's 26-yard run, Payne's pass to Bernie Sizemore for 8 yards, Payne's 2-yard blast, and a pair of touchdowns by Basil Drake. A fullback who had escaped notice for much of the season, Drake enjoyed his coming-out party at Dudley Field.

Led by the resolute Jack Stroud, later to become All-Pro, the UT line made it relatively easy for Lauricella and Company to thread through the Commodores. Losing coach Bill Edwards was suitably impressed. "Tennessee has a very fine football team," he observed. "It has depth and power, and those boys block and tackle."

Weather conditions were far from ideal, including wind that was a big factor in the Commodores' paltry 17.5-yard punting average. But it didn't affect the ground game, an area in which Tennessee piled up impressive yardage led by Kozar's 74 yards and Payne's 72.

Tennessee	7	3	13	20	43
Vanderbilt	0	0	0	0	0

UT   Kaseta, pass from Lauricella 27 (Shires kick)
UT   Shires, field goal 27
UT   Payne, run 16 (kick failed)
UT   Sizemore, pass from Payne 8 (Shires kick)
UT   Payne, run 5 (Shires kick)
UT   Drake, run 2 (kick blocked)
UT   Drake, run 1 (Shires kick)

Dick Ernsberger Remembers

"This game was sort of the kickoff for the 1951 national championship because it seemed like everything came together then, both offense and defense. We were still trying to prove ourselves to some extent. We had lost that game to Mississippi State early in the year, which made us realize we had work to do. So we had to start over and get it back together.

Bill Dyer's cartoon in the *Knoxville News Sentinel* saluted Vols defensive backfield star Jimmy Hill.

"Even after the big Kentucky game, we didn't have any trouble getting up for Vanderbilt. There were several factors involved. For one thing, Vanderbilt had a good season. They went 7–4 that year. Of course, Vanderbilt always wanted to beat Tennessee. They were always the underdogs.

"We had already accepted the Cotton Bowl invitation, and we didn't want to go into the bowl coming off a loss to Vanderbilt. They had a topnotch quarterback in Bill Wade and an excellent receiver in Bucky Curtis. But we had gone up against Babe Parilli of Kentucky the previous week, and we were prepared for facing good quarterbacks.

"General Neyland didn't like the passing game on the basis of too many bad things can happen when you put the ball in the air. He always felt that we were at an advantage any time we played a team that passed a lot. He didn't like the passing game. If he hadn't thought it was bad, he would have put more passing into his offense.

"We had three guys back there in the secondary— J. W. Sherrill, Jimmy Hill, and Bert Rechichar—who were

about as good as you could ever ask for. The General felt that when the ball was in the air, it belonged to us. I think Sherrill had something like 10 career interceptions, which is an amazing statistic considering the passing game was just starting to really come into its own in college football.

"Tennessee hadn't been to a bowl since 1946, so we were very excited about getting to go to the Cotton Bowl. The General just told us we were going to the Cotton Bowl to play Texas. But Texas was a good team to meet in a bowl because Texas was ranked third, and we were fourth.

"Vanderbilt was a good team, not what you would call an outstanding team, but still a good team. They scored a lot

of points and were hard to handle, but we had a good game that day, partly because we had a lot of incentive, wanting to win the game that would carry us over to the bowl game."

Vols 20, Texas 14 (Cotton Bowl)

Outweighed 25 pounds a man in the line but never out-gamed, Tennessee drove for a pair of fourth-quarter touchdowns to defeat Texas in the Cotton Bowl, 20–14, and set the stage for a consensus national championship in 1951.

After the Cotton Bowl, the Vols celebrate in the dressing room with Head Coach Bob Neyland, right.

Decided underdogs against the hefty Longhorns, the Vols staged a comeback from a 14–7 deficit that many old-timers vow to this day provided the most thrilling victory in school history. Ironically, a missed extra point by the usually reliable Pat Shires may have tipped the scales in Tennessee's favor.

When Shires misdirected the kick after the Vols' second touchdown, leaving the score at 14–13 in Texas's favor, Coach Bob Neyland buttonholed the crestfallen West Virginian as he returned to the bench. "Son, don't worry," he said. "We didn't come out here to tie."

Strange as it may seem, Texas blamed the flawed kick for its eventual demise. "When we had that one-point lead, we played too conservatively," a Longhorn assistant said, suggesting with some degree of logic that his team was guilty of sitting on the lead rather than taking risks to expand its advantage.

A one-touchdown underdog, based largely on a weight chart showing a gaping size deficit, the Vols proved that Goliath-like dimensions aren't a necessary adjunct of championship football. The visitors drew first blood and last in the widely ballyhooed intersectional match-up.

Hank Lauricella, aided no little by picture-perfect blocking, made a beautiful 75-yard run in the first quarter to break up the uneasy sparring that marked the early stages of the contest. Winded, Lauricella went to the sidelines, yielding his place to teammate Herky Payne, whose pass to end John Gruble covered the remaining 5 yards. Shires's point-after split the goalpost.

After Texas scored twice in the second quarter to lead by 14–7 at halftime, the Vols came back to score two hard-earned touchdowns in the final quarter. Andy Kozar, who accounted for 52 of the first drive's 83 yards, surged across from the 5, at which point Shires's crucial missed kick took place.

Jimmy (Cowboy) Hill, a brilliant defensive back from Maryville, Tennessee, had to make two key plays to set up the final opportunity. After the Vols kicked away a good scoring chance when Hill intercepted a pass and returned it to the Texas 46, Cowboy came through again by recovering a fumble at the Longhorn 43.

This time there was a payoff. Kozar picked up 6 yards, Lauricella's pass to Bert Rechichar netted 23, Kozar got 1, and Lauricella gained 11. From the 2-yard line, Kozar scored over left tackle, and Shires added the extra point.

Still, Texas wouldn't quit, scaring UT fans out of their wits by unleashing a passing attack that carried to the Tennessee 16 before the drive ran out of steam.

Tennessee	**7**	**0**	**0**	**13**	**20**
Texas	**0**	**14**	**0**	**0**	**14**

UT	Gruble, pass from Payne 4 (Shires kick)
Texas	Townsend, run 5 (Tompkins, kick)
Texas	Dawson, pass from Tompkins 34 (Tompkins kick)
UT	Kozar, run 5 (kick failed)
UT	Kozar, run 2 (Shires kick)

Hank Lauricella Remembers

"The whole time I was at Tennessee, I don't believe the General expressed himself as much before or after a game as he did this one. The General is so revered, I hate to use any slang talk by him.

"Going into the game, he told us, 'We are going against a team that is bigger than we are. Their size and strength may find us trailing at halftime. But we are faster and *better conditioned. So don't be disappointed if we are trailing at halftime.'*

"Then with all the noise going on before the game, the Texas band marches past our locker room, and they are playing 'The Eyes of Texas Are Upon You.' And Neyland says to us, 'When this game is over, they'll be playing "The Tennessee Waltz."'

"At halftime I don't remember exactly what he said, but it was to the effect, 'I told you about what the score might be like at halftime.'

"On the 11-yard run I had, leading to Kozar's touch-down, I took my three steps to the left, and I put my hand on John Michels' uniform after he had pulled, and I literally just followed him down the field.

> "When the game ended, I never saw such joy and exhilaration. This was the only time I remember the General talking to us after the game the way he did after this one."
>
> —Hank Lauricella

"On the 75-yard run, Kozar and Hahn were the lead blockers on the end. They were able to fake as if I was going outside. As I turned upfield, it was a perfectly blocked play. A Tennessee man was in pursuit of every Texas defender. I was so anxious to run, I kind of lost my footing, or else I would have scored. Some of our guys made more than one block during that play. It was almost a perfectly executed play, other than my losing my footing and having to rely to some extent on instinct. There was a great picture that showed how good the run was.

"Herky Payne, of course, threw the touchdown pass on fourth down.

"When the game ended, I never saw such joy and exhilaration. This was the only time I remember the General talking to us after the game the way he did after this one. The General turned to us, and said, 'I love every one of you sons of bitches for what you did.' I hope that quote isn't demeaning to him at all. He was just that exhilarated. Normally, he'd just walk around and make comments to individuals.

"That game brought more joy to the team than any other. The Athletic Department arranged us a little party that night. I never saw such happiness. Have you ever seen Gordon Polofsky with tears in his eyes? He had tears in his eyes that night, crying.

"If the voting had been done after the bowls, we would have been first because Kentucky beat the number-one team, Oklahoma, in the Sugar Bowl. That's the game our bunch always remembers, the bowl win over Texas.

"We had the two-platoon system going good in 1950, but 1949 was the first year of it. So we all practiced at one offensive position and one defensive position because we didn't know how well the two-platoon deal would work out."

1950 National Review

Notre Dame began the season as the number-one team in the nation. And why not? The Fighting Irish of Coach Frank Leahy had gone 38 straight games without a loss and had been a nearly unanimous choice for the 1949 national title.

But the new season developed into a disaster as the men from South Bend couldn't maintain the pace of their recent predecessors. The Fighting Irish's Waterloo came in only the second game of the season when archrival Purdue beat them, 28–14.

Before the year was over, Indiana, Michigan State, and Southern California had also overcome Notre Dame, which ended the season with a surprisingly poor 4–4–1 record. All of the losses were close, but the cumulative effect was that Notre Dame dropped out of the top 20 altogether.

Bud Wilkinson's Oklahoma Sooners won the AP vote as national champion, but in that era the final vote was taken before the bowl games. Otherwise, the Sooners would have been dislodged on the basis of a 13–7 Sugar Bowl defeat at the hands of Kentucky.

Oklahoma had roared through the regular season unbeaten, running its winning streak to 31 before bowing to Paul Bryant's Wildcats. Three Sooners to land Hall of Fame enshrinement were coach Wilkinson, halfback Billy Vessels, and tackle Jim Weatherall.

Another outstanding team in 1950 was Army, which under Coach Earl (Red) Blaik ran its undefeated string to 28 games. The average score per game was 33–3, but all that meant nothing to Navy going into the annual match-up between the service academies at the close of the season. The Midshipmen built a 14–0 halftime advantage and hung on for a 14–2 victory.

With Army losing at the end of the year and Oklahoma being defeated in the Sugar Bowl, it was widely agreed that Tennessee's 20–14 win over Texas in the Cotton Bowl would have vaulted the Vols into the number-one position if a post-bowl vote had been conducted.

The Vols had learned one indelible lesson: If you must lose a game, do it early and get it out of the way. UT's one defeat in 1950 came in the second game of the season, against Mississippi State, giving voters plenty of time to forget about it.

The 1951 Vols

Chapter 4

1951

*T*he victory over Texas was what did it, vaulting Tennessee to the top of the preseason rankings for 1951 and putting the Vols into the national championship picture as the team to beat.

And why wouldn't the Vols be favored? Everything pointed to their dominance after they edged Texas 20–14 by coming back from a 14–7 deficit. The way Hank Lauricella and Andy Kozar pounded the Longhorns defense in the final quarter left the impression the Vols won the game going away.

The Cotton Bowl triumph finally silenced once and for all the doubters who had said that while Neyland had once been a great coach, a Hall of Famer to be sure, he was a man lost in the wake of two-platoon football, the T formation, and numerous other innovations thought to be the wave of the future.

But now the 1951 season was at hand. Although Tennessee's losses were slim, the impact could be immense with the departure of offensive lineman Jack Stroud, defensive end Bud Sherrod, and secondary stars Jimmy Hill and J. W. Sherrill.

The 1951 coaching staff. Seated, from left, are Al Hust, Harvey Robinson, Bob Neyland, L. B. (Farmer) Johnson, and Ike Peel. Standing, from left, are Ralph Chancey, Chan Caldwell, Hodges (Burr) West, Mickey O'Brien, John Sines, and Emmett Lowery.

1951 SCHEDULE

UT 14	Mississippi State 0	Knoxville
UT 26	Duke 0	Knoxville
UT 42	Chattanooga 13	Knoxville
UT 27	Alabama 13	Birmingham
UT 68	Tennessee Tech 0	Knoxville
UT 27	North Carolina 0	Chapel Hill
UT 60	Washington & Lee 14	Knoxville
UT 46	Mississippi 21	Oxford
UT 28	Kentucky 0	Lexington
UT 35	Vanderbilt 27	Knoxville
UT 13	Maryland 28 (Sugar Bowl)	New Orleans

wart captain. Up front, the Vols would have John Michels, Bill Pearman, Doug Atkins, Jim Haslam, Ted Daffer, Bob Davis, and a host of other seasoned veterans.

Fed by the 1950 win over Kentucky and the improbable defeat of Texas, optimism, enthusiasm, and expectation had never been more evident in the history of Tennessee football.

Vols 14, Mississippi State 0

By going head-to-head with the one team to trim them in 1950, the Volunteers hoped to expurgate the only foul memory of a season in which they had slowly built momentum to

It was correctly assumed that those all star–caliber players would be missed, but the cast of returnees was so impressive that football predictors from coast to coast agreed that Tennessee's reservoir of talent, combined with Neyland's coaching genius, would pave the way for a championship season in Knoxville.

Lauricella and Kozar, the one-two offensive punch that blew away Texas, would return along with their backups, Herky Payne and Dick Ernsberger, respectively. Bert Rechichar would be there to serve as the stal-

The national championship backfield of 1951 included, from left, wingback Bert Rechichar, fullback Andy Kozar, tailback Hank Lauricella, and blocking back Jimmy Hahn.

1951
T

the point that a post-bowl analysis would have ranked them best in the nation.

Scarcely a thing of beauty, however, the Tennessee victory over Mississippi State was tied to their opponents' mistakes in the opening period, both of which led to touchdowns. From that point, the game was essentially a standoff in which the UT defense played well enough to thwart the Bulldogs' offensive plans.

Mississippi State coach Arthur (Slick) Morton's pregame comment that his team's chances depended on avoiding any grievous mistakes was prophetic. State appeared a little jittery on the opening kickoff, fumbling and consequently starting from its own 20.

Two plays into the game, Norman Duplain fumbled the ball into the hands of UT's Roger Rotroff, who made the recovery at the State 35. The bobble completed quite a turnaround for Duplain, who had been a hero of State's 7–0 victory in 1950. A 17-yard scoring pass from Hank Lauricella to Vince Kaseta, streaking across the goal at full speed, accounted for the opening touchdown.

A short time later, the second score developed, again involving a major mistake by the visitors. Ted Daffer blocked a punt, which was scooped up by hard-charging linebacker Gene Moeller at the State 18. Again the Vols turned opportunists with fullback Andy Kozar doing the honors in two plays.

First, the big Pennsylvania-born running back found a sliver of daylight that moved the ball to the 2-yard line. As the sportswriters quipped, there was no stopping Kozar once the smell of the goal line was within his range. He drove across for the second, and last, touchdown of the day.

Captain and wingback Bert Rechichar kicked both extra points, which in the post-game analysis probably didn't do much to offset the sorrow he felt when his nifty 73-yard

punt return, also in the first period, was nullified. As Rechichar exploded toward the sidelines, an official detected a clip and brought the ball back. Bob Wilson, covering the game for the *Knoxville News-Sentinel*, reported that Rechichar had already reached the open field when the needless infraction occurred.

At that point, the UT offense went into a swoon, a lapse fortunately not shared by the defense. The Bulldogs got past the 50-yard line only three times and never penetrated beyond the Tennessee 40.

Mississippi State	0	0	0	0	0
Tennessee	14	0	0	0	14

UT   Kaseta, pass from Lauricella 17 (Rechichar kick)
UT   Kozar, run (Rechichar kick)

Jimmy Hahn Remembers

"I don't feel our 7–0 loss to Mississippi State in 1950 caused us to play any harder when we met State again the following season. We knew this time we had the home advantage and that we were a much better team than had played at Starkville in 1950.

"All these years I've never heard mentioned some of the important changes General Neyland introduced to our offensive system after the Mississippi State game. During that week of the Duke game, down on the river field, with heavy security in place against unwanted observers, even across the river and up the high banks, our offensive team spent hours working on what was called the buck-lateral series.

"I had seen in movie newsreels of that period Michigan State using the buck-lateral series very effectively. So I knew what was coming when it was introduced to us. The procedure

was for our center, Bob Davis, to snap the ball directly to the fullback. I as blocking back hopped around with my back to the line of scrimmage.

"The fullback then rushed by me on his way to the hole with the option of handing me the ball, depending on what play had been called in the huddle. I could then run with the ball or lateral it to our tailback, either Hank Lauricella or Herky Payne, running wide. Then they would either run the ball or pass.

"The following Saturday against Duke we used this series for just a few plays. We won the game, 28–7, and then used the buck lateral the rest of the 1950 season just occasionally. Against Texas in the Cotton Bowl it really paid off. I would say we used it that day on about every third play. I believe even as blocking back I got enough yardage that the sticks were moved for first downs on four carries. They were third- or fourth-down situations. It helped allow Andy Kozar to have a really great game against the Longhorns.

"In the 1951 season we used it quite a bit, trying to mix things up. So I thought we would beat Mississippi State, but I thought it would be by a more decisive score than 14–0.

"We were preseason number one in 1951, but I think our team was wondering if we were really that good. Sure, we had some important victories in 1950 over high-ranked teams like Alabama, Kentucky, and Texas. But we also knew those games were close. At the start of 1951 we were soberly hopeful we could win all our games, but we were far from feeling invincible.

"I remember General Neyland telling us that we should disregard any news articles about our being ranked number one. He didn't want us to pay any attention to such talk.

"One of the General's maxims that he reviewed on the chalkboard before every game was, 'Play for and make the breaks, and when one comes your way, score.' That meant blocked kicks, interceptions, fumbles, and the like. As I remember, we got a number of breaks and scored off two of them in the first quarter.

"We had other breaks as the game went along, but we didn't capitalize. With all those opportunities, we didn't get any more points. So there were times when we didn't carry out all the General's aspirations. We were supposed to, but we didn't always do it.

"As a punt returner, Billy Blackstock wasn't real fast, but he didn't mess up catching it. There is a knack to running the ball in getting past the second and third tacklers. Blackstock was very good at that.

"Bert Rechichar's contribution to our success in 1951 was tremendous. Somehow he seemed more mature than the rest of us, but he wasn't really. He was a man of few words but a man of performance and action. He was one of the few men the General would play constantly—on offense or defense—when the pressure was on.

"Bert had a long stride with good balance. He was our team captain and had every player's complete loyalty and support, not only because of his ability as a football player but because of his unassuming, laid-back, humble demeanor and personality. He would never accept any credit for the success of that team even though he was a major contributor. We would not have been national champion without him.

"General Neyland always emphasized in squad or other group meetings that our team didn't have individual stars, that we were all stars, and that we were a team. I really think he was trying to train us to become future coaches.

"In that Mississippi State game, I don't feel we had developed full confidence in our running game like we did later. In other games, I think we did feel that we were invincible and couldn't be stopped. I think the General decided after we took the early lead to play conservatively, partly because we had a good defense. I think he settled for a low-key win. His objective

> "General Neyland always emphasized in squad or other group meetings that our team didn't have individual stars, that we were all stars, and that we were a team."
>
> —Jimmy Hahn

was to win, never to roll up the score. With good punting and a superior defense, he challenged opponents to drive the length of the field and score.

"Hank Lauricella was very valuable in helping us have good field position. When our bus got to the practice field during the season, Hank would already be out there working on his punts. He would stand at midfield and practice punting the ball out of bounds near the corner of the end zone. He developed great accuracy and also practiced quick-kicking.

"He quick-kicked one time from inside our 30 in the State game, and the ball died at about the 1-foot line. The rest of the game was played on Mississippi State's side of the field. This helped the General win games. Our coverage team still holds NCAA records for covering punts and keeping the opponents way down the field."

tory of the young season. Murray's forces had disposed of South Carolina in a previous game.

Tennessee was also unbeaten, but Coach Neyland anticipated that "our boys might be in for a real letdown." Whatever letdown might have occurred must have been left in the dressing room as the Vols capitalized on a Duke fumble to set up a score before the end of the first period.

After the ubiquitous Gene Moeller snatched a fumble in midair and gave UT possession at the Duke 48, the offense turned it over to Hank Lauricella for the final 29 yards. The dazzling All-America from New Orleans crashed through left guard and scampered across the goal line untouched. The only Blue Devil with a shot at him was obliterated by Vince Keseta's shattering block.

Vols 26, Duke 0

With coaches of both teams bemoaning their prospects and seeing their chances at victory somewhere between slim and none, the South's top early-season showdown was settled decisively in Tennessee's favor, 26–0, over Duke.

Leading sportswriters from every daily in North Carolina were on hand at Shields-Watkins Field as Duke coach Bill Murray and his Blue Devils sought their third vic-

The Duke Blue Devils were victims of the Vols' single-wing formation and 6-2-2-1 defense in both 1950 and 1951.

Duke then allowed Bert Rechichar's ensuing short kickoff to bounce around as a free ball, which the Vols' John Michels recovered. This time, second-team tailback Herky Payne was at the controls, sending the team downfield to the one, at which point Dick Ernsberger carried it across.

Evenly dividing its touchdowns between the first two quarters, Tennessee scored again in each of the final two segments. Bert Rechichar made both scores possible with scintillating punt returns into the Blue Devils' territory.

Moeller was labeled ubiquitous for good reason. The backup junior linebacker recovered two fumbles and intercepted two passes, earning him the *Knoxville News-Sentinel*'s designation as the top defensive player for the Vols. With those kinds of statistics, no one could deny that the Iowa farm boy was the star of the game.

Two Knoxville High School alums, backs Ray Byrd and Billy (Bye Bye) Blackstock, contributed to Tennessee's display of depth, playing behind first- and second-teamers Lauricella, Payne, Ernsberger, and Andy Kozar. Lauricella led all runners with 90 yards, but Byrd edged out the others with 49 yards on eight carries.

Tennessee might have been even more dominant had their overeagerness not drawn 10 penalties. On the other hand, the Blue Devils committed an equal number of infractions. The result was a game in which sloppy play marred an otherwise classic match-up.

Duke	0	0	0	0	0
Tennessee	**7**	**6**	**7**	**6**	**26**

UT   Lauricella, run 29 (Rechichar kick)

UT   Ernsberger, run 1 (kick failed)

UT   Payne, run 4 (Rechichar kick)

UT   Alexander, pass from Payne 17 (kick failed)

Mack Franklin Remembers

"At the time of the Duke game, I was a sophomore playing as a regular with the special teams and backing up Roger Rotroff at defensive end. Duke was a top opponent. The Vols–Duke series was pretty close to even at that time, Tennessee with a slight edge but Duke very competitive. The Blue Devils were always a good team, and Coach Bill Murray invariably had them ready.

"We went into the 1951 season with confidence we would have a good team. Defensively, we expected to be strong, but we didn't foresee holding a team like Duke scoreless. Eventually, we had five shutouts that season, and we were very pleased with that.

"Duke was a real challenge, a consistently strong football program, but we had a good blocking team that season and managed to move the football. I feel like I was something of an expert on our blocking, even though I was with the defensive team. The previous year, as a freshman, I practiced against our offense. Jimmy Hahn and Dick Ernsberger were probably the two best kick-out blockers in the United States. That was the old 10 play where they came out and double-teamed me.

"Of course, you had other great blockers like John Michels and Bert Rechichar and Vince Kaseta. General Neyland emphasized blocking and would run a play 100 times before he thought the team was ready to use it in a game.

"Gene Moeller had a tremendous day. He was at the right spot at the right time. He was kind of a laid-back guy, but extremely competitive. Two interceptions and two fumble recoveries, that would be a season's production for most people.

"We had too many penalties, but the General didn't mind them too much if they were caused by aggressiveness. What bothered him was for penalties to be caused by lack of

concentration or lack of alertness. He didn't want mental mistakes. Most of our talking came from Farmer Johnson, who headed up the defense. You knew if you had to talk to General Neyland, you were in trouble.

"Bert Rechichar was the best athlete on the 1951 squad. He did it all—he returned punts and kickoffs, he kicked extra points and field goals, he kicked off, he ran the ball, and caught passes and was a good blocker. And he did them all well. Bert was all business on the football field. He didn't make the All-America teams, but as far as I'm concerned, he was the workhorse.

"It was a privilege and a thrill for me to be part of such a great team."

Vols 42, Chattanooga 13

As all hands agreed, the Volunteers' 1951 performance against Chattanooga was uninspired. Still, it was enough to move them past the Moccasins, 42–13, despite heroic play by Chattanooga quarterback Hal Ledyard.

Jimmy Wade, playing his first game for Tennessee as a third-team safety, helped to keep the Vols on top with a pair of spectacular fourth-quarter touchdowns on an intercepted pass and a punt return.

But it was Ledyard's passing wizardry that stole the show for most of the afternoon. A Chattanooga native, he represented his hometown well against the deeper Tennessee squad, connecting on passes that set up both of his team's touchdowns.

Tennessee coach Bob Neyland went all out in his praise of the rubber-armed Ledyard, whom he described as tops among T-formation quarterbacks he had seen. "His passing was superb, and his running effective," Neyland said. "His poise and selection of plays were excellent."

On the other hand, newspaper accounts indicated that the Vols hardly excelled in any phase of play. Blocking was below par, tackling was less than vicious, and the defense was fooled repeatedly by Ledyard's deft ball-handling.

For three quarters, Tennessee defenders were at Ledyard's mercy, coughing up ground in impressive chunks. But then, in the final period, Joe Maiure and Wade got the bead on Ledyard's bullet-like passes and made the Vols' first two interceptions of the season.

Andy Kozar had two touchdowns for Tennessee, while John Davis and Herky Payne scored one each before Wade took over. The first of Jimmy's two scores covered 34 yards on an interception. The second was a punt return for 54 yards.

Only 15,000 spectators showed up at Shields-Watkins Field to see the Vols take on the team of Coach A. C. (Scrappy) Moore, who did an outstanding job of preparing the Mocs for battle. One area in which Tennessee appeared to have improved was passing, with nine completions in 12 tries for 149 yards.

Chattanooga scored one touchdown each in the second and third periods. Both came on the ground but were set up by Ledyard's passing.

Chattanooga	0	7	6	0	13
Tennessee	14	7	7	14	42

UT	Kozar, run 1 (Kolenik kick)
UT	Kozar, run 2 (Kolenik kick)
C	Dukes, run 1 (Medich kick)
UT	T. Davis, pass from Lauricella 34 (Kolenik kick)
C	Hostetler, run 7 (kick failed)
UT	Payne, run 6 (Kolenik kick)
UT	Wade, interception return 34 (Kolenik kick)
UT	Wade, punt return 54 (Kolenik kick)

1951

"Jimmy Wade had been on the scout team and hadn't played in the first two games of his freshman season. He told Coach Harvey Robinson that if he didn't play against Chattanooga he was going to transfer. So they played him, thank goodness, and Jimmy turned out to be one of the best tailbacks who ever played for Tennessee. He wouldn't have been in there against Chattanooga, otherwise. All Jimmy did was intercept a pass and return it for a touchdown and return a punt for a touchdown.

"Hal Ledyard was the only quarterback I ever saw General Neyland go onto the field after the game and shake an opponent's hand. We were playing a three-deep zone, and Ledyard just kept putting it out there and completing passes. He had a great ball game against us. He stole the show.

"Neyland praised our opponents before and after the game. Before a game, you would have thought we were playing the New York Yankees, no matter who we were playing—Chattanooga, TPI, or anybody else.

"Neyland and Scrappy Moore were big buddies. Chattanooga was great for getting us ready to play Alabama. Chattanooga had good football players, a good head coach, and a good line coach in Andy Nardo. Scrappy got more out of less than anybody I know. They were well coached, and he had a good offensive mind. He would give you problems.

"In that game we fumbled five times. We rushed for 103 yards. Chattanooga got penalized 105 yards. They might have beaten us if they hadn't been penalized that much. Obviously, we had a letdown after the Duke game.

"We didn't give a lot of thought to being ranked first. The General told us not to read our newspaper clippings. Apparently, Chattanooga hadn't read our clippings either, because they gave us all we could handle."

Vols 27, Alabama 13

The Alabama-Tennessee series is a giant attraction at any time—whether in those years when both teams are powerhouses, or when one is riding the crest and the other is down on its luck.

In 1951, packed stands awaited the October 20 confrontation at Birmingham's Legion Field. Tickets were hard to come by, despite the disparity in the opponents' season records: Tennessee came to town as a contender for the national championship, while the Crimson Tide had been beaten three times already.

Hank Lauricella emerged as the star of stars, taking his place with fabled Tennessee tailbacks of other Neyland-coached teams. Running, passing, and punting, he fired the Vols to a 27–13 conquest of a revved-up Alabama squad that refused to go quietly.

In the aftermath of the blood battle between the two Southeastern Conference stalwarts, it was neither a run nor a pass that decided the contest for Tennessee. It was a punt—a quick kick, to be specific—that did in the Red Elephants.

Alabama had pulled into a 7–7 tie and stunned the Vols with a drive that carried to the UT 17. Linebacker Gordon Polofsky met Tide halfback Bobby Marlow head-on, knocked the ball loose, and grabbed the fumble. Two plays later, Lauricella's quick kick died at the Alabama four.

And that was the ballgame. Tennessee scored two touchdowns before Alabama could cross midfield again. A relieved Bob Neyland told reporters outside the dressing room, "I'm glad we've got that one behind us. Man, those fellows were tough. I knew they would be. They've had some tough luck."

Among his many accomplishments that firmly established him as an All-America, Lauricella ran for 108 yards

on 15 carries and completed nine of 16 passes for 108 yards. He also made a 35-yard touchdown dash that was considered the most spectacular play of the afternoon. Dick Ernsberger and Ed Morgan recorded other outstanding plays for Tennessee.

A 20-yard touchdown pass from Lauricella to Bert Rechichar was the play that opened the Tennessee scoring.

In the long run, vicious defensive play probably spelled the difference between winners and losers. News accounts glowed with reports on the contributions of Tennessee defenders Ted Daffer, Bill Pearman, Doug Atkins, Bob Fisher, Roger Rotroff, Polofsky, Gene Moeller, Bill Jasper, Joe Maiure, and Jerry Hyde.

Tailback Hank Lauricella, at far left with ball, follows John Michels's block in the 1951 Alabama game at Legion Field in Birmingham.

Tennessee	0	7	7	13	27
Alabama	7	0	0	6	13

UA	Marlow, run 1 (Conway, kick)
UT	Rechichar, pass from Lauricella 20 (Rechichar kick)
UT	Kaseta, pass from Payne 20 (Rechichar kick)
UT	Ernsberger, run 3 (Rechichar kick)
UA	Marlow, run 1 (kick failed)
UT	Lauricella, run 35 (kick failed)

"Alabama was an outstanding team. We always have had a great rivalry with them, and it was a game we always looked forward to. There was tremendous sportsmanship displayed by both sides, a quality I think was due to the caliber of coaches and the caliber of players representing both schools. There was no trash talk or anything like that. We just enjoyed the competition.

"General Neyland required total commitment and discipline, and he got it. Red Drew was the Alabama coach at that time.

"Hank Lauricella and I were tailbacks at that time, and we got along very well. We lived in the same dorm for four years, we went to classes together, we practiced together. We were good friends and still are. My wife and I had a son who was married in Baton Rouge in the winter of 2002, and Hank and his wife, Betty, drove over from New Orleans for the wedding.

"Our team was really a happy family, with very few problems. To this day, we still greatly care about each other.

"Football is a lot different today than then. In 1949 we played four tailbacks, a position that is the equivalent of quarterback today. Nowadays the quarterbacks generally play the whole game. The coaches back then received a lot of credit for playing a bunch of kids. Today, on the other hand, a guy like me might as well transfer out.

"The General played two teams. We had an abundance of backs, but not as many linemen. We had Ed Morgan and Bert Rechichar, Andy Kozar and Dick Ernsberger, Jimmy Hahn and Bernie Sizemore. It was more difficult to recruit outstanding linemen than backs. Francis Holohan was the toughest guy in our line.

"That game was Lauricella's best. I think I contributed less that game than just about any game all season. But Hank was tremendous. He ran and passed very well, and he kicked well. He was probably the best punter in the league. He could kick toward coffin corner, and he quick kicked.

"The quick kick isn't all that difficult. It's a matter of getting the roll. It's a matter of practice, and we kicked out of bounds more successfully than they do today. We'd go out and work early on our punting because you didn't have punting specialists. What you'd do on the quick kick is keep it low to get the good bounce. You'd drop the ball at a lower spot and you'd get contact with it lower.

"Our position coach, Harvey Robinson, was a perfectionist. He said he knew we couldn't be perfect but that he would stay on our backs until we got the closest thing to it. He made it a little difficult at times, but we all loved Coach Robinson. He ran the offense for the General because the General spent more time on fundamentals and as a defensive strategist. Harvey stayed on us all the time. If you're not careful, that could take a little fun out of the game.

"Gordon Polofsky was a great linebacker, backed up by Moose Barbish and Gene Moeller. Roger Rotroff probably made more tackles from his end position than Doug Atkins did, but that was because they ran away from Atkins. They wanted to stay away from Doug. Rotroff was a super player. The year before, though, we were saying Atkins and Bud Sherrod were the best pair of ends in the country. Then Roger stepped in 1951 and did a great job for us.

"Of course, Atkins was a terrific athlete. The 1950 team was probably better defensively, and the 1951 team because of experience was probably better on offense. Another thing. On defense, we had lost defensive backs Jimmy Hill and Bud Sherrill.

"Alabama about that time was having a little trouble recruiting. They may have been down from their usual standards. They had recruiting problems until Bear Bryant came back in 1958.

"It seems to me that probably General Neyland hasn't received as much credit throughout the country as he deserved. Of course, he did here in Tennessee. But he did so many things for the game of football, like the way he organized the sidelines and had everybody assigned to a certain area on the bench.

"His organization of practice and his defensive strategies were 50 years ahead of his time. He did so much for the game itself. They're still doing things like the General did them. He emphasized fundamentals more than most.

"Looking back on my own career, I actually gave thought to transferring out in my freshman year, 1948. I thought about transferring to another SEC school, maybe Georgia Tech or Ole Miss. The General was very fair because I told him I was unhappy. The problem was I was homesick rather than being mad at anybody. I told Coach Robinson not to put me in that season.

"Florida might have figured in since it was close to my home in Pensacola. But Florida wasn't very good back then,

and I would have been crazy to have gone there at the time. It took me a while to adjust. General Neyland told me that by Christmas they couldn't run me off with a shotgun. And he was right. I felt good about Tennessee by that first Christmas."

Vols 68, Tennessee Tech 0

For the game with Tennessee Tech, the UT first team enjoyed a virtual day off, as the reserves filled in for all but the first period. Even so, the Vols had no trouble mowing down Tech, 68–0, before a slim gathering of 15,000 at Shields-Watkins Field.

Hank Lauricella, who was well on his way to All-America honors, earned rest-and-relaxation time by making the most of his opportunities on the two occasions he was handed the ball. In the first period, he set sail on center Bob Davis's snap and ran 76 yards to pay dirt. A few plays later, he went 34 yards on a carry that barely missed being another touchdown.

Two Tennessee starters were ruled out of the game during the week leading up to the intrastate match, both victims of practice-field injuries. Linebacker Gordon Polofsky, hurt in a Wednesday scrimmage, was replaced by freshman Lamar Leachman. The day after Polofsky's mishap, offensive end Vince Kaseta injured his arm and gave way to another freshman, Vic Kolenik.

Then as now, the Alabama game was always key to Tennessee's success.

Tennessee Polytechnic Institute, as it was known in the 1950s, was helpless before the finely tuned Tennessee single-wing offense. A partial list of the indignities that Neyland's troops perpetrated against the visitors from Cookeville included the following: a pair of touchdowns each by Herky Payne and Andy Kozar, two touchdown receptions by the rookie Kolenik, a 73-yard punt return for a touchdown by Billy Blackstock, and a 63-yard run from scrimmage by Ray Byrd.

The Golden Eagles managed only one drive that scared the UT defenders. A score was averted when Don Francisco, a former star at Dobyns-Bennett High School in Kingsport, Tennessee, fumbled the ball at the 1-yard line. UT's Mack Franklin pounced on it.

The Vols rolled up the score with 20 points in the first quarter, 13 in the second, 14 in the third, and 21 in the fourth. Overall, the cakewalk against the Golden Eagles was deemed valuable in getting out any kinks before the following Saturday's outing at North Carolina.

Tennessee Tech	0	0	0	0	0
Tennessee	20	14	13	21	68

UT	Ernsberger, run 1 (Rechichar kick)
UT	Lauricella, run 74 (kick blocked)
UT	Payne, run 4 (Rechichar kick)
UT	Kozar, run 4 (Kolenik kick)
UT	Kozar, run 1 (Kolenik kick)
UT	Payne, run 18 (kick failed)
UT	Kolenik, pass from Crowson 50 (Kolenik kick)
UT	Kolenik, pass from Crowson 9 (kick failed)
UT	Blackstock, punt return 72 (kick failed)
UT	Williams, field goal 21
UT	Byrd, run 63 (kick blocked)

Pat Shires Remembers

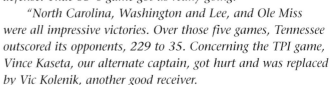

"We may have started peaking with the TPI game and culminated in our 28–0 victory at Kentucky on a terribly cold day in Lexington. Between TPI and Kentucky, Tennessee played good offense and good defense. That 68–0 game got us really going.

"North Carolina, Washington and Lee, and Ole Miss were all impressive victories. Over those five games, Tennessee outscored its opponents, 229 to 35. Concerning the TPI game, Vince Kaseta, our alternate captain, got hurt and was replaced by Vic Kolenik, another good receiver.

"Billy Blackstock and Ray Byrd were the two old Knoxville High School boys who came along that year. Blackstock did a lot of punt returns. He wasn't awfully fast, but he could see the field and he got behind the wall and used his blockers. His average for return on punts, about 26 yards, still stands as an NCAA record.

"General Neyland scheduled TPI because Mercer and Sewanee and Southwestern had quit football after the war. He was looking for somebody to play that Tennessee could beat easily. Chattanooga was too tough to be classified as a real breather. And they had a good coach in Scrappy Moore.

"So Tennessee had Tennessee Tech as a breather. Sometimes you could use subs against Chattanooga, but sometimes you couldn't. Against TPI, there was an opportunity to use everybody.

"Our blocking by this time was real good. Vince Kaseta, an end, was one of the best. Jim Haslam could hold a block and had good speed. Jimmy Hahn was as good as we've had. John Michels was great. Bob Davis never had a bad snap. Whig Campbell was good.

"The blocking was unbelievable, and so was Lauricella as a runner. He was probably the fastest man on the team, an outstanding sprinter in track as well as a great football player.

"Kozar was a better runner than Ernsberger, but Ernsberger was probably a better blocker. Kozar was a good blocker, too.

And don't forget Buddy Lyons. He played a lot, partly because he was so smart. I remember one time he came up to me to suggest a play, We ran it, and darned if Ernsberger didn't run 35 yards for a touchdown.

"That year I was mostly the quarterback on the scout team. I had had some injuries.

"We were all very close, partly because we all lived in East Stadium dormitory. We were pals with basketball players and other people in the various sports. I enjoyed living there and having those meals at the training table.

"We ate pretty well under Mr. Jim Thompson, who ran the training table in the stadium. He'd have spaghetti on Saturday, liver on Wednesday, steaks on Friday. Roger Coggins used to say that other people didn't like liver, so could he have their liver? He would eat anything.

"We had fish at lunch on Friday. I guess that was because we had so many Catholic boys on the team. Guys like Lauricella, Rechichar, Kaseta, Michels, Kozar, Sekanovich, Laughlin.

"We had a lot of good football players. And our coaches were great. Harvey Robinson was a perfectionist who would run players at night over on the track.

"I thought it was a good thing having the players live together for four years. I think they'd be better off if they still did that with our teams now.

"Part of the reason I came to Tennessee from West Virginia was that my brother Abe talked to me about it. That, and the fact Tennessee was using the single wing, and I was a single-wing tailback in high school."

Vols 27, North Carolina 0

Hank Lauricella made a strong case that he should have both All-America and Heisman Trophy honors when he had a hand in all four Tennessee touchdowns in the Volunteers' victory, 27–0, over North Carolina, an event that drew a bevy of Eastern sportswriters who were visiting the Tar Heel State to cover Ryder Cup golf.

The reporters left Kenan Stadium in Chapel Hill singing the praises of the wily Tennessee tailback, who was locked in an exciting battle with Princeton's Dick Kazmaier for the affections of the Heisman voters. (Kazmaier eventually won the trophy, a verdict that didn't sit well with Tennessee fans, who later were incensed by other Heisman snubs to Johnny Majors and Peyton Manning.)

Lauricella ran for two touchdowns, passed for one, and set up the other with a 31-yard dash that took the ball to the North Carolina 21. His compilation of rushes from scrimmage included jaunts of 45, 31, 27, 14, and 12 yards.

Lauricella's statistics had to impress the heavy turnout of Eastern writers. He completed three of eight passes for 71 yards, while picking up 150 yards on 13 carries. Team captain Bert Rechichar also had a big game, catching passes from Lauricella and contributing substantially as a punt-return specialist.

Seven minutes into the game, Rechichar caught a 25-yard pass from Lauricella at the goal line to lead the way to a shutout victory. Just before the half, Lauricella ran 27 yards for the second touchdown.

All-America Hank Lauricella, seen here with his father, John Lauricella Sr., was the starting tailback on the national championship teams.

In the third quarter, after connecting with John Davis for a 28-yard pass that carried to the one, Lauricella picked up the final yard to give Tennessee its third touchdown. Fullback Andy Kozar accounted for the fourth, blasting over the right side of the line.

North Carolina found Tennessee's defenders too stubborn to overcome. Two drives, mounted mainly against reserves, reached deep into UT territory, but Coach Neyland responded by sending his starting players back into the fray to turn back the threats.

Herky Payne, playing behind Lauricella at tailback, picked up some impressive yardage, but his unit never could get across the double stripe.

Statistics told the story, something that wasn't always true with Neyland-coached teams. While the Vols were piling up 280 yards on the ground, North Carolina could manage only 80. The Vols also enjoyed an advantage in passing yardage, amassing 90 yards against only three for the Tar Heels.

Tennessee	13	0	14	0	27
North Carolina	0	0	0	0	0

UT	Rechichar, pass from Lauricella 25 (kick failed)
UT	Lauricella, run 27 (Rechichar kick)
UT	Lauricella, run 1 (Rechichar kick)
UT	Kozar, run 9 (Rechichar kick)

Gordon Polofsky Remembers

"I didn't get to play in this game, or the Tennessee Tech game before North Carolina or the Washington and Lee game after it. I had some muscle pulls in my leg and didn't play. But I did make the trip.

"North Carolina was a great place to play, a very picturesque place for a game. Walking through the pine woods, I remember being very impressed by the campus. It was really gorgeous. That stands out in my mind.

"Either Moose Barbish or Gene Moeller started in my place. I remember a whole bunch of writers coming over to see if Lauricella was the real deal, and they wanted to compare him to Dick Kazmaier, the other Heisman Trophy candidate.

"Not knowing too much about Kazmaier, I would just say that Lauricella was an all-around football player. He threw well, he kicked, he ran, and he had a good mind. He was what it takes, a perfectionist with a good head on him. Also, he was my roommate. One of the best people on the face of the earth.

"It was sort of a runaway game, two touchdowns in each half. It seems like North Carolina threatened a couple of times, but they couldn't score. They were coached by Carl Snavely. There was good balance by us on offense and defense, but I felt this particular game was more of an offensive show.

"I had started out at UT as a fullback, but I liked switching to linebacker. I felt defense was more of a natural way to play football. You found the ball and went to it, and you knocked somebody's ass off. But I played a lot of offense in 1949. I was part of what was called the bull backfield, Herky Payne and I. He weighed about 195, and I weighed 215, which was pretty big back then.

"So when we got inside their 10, they often put Herky and me in the game. We were two big backs, and we were the scoring machine because of our size. Anybody who says they don't enjoy the notoriety of scoring touchdowns isn't telling the truth.

"Over the years the association has been great. Now after practice, players go their separate ways. They talk about us being a family back in 1951. Well, we were a family. We lived in the stadium together; we ate every meal together. We couldn't have a car; we couldn't get married. So we had each other, and that was the size of it.

"Everybody knew everybody else's parents, their sisters, brothers, and cousins. That was a wonderful way to have good relationships. The guys I played with like Moeller, Davis, Kozar, Haslam, all of them. They'd do anything for me, and I'd do anything for them.

"One of the best things I've ever been involved with is the Wall of Fame outside the football building, with the names of all the UT letter winners on it, from all sports, men and women. I wish it had generated more publicity when it opened, but it is something that won't ever be forgotten. Everybody that sees it loves it."

Vols 60, Washington & Lee 14

Fearful they could get bogged down by Washington & Lee the way they did in 1950, the Vols came out against the Generals in a dominating mood, posting 28 points in the first quarter en route to a 60–14 victory.

All-America tailback Hank Lauricella directed the offense to quick first-period touchdowns, but the ease with which Tennessee took command inspired Coach Neyland to pull his starter and replace him with another gifted signal-caller, Herky Payne.

The heady senior from Pensacola, Florida, made the most of his opportunity, scoring four touchdowns, passing for another and ripping through the Generals for 151 yards on 18 carries. So decisive was Tennessee's superiority that Neyland decided to play Ray Byrd, his third-team fullback, almost all of the second half.

Filling in behind Andy Kozar and Dick Ernsberger, the former Knoxville High School star picked up 84 yards on 14 tries.

Tennessee didn't want a repeat of the close call it survived the previous year. The Vols were able to nudge the Generals by a 27–20 count in 1950, a near-upset that showcased the brilliant work of a talented W&L quarterback, Gil Bocetti.

Bocetti again made himself a nuisance, passing for 121 yards and running for 57, but the Vols obliterated the visitors' dreams of an upset by amassing 513 yards (as of 2003, still a UT record) on the ground and chalking up 24 first downs. Overall, it was a masterful performance as the Vols raced to their 17th straight victory since the Mississippi State loss of the 1950 season.

The last Tennessee scoring march covered 62 yards and involved Byrd, Larry Crowson, Billy Jack Cunningham, and Hal Hubbard as the backfield. The cast of reserves put together a nifty drive that ended with tailback Crowson slipping across the from the 1-yard line.

Washington & Lee	0	7	0	7	14
Tennessee	28	7	18	7	60

UT   Lauricella, run 20 (Rechichar kick)

UT   Ernsberger, run 8 (Rechichar kick)

UT   Payne, run 6 (Rechichar, kick)

UT   Payne, run 5 (Rechichar kick)

W&L   Thomas, pass from Bocetti 11 (Lafferty kick)

UT   Kolenik, pass from Payne 11 (Williams kick)

UT   Lauricella, run 54 (kick failed)

UT   Payne, run 5 (kick failed)

UT   Payne, run 2 (kick failed)

W&L   Thomas, pass from Bocetti 35 (Lafferty kick)

UT   Crowson, run 1 (Kolenik kick)

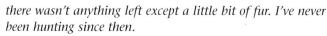

"The close call we had with Washington & Lee the previous year had a lot to do with us being ready to play them in 1951. We didn't want to have a close call again, and we sure didn't want to lose the game. So the coaching staff had us ready to play a good game.

"I don't remember a lot about the game, but one thing I do remember is Ray Byrd getting the chance to play and having a real good game. I guess when we scored 28 points the first quarter the coaches felt there would be an opportunity to let a lot of people play. Ray was a strong runner with good speed. He ran straight up.

"Herky Payne was such a powerful runner and so dependable down deep that coaches felt they could take Lauricella out when the ball got down to the 20 and then let Herky help take it on in.

"One thing I can say about my years at Tennessee is that I'm the only guy I know that went through five spring practices. That was because they let me come over there during my senior year at Knoxville High School and participate in the spring. In one practice they put me out there, just me, against Paul Gearing, Jack Stroud, and Ken Donahue. They like to have knocked me in the damn river over there. I was still in high school. They must have been trying to run me off.

"W. C. Cooper, the tailback, was another old Knoxville High School teammate of mine. He took me hunting one time, found me a rabbit, and handed me a shotgun. It was a little old rabbit. I fired the shotgun, and when I got to the rabbit,

there wasn't anything left except a little bit of fur. I've never been hunting since then.

"That reunion in the fall of 2001 was a testament to the brotherhood we felt on that team. If somebody got out of line—smoked or drank or something—one of the older guys would get after him and tell him to cut it out. We had discipline among ourselves.

"That year I would go into the defensive line as a sub for Ted Daffer. He ran so much sideline-to-sideline he would wear himself out.

"One player I remember very well was Francis Holohan, who was so tough in the defensive line that one time I thought a guy on the other side was going to bleed to death. When I got in, the other guy said, 'Thank God, you're here.' Everybody thought Doug Atkins was tough. He was, but I would like to have seen Atkins and Holohan go at it. They were both tough guys."

Doug Atkins, seated at center, is one of the few athletes who was inducted into both the college and professional Halls of Fame.

1951

T

Vols 46, Mississippi 21

Only five minutes into the game, fullback Dick Ernsberger burst over left tackle for a 53-yard touchdown run that opened the floodgates for an impressive 46–21 victory over the Mississippi Rebels.

Going into Oxford, the Vols were determined they wouldn't suffer the same fate as Kentucky earlier in the season, when the heavily favored Wildcats lost to the Rebels, 21–17. The Tennessee players weren't going to let their pristine 1951 record suffer the blemish of an upset if they could help it.

So, when Ernsberger went all the way, other players fell in line and made their contributions as well: Hank Lauricella, 25 yards for a touchdown; Herky Payne, a 14-yard score; Andy Kozar, 51 yards, setting up still another touchdown.

The winning formula extended beyond Ernsberger, Lauricella, Payne, and Kozar to the fierce-charging offensive unit that included center Bob Davis, tackle Jim Haslam, end Vince Kaseta, guard John Michels, blocking back Jimmy Hahn, and the captain of the team, Bert Rechichar.

But Rechichar's abilities reached far beyond the toughness he acquired as a youngster growing up in Pennsylvania. Against Ole Miss, for instance, he exemplified his value in his uncanny savvy while running with the football. He carried the ball five times for 67 yards, with his reverses setting up touchdowns and giving the Rebels a change of pace to worry about.

While Lauricella experienced no more than an average game in his final appearance against Ole Miss, the Tennessee victory bore his unmistakable handprints. Or, more appropriately, footprints. Hank's coffin-corner kicking helped keep the Rebels penned up in their own territory.

On defense, press-box experts agreed that end Doug Atkins had his best game of the year, a day's work that included a tide-turning pass interception in the third quarter.

Jimmy Hahn supplies a block for Andy Kozar. Hahn was a two-time winner of the Jacobs Trophy for best blocker in the Southeastern Conference.

A dispute over future sites for Vols–Rebels match-ups made this the last Tennessee–Ole Miss game until 1956. Bob Neyland took exception to a proposal by Rebel authorities that the game be alternated between Memphis and Oxford.

Tennessee	13	6	6	21	46
Mississippi	7	7	0	7	21

UT	Ernsberger, run 53 (kick failed)
UT	Lauricella, run 24 (Rechichar kick)
UM	Boykin, run 1 (Lear kick)
UT	Payne, run 12 (kick failed)
UM	Boykin, pass from Lear 28 (Lear kick)
UT	Kozar, run 1 (kick failed)
UT	Payne, run 1 (Rechichar kick)
UT	Kozar, run 1 (Rechichar kick)
UT	Payne, run 34 (Rechichar kick)
UM	Bridges, pass from Lear 17 (Lear kick)

Vince Kaseta Remembers

"I have always felt that we were successful—except for the Maryland game—because we had some people who were overachievers, we had some people with talent, we had some luck, and, starting with General Neyland, we had some great coaches.

"General Neyland always emphasized the importance of good blocking. He didn't like the passing game because he believed that, once the ball was in the air, it was anybody's ball. The single-wing formation required good blocking to move the ball. Basically, it was a running system.

"If I'm not badly mistaken, the 1951 Tennessee team made more yardage on the ground than any other University of Tennessee team, before or after. To the best of my memory,

the opponents' defensive lines outweighed our offensive line, man for man.

"General Neyland was a believer in good blocking technique. He said one good blocker was worth two good ball-carriers.

"We spent a lot of time on what today would be called special teams. That included coffin-corner kicking. You don't hear much about coffin-corner kicking these days. George Cafego later was a great Tennessee coach for kickers, but I am sure he learned it all from the General.

> "General Neyland was a believer in good blocking technique. He said one good blocker was worth two good ball-carriers."
>
> — Vince Kaseta

"I didn't realize General Neyland didn't want to play at Memphis and Oxford. It seemed to me Oxford was a pretty nice town when we played down there in 1950. But it wasn't that way at Starkville where Mississippi State fans tried to tip over our bus after they beat us in 1950. Starkville was the pits. We stayed over at West Point and came to a movie Friday night in Starkville.

"Bert Rechichar was deceptively fast, especially for a guy his size. He had a lumbering style, which made him look slower than he was. You had to have some speed to run the reverse, and Bert ran it very well.

"But then he didn't need much speed when the offensive line cleaned out the defensive tackles.

"Doug Atkins had a great game against Ole Miss, which is not surprising when you consider how good Atkins was. He was the best defensive lineman I ever saw.

"You know, I said the 1951 team had overachievers on it. But when we had our reunion in the fall of 2001, I read everybody's biographies, and it happened in life, too. Many overachieved, which suggests they worked hard at what they did and were successful. In my opinion, that's a carryover from what they learned on the football field.

"General Neyland's game maxims included, 'Play for and make the breaks and when one comes your way, score.'

That applies to football, but it also applies to life. You see guys wait for the break to come or wait for the gravy train to come along. They don't do anything to make it happen. Somebody who coaches like General Neyland coached will drill that into you."

Vols 28, Kentucky 0

Tennessee's remarkable string of victories over Kentucky extended to 19 when the number one–ranked Vols disposed of Paul (Bear) Bryant's Wildcats, 28–0, on a bitterly cold afternoon at Stoll Field.

For the third straight season, Kentucky's great All-America quarterback, Babe Parilli, left the field in a state of frustration after having failed not only to beat the Vols but to score any points against the Wildcats' neighbors to the south.

But as Bryant said in a salient wrap-up to the game: "We had a few men. They had 50." That wasn't a bad summary, considering the Vols won the game on equal parts offense and defense. Twin tailback terrors Hank Lauricella and Herky Payne wouldn't be stopped, and the defense kept alive its streak of shutting out the Wildcats for a third straight time.

Bryant and Bob Neyland suggested that the game hinged on a Tennessee goal-line stand in the third period. The Vols led by 14–0 at that point and needed a big play to thwart the threat of a Kentucky rally. Parilli was stopped on fourth down when he attempted to sneak across from the one.

Defensive statistics hadn't been refined to include sacks back in those days, but Tennessee's linemen harassed the gifted Parilli throughout the afternoon, with leadership up front provided by Bill (Pug) Pearman, Mack Franklin, Doug Atkins, and Ted Daffer.

Andy Kozar could always be depended on for short yardage during the two championship seasons in which he participated, 1950 and 1951.

The pressure applied by the line helped Bill (Moose) Barbish rake in a pair of interceptions, adding to Parilli's misery index.

Lauricella, running around and through Kentucky defenders, accounted for 133 yards in 17 carries on the ground. Payne carried the ball 12 times for 48 yards. Andy Kozar, Dick Ernsberger, and Bert Rechichar also contributed standout performances.

The Volunteers' best performance of the season was also the most consistent. Tennessee tallied a touchdown in each period. Another string that stayed intact was Neyland's success against Kentucky. He ended his career a year later without ever having lost a game to the Wildcats.

Tennessee	7	7	7	7	28
Kentucky	0	0	0	0	0

UT   Payne, run 6 (Rechichar kick)

UT   Kozar, run 1 (Rechichar kick)

UT   Kaseta, pass from Lauricella 8 (Rechichar kick)

UT   Kozar, run 3 (Rechichar kick)

Bill (Pug) Pearman Remembers

"It was frustrating to Kentucky people that they got shut out three straight years—1949, 1950, and 1951—when Babe Parilli played up there. It still is. I have a lot of friends who played there, and they haven't gotten over the fact that we beat them all three years. And didn't just lose—they got shut out.

"It was a game that had two master coaches going after each other, Bryant against Neyland. We never really prepared especially for Kentucky, except the week of the game. We got the breaks, and we were coached very well. But Kentucky was well coached, too, of course.

"We prepared the same way for every game. Kentucky was the best team on our schedule at that time. Emmett Lowery was the man who scouted Kentucky for Neyland. He was the basketball coach at UT, but he always scouted Kentucky for the General. Lowery was great at doing that. He always had a few helpful thoughts about some players that wouldn't be included in most scouting reports. He was extremely thorough.

"Kentucky had a bunch of great players, guys like Parilli, Walt Yowarsky, and Bob Gain, and we never figured we could beat them 28 points.

"Tennessee had some excellent goal-line stands, with key plays from guys like Gordon Polofsky, Mack Franklin, and Francis Holohan. One of those times, when it looked like Parilli was about to score from the one, I had lined up wrong. I normally lined up between the end and the tackle, but this time I had lined up between the guard and the center.

"I turned around and said to Gordon, 'Polofsky, I'm in the wrong defense.' He told me to shut up and do it. Well, as it so happens, Parilli ran right toward me, so I wound up chasing him backwards all the way almost to midfield. It was fourth down, and he finally fumbled.

"When you played between Bud Sherrod and Francis Holohan, like I did in 1950, you didn't have a whole lot to do. Holohan was strong, he was determined, and he was a hell of a teammate.

"It was cold up there that day, but not as cold as the year before at Knoxville. That was the time we had the huge snow. Gus Manning was told by General Neyland to round up some students, and we would pay them to shovel snow off the field. They did okay up until about midnight, and by that time some of them had started drinking and weren't too handy with the shovel from that point.

"That game was the end of our season. We never played worth a damn after that, Vanderbilt almost beat us, and we lost to Maryland in the Sugar Bowl. That one was a shock. I don't know what in the hell happened."

Vols 35, Vanderbilt 27

As dominant as the Vols were against Kentucky the preceding week, they were far more vulnerable in the regular season windup against Vanderbilt at Shields-Watkins Field. Tennessee, which led by as much as 21–0, hung on for dear life in the fourth quarter, and emerged with a 35–27 win over the fired-up Commodores.

So impressive was the Vanderbilt rally that a Knoxville sportswriter was moved to dub the loss a "glorious defeat." The Vols had everything going their way until the third period when Vanderbilt's superb passer, Bill Wade, brought his team back to within a point of the lead.

Completing 16 of 24 throws for 251 yards, Wade set every Commodore scoring drive in motion and sustained it with his memorable striking power. Surprisingly, however, the scoring plays were all posted on running plays. But it was clearly Wade's passes that made the comeback a reality.

Most spectacular of his throws was a 64-yard bull's-eye to Jimmy Ray that put the Commodores in position for their third touchdown. It was dread of what Wade might do with his next opportunity that caused 40,000 fans to exit the stadium on rubbery legs.

As time expired, Tennessee scored the touchdown that wrapped up the undefeated regular season. With the Vols driving goalward, Coach Neyland substituted Herky Payne at tailback for Hank Lauricella. The fans expected a run by the powerful Payne, but Neyland crossed them up by letting fullback Andy Kozar barrel across the goal line.

On an unseasonably warm November afternoon, tempers flared at this point, indicative of the emotional level that prevailed for the traditional intrastate battle. Players rushed from the benches toward the Vanderbilt goal, but cooler heads prevailed to prevent a melee.

It's a good thing, too, because nothing should have been allowed to detract from a tense, ferocious, and spirited struggle between the two teams. A couple of players had been banished earlier in the game for letting their tempers get the better of them.

Kozar enjoyed an outstanding game as Tennessee stuck to the ground and left the passing to Wade and his Commodore teammates. Andy riddled the Vanderbilt defense for 111 yards on 19 carries; Payne came next with 68 yards on 15 carries.

Lauricella's day was far from typical in that he spent most of the game rooting hard for his replacement, Payne, rather than providing the offensive fireworks in his own right. Of course, Lauricella continued to punt the ball masterfully, forcing Vanderbilt to drive long distances.

Any acrimony that built up during the contest dissipated when players from both teams marched to midfield at game's end and shook hands in a display of sportsmanship.

Vanderbilt	0	0	20	7	27
Tennessee	7	7	7	14	35

UT	Kozar, run 1 (Rechichar kick)
UT	Payne, run 17 (Rechichar kick)
UT	Atkins, punt return 6 (Rechichar kick)
VU	Allen, run 1 (Foster kick)
VU	Allen, run 4 (Foster kick)
VU	Duncan, run 4 (Foster kick)
UT	Payne, run 2 (Kolenik kick)
UT	Kozar, run 1 (Kolenik kick)
VU	Duncan, run 1 (Foster kick)

<u>Doug Atkins Remembers</u>

"Bill Wade and Bucky Curtis just about beat us. They passed us silly. We hadn't seen that kind of passing. I tried to get in Curtis's head with the idea of slowing him down. But I don't think I've slowed him down yet.

"Wade and I were teammates with the Chicago Bears. Bill was a nice guy, and I never heard him say a bad word about anybody. He was a very underrated quarterback. He may not have been as spectacular as some quarterbacks, but he didn't make any mistakes. That was his secret.

"Bill was a smart quarterback and tough as nails. I don't think he ever missed any time in the NFL because of being hurt. If you needed a quarterback to run for five or six yards, I don't think there was anybody who was better in the clutch than he was. The Bears won the NFL championship in 1963 against the Giants with Wade at quarterback. The score was 14–10.

"I don't know what happened to us. Some people may have thought we let up after getting ahead 21–0. But Neyland wouldn't allow you to let up, even if you were ahead, 50–0. I think Wade and Vanderbilt just had our number. They got a little better as the game went along.

"I don't remember anything about the melee at the end of the game. I know that Neyland wouldn't allow you to fight.

"Although I played basketball some while I was at UT, I had quit by this time and didn't take basketball up again until I finished my senior football season and joined a team called the Detroit Vagabonds. Our best-known player was Bill Spivey, the center from Kentucky.

"In 1951, though, I was just playing football. I liked basketball better than football because you didn't get beat up. But coaches encouraged me to give up basketball and spend all my time in football. It worked out for the best.

"That was a good reunion we had during the 2001 season at Club LeConte in downtown Knoxville. I guess we've done pretty well. We've stayed friends for a long time."

Alternate captain Vince Kaseta and captain Bert Rechichar provided the necessary leadership for the 1951 Vols.

Maryland 28, Vols 13 (Sugar Bowl)

And then, after an unbeaten regular season, everything came crashing down in a numbing Sugar Bowl loss to Maryland. The Terrapins' 28–13 victory over the Vols deflated longtime college football watchers—and not just those in Tennessee—who had rashly stated that UT's 1951 squad may have been the greatest team of all time.

The precision blocking, the perfectly executed offensive formations, and the stingy, senior-dominated defense were hard to find against a Maryland squad led by All-America

Ed (Mighty Mo) Modzelewski on offense and, among others, his brother Dick on defense.

In fact, they were non-existent or at least bore no resemblance to the Tennessee machine that had pulverized practically every opponent in the march to the national championship. (Fortunately for UT, the final AP and UP voting was done before the bowl games were played.)

Both coaches, Tennessee's Bob Neyland and Maryland's Jim Tatum, tried to outdo each other before the game in proclaiming the hopelessness of their respective causes. Said Neyland: "We would have to score four touchdowns, and I don't think we can do it." Similarly pessimistic, Tatum responded, "Our only consolation is that Neyland doesn't try to run up a score. I hope he still doesn't."

Tennessee's single-wing attack, which many thought unstoppable, never got untracked. All those heralded orange-shirted runners put their massive talents together for a grand total of 81 yards, little more than half as much as the Mighty Mo's 153.

The Vols weren't sharp, continuing a decline in their play that was first noticeable when they nearly blew a lead to Vanderbilt in the second half of the season finale. Whether it was the eight-man line Maryland employed or just some inexplicable letdown by the Vols, Tennessee didn't reach the peak it last displayed in its methodical win over Kentucky on Nov. 24.

Defensively, the Vols also sagged. Maryland was paced by Ed Modzelewski from his fullback slot, but there were other Terrapin heroes, such as quarterback Jack Scarbath and the entire offensive line, centered around All-America guard Bob Ward.

Maryland jumped ahead 7–0 in the first quarter, pushed its advantage to 21–6 at halftime and coasted to victory by taking a 28–6 lead into the final period. Not even another evening on Bourbon Street could ease the pain suffered by Tennessee's large contingent of fans who showed up in the Sugar Bowl audience of 82,000.

Tennessee	0	6	0	7	13
Maryland	7	14	7	0	28

UM	Fullerton, run 2 (Decker kick)
UM	Shemonski, pass from Fullerton 6 (Decker kick)
UM	Scarbath, run 1 (Decker kick)
UT	Rechichar, pass from Payne 4 (kick failed)
UM	Fullerton, interception return 46 (Decker kick)
UT	Payne, run 2 (Rechichar kick)

John Michels Remembers

"I still have a scab over my brain about that game. It bothered me then, and it still bothers me. Why that would stick in my craw after losing four Super Bowls I don't know, but the Maryland game still gripes me like nothing else.

"We had a great football team, but Maryland did an outstanding job of coming up with something that completely surprised us, coaches and players alike. They ran a defense called the Eagles defense that the Philadelphia Eagles had. They covered the center and both guards. What it amounted to was that nearly everybody along the line was covered. We couldn't make the adjustments we needed.

"It was a defense we had not seen, and we weren't prepared for it. Later, teams started throwing the ball on the Eagle defense, and that cut down on its effectiveness. Of course, Maryland had some exceptional personnel in the Modzelewski brothers and Bob Ward and a bunch of others.

"But in my mind the thing that beat us was that defense we had never seen and weren't able to handle.

We may have been on a downslide after the Kentucky game, but to me it was not very obvious. I think the other players felt the same way.

"Offensively, we let our defense down. We just didn't sustain anything. Three downs and out. Maryland had an excellent football team. They did a really good job against us.

"We were undefeated, riding high, and somebody stuck a pin in our balloon. It's still hard to take. That day we met somebody who outfoxed us.

"After the game, Neyland and Maryland coach Jim Tatum were roommates at a convention up north. You can bet Neyland was picking his brain about that defense. The only time you saw that defense was when pros used it. Colleges didn't at that time. Passing might have cut down on it, but Maryland knew we were a running team.

> "We were undefeated, riding high, and somebody stuck a pin in our balloon. It's still hard to take."
>
> —John Michels

"I think the key to how General Neyland took it was that he didn't say much of anything in the locker room after the game. I never felt sorrier for anybody in my life. I felt like I had let the man down tremendously, and there was no way to make up for it. The rest of the team felt the same way.

"Hank Lauricella damn near died. Here he was back in New Orleans. We felt the same way he did. We wanted to make this a great going-away present for him. It would have been wonderful if we had one, but the great fairy tale didn't work out.

"I've never met a greater bunch of guys than the ones on that team. The loss just crushed us.

"We had practiced at LSU and didn't go from Baton Rouge to New Orleans until the day before the game. We worked out five days at LSU. Later some people tried to imply that had something to do with our loss, that if we had been in New Orleans, closer to the action, it wouldn't have happened. But that's garbage."

1951 National Review

Although two of Tennessee's championships (1951 and 1998) bore the AP and coaches' polls seal of approval, the 1951 title was mired in controversy.

The Vols' shocking loss to Jim Tatum's Maryland Terrapins in the Sugar Bowl was a body blow to UT's claims of supremacy. It was a situation the opposite of 1950 when the Vols finished fourth in the AP balloting but were the only top-five team to win its bowl game.

When the Vols bowed to Maryland at New Orleans, several teams stepped forward to stake their claim to the top ranking.

The most persistent team in pursuit of Tennessee most of the season had been Michigan State. The Spartans were voted into Big Ten membership in 1950 but weren't eligible for the Rose Bowl until two years later.

Biggie Munn's Spartans finished the season unbeaten, their path to a perfect season leaving a trail of victims in their wake that included Michigan, Ohio State, Penn State, and Notre Dame. But there was no bowl game for the Spartans to bolster their claim.

Maryland was equally vocal in presenting its case for recognition as the nation's most deserving team. The bowl win over Tennessee was the icing on the cake in an unbeaten season that saw the Terrapins roll past Georgia, North Carolina, and LSU.

Illinois and Georgia Tech suffered only a solitary blemish, their only stain a tie.

Ray Eliot's Fighting Illini defeated UCLA, Syracuse, and Michigan, but fought to a scoreless deadlock with Ohio State. Illinois crushed Stanford in the Rose Bowl, 40–7.

Georgia Tech, under Bobby Dodd, finished 11–0–1, playing Duke to a 14–14 tie and winning every other game, including the Orange Bowl meeting with Baylor, 17–14.

Princeton enjoyed a banner season, but the Heisman Trophy won by Dick Kazmaier was the only hardware the Tigers had to show for their 9–0 record. By that era in football history, the Ivy League was no longer given serious consideration in national championship calculations.

The Heisman Trophy award to Kazmaier was hotly disputed by Tennessee fans, who believed the trophy should have been presented to Vols tailback Hank Lauricella.

UT fans were later disillusioned when Johnny Majors (1956) and Peyton Manning (1997) were passed over for the prestigious award, convincing Tennessee partisans that something reeked of foul odor in the Heisman process.

The 1967 Vols

Chapter 5

1967

*T*ennessee's wise selection of Doug Dickey as head coach in 1964 can be traced back to 12 years earlier when former UT star Bob Woodruff was head coach at Florida and Dickey was his bright, over-achieving quarterback. Woodruff, who in 1963 became athletic director at Tennessee, recognized Dickey's coaching potential and, after the close of the '63 season, hired his astute onetime signal-caller away from Arkansas, where Dickey was an assistant on Frank Broyles's staff.

Dickey, later to be inducted into the College Football Hall of Fame, took the struggling Vols and directed them to two Southeastern Conference championships in 1967 and 1969. And it was in 1967 that Dickey's orange-clad troops also earned the national number-one spot in the Litkenhous ratings.

Because of a razor-close loss in the season opener and a narrow defeat in its bowl game, the 1967 Tennessee team hasn't received the acclaim it was due as a national champion. But a close look at that season as it unfolded reveals that the Volunteers made a spirited bid for number one in mid-November but fell back in both wire-service polls because of a strong finish by Southern California.

The 1967 coaching staff. Seated, from left, are Bill Battle, Doug Knotts, Head Coach Doug Dickey, Jimmy Dunn, and Ray Trail. Standing, from left, are Jack Kile, George Cafego, Bob Davis, George McKinney, and P. W. Underwood.

UT 16	UCLA 20	Los Angeles
UT 27	Auburn 13	Knoxville
UT 24	Georgia Tech 13	Knoxville
UT 24	Alabama 13	Birmingham
UT 17	LSU 14	Knoxville
UT 38	Tampa 0	Tampa
UT 35	Tulane 14	Knoxville
UT 20	Mississippi 7	Memphis
UT 17	Kentucky 7	Lexington
UT 41	Vanderbilt 14	Knoxville
UT 24	Oklahoma 26 (Orange Bowl)	Miami

The *Knoxville Journal*'s Ben Byrd wrote that first place was up for grabs after the Vols defeated Ole Miss convincingly, 20–7, on November 18, but Southern California's victory over highly regarded UCLA that same weekend tipped the scales in favor of the Trojans.

So, despite season-ending wins over Kentucky and Vanderbilt, Tennessee finished second in both the AP and UP polls and settled for the Litkenhous ratings as its sole claim to a national championship. Nevertheless, the turnaround the Vols made after a season-opening loss to UCLA in Los Angeles will be remembered as one of the most striking reversals of form in UT history.

With an extra week to get ready for Auburn because of an open date, Dickey drastically revamped the defense. The Vols stopped the Tigers' heralded offense, badly disappointing Auburn coach Shug Jordan, who came to Knoxville oozing with confidence.

The amazing progress Tennessee made in Dickey's fourth season as head coach not only resulted in an SEC championship and gave them a claim to the national title but also broke Alabama's dominance of the Vols that had begun in 1961 under Coach Paul (Bear) Bryant.

One of the keys to UT's success was the teaming of Steve Kiner and Jack Reynolds at linebacker. From 1967 through 1969, the two headhunters perhaps constituted as formidable a pair of linebackers as ever played the college game.

UCLA 20, Vols 16

Gary Beban launched his successful Heisman Trophy campaign by making the play of the game, but it was teammate Greg Jones who carried the brunt of the offensive load as UCLA defeated the Vols, 20–16, at the Los Angeles Coliseum.

As UCLA riddled the Tennessee defense for 412 yards—with 305 on the ground—Jones pounded out 135 yards on 15 carries, easily earning him back-of-the-game recognition over the returning Bruins quarterback, Beban.

Some of UCLA's women students greet Captain Bob Johnson as the Vols arrive in Los Angeles for the season opener against the Bruins.

But Beban's Heisman hopes were boosted when he made the play that decided the game. The scene was classic Heisman material. Trailing 16–13 in the fourth quarter, the Bruins needed 2 yards on fourth down at the Tennessee 27. It could have been his team's last opportunity to pull the chestnuts out of the fire against the visitors from the South-eastern Conference.

UCLA called a timeout during which the weary Beban told his coach, Tommy Prothro, that he had enough stamina left to get the necessary yardage for the first down. And then some, he could have added.

Because that's what the Bruin great did. He pulled the ball from center and then took an "S path," as a newspaper called it, into the end zone for the decisive points.

As close as they came to winning the intersectional battle, the Vols were disappointing in a number of respects, revealing shortcomings Dickey would correct during the open-date period that preceded the next game.

Tennessee	7	0	6	3	16
UCLA	0	3	7	10	20

UT	Fulton, run 1 (Kremser kick)
UCLA	Andrusychyn, field goal 37
UT	Pickens, run 1 (kick failed)
UCLA	Beban, run 5 (Andrusychyn kick)
UCLA	Andrusychyn, field goal 27
UT	Kremser, field goal 35
UCLA	Beban, run 27 (Andrusychyn kick)

Charles Rosenfelder Remembers

"The 1965 Rosebonnet game with UCLA in Memphis got everybody excited, and the fans wanted some more of that. It's

been a great series. I remember my parents talking about the 1965 game and telling me that when it was over everybody just gave a sigh of relief and the band played for about a half hour.

"The 1967 game was like a bowl game. We went out several days early, toured Disneyland, and enjoyed ourselves on the West Coast. The result wasn't what we wanted, but it probably set the stage for us to have the good season we had.

"I remember the two weeks following the UCLA game including an open date before Auburn. Coach Dickey told us we were out of shape. He really put us through the paces for those two weeks. He made a lot of changes, especially in the defense.

"I remember that run by Gary Beban. It looked like we were playing two-handed touch below the waist. I think everybody on the defense had a crack at Beban and touched him before he reached the end zone. He ran like an S through the whole defense.

"Greg Jones made tremendous yardage, being one of those big tailbacks UCLA always had. They also had a big defensive line, not only big but one of the strongest and most physical I played against at UT.

"I thought for the first game we played okay, but you can't let down any time. UCLA was a good team, not quite as good as Southern Cal that year.

"We were coming off the Gator Bowl win over Syracuse. Our offensive line had played together two years. Joe Graham played with pain and was a heroic figure. We knew we would carry the load early in the season. But we felt we were of championship caliber. Ray Trail was our coach, still young in the profession, and he did a good job considering the circumstances. He had come in as a replacement for Charlie Rash, who had died in the car-train collision that also took the lives of two other coaches.

"I have the highest respect for Coach Dickey. Things I learned from him I still use in my business life and my home life. The maxims he dwelled on apply to everything you do. He was young at the time, but he always managed

to say the right thing at the right time. He had a good perspective on the whole thing. He surrounded himself with good coaches because he knew they could make him or break him. Coach Dickey had a quick mind.

"We could have been recognized as the national champions if we had done a little better in a couple of games. It's like a big family with our camaraderie, and that's something you really are reminded of when you have a reunion like we had in 2001. When you're part of an organization like UT, you have to be happy about it.

> "I have the highest respect for Coach Dickey. Things I learned from him I still use in my business life and my home life."
>
> —Charles Rosenfelder

"We had a lot of guys who were tough and a lot of guys who were both smart and tough. We had a good mixture, but none of the guys ever got in serious trouble."

Vols 27, Auburn 13

Wholesale changes in the defense, notably a new attitude of toughness, transformed the Vols into a powerhouse capable of national-title aspirations two weeks later against the Auburn Tigers.

The 27–13 victory reflected a different defensive personality, evidenced by contrasting statistics: Whereas UCLA had pounded the Vols for 305 yards on the ground, the Tigers were held to a measly 78.

The insertion of Jack Reynolds at linebacker in the starting lineup and the return of Nick Showalter to end were key moves Dickey orchestrated during the extra time he had to prepare for Auburn. Never again during the championship season would Tennessee lose its newfound defensive purposefulness.

None of the Volunteers' four touchdown excursions came cheaply. Representing scoring marches of 74, 80, 48,

and 82 yards, much of the terrain was covered by Charley Fulton, who took over at quarterback in the third period, replacing the injured Dewey Warren.

Fulton, the senior from Memphis who divided his time at Tennessee between tailback and quarterback, behaved more like a running back despite his location behind center. The diminutive veteran carried the ball 22 times and netted 103 yards.

While the most notable improvement for the Vols came on defense, the line blocked with more authority than it did against UCLA. Dickey credited captain Bob Johnson, John Boynton, Elliott Gammage, Charles Rosenfelder, and Joe Graham for their bone-crushing contributions.

Fulton received some help in making Auburn's line porous against the running attack. The three of them—

As quarterback for the 1967 Vols, the colorful Dewey Warren was not only a deadly passer but also more nimble afoot than many suspected.

Fulton, Walter Chadwick, and Richard Pickens—amassed 269 yards.

But the one statistic that more than anything else portended well for the future pertained to the defense: Auburn was able to grind out only one first down by rushing. Coach Dickey, offensive coordinator Jimmy Dunn, and defensive coordinator Doug Knotts knew they had the makings of an outstanding team, as revealed in the events that had just unfolded at Neyland Stadium.

Auburn	0	13	0	0	13
Tennessee	7	7	6	7	27

UT	DeLong, pass from Warren 3 (Kremser kick)
AU	Carter, run 1 (Wiley kick)
UT	Warren, run 1 (Kremser kick)
AU	Riley, field goal 46
AU	Riley, field goal 44
UT	Chadwick, run 6 (kick failed)
UT	Chadwick, run 8 (Kremser kick)

Coach Doug Dickey Remembers

"In the UCLA game we did not play effectively on defense. We had moved Nick Showalter from end to linebacker, and that didn't work out for us. Nick wasn't big enough to handle the linemen you face at that position. We needed to move him back to defensive end where he played very well.

"That position now is often referred to as outside linebacker. Nick was outstanding there. So we put Jack Reynolds, a much burlier guy, at Nick's old position, and the changes worked very well. In the Auburn game—and I don't remember how good they were that year—we drastically reduced the amount of yardage we gave up on the ground compared to what we had done against UCLA.

"We were lucky we had two weeks to make our alignment different. From the Auburn game on, we were a pretty good football team. In the UCLA game, we missed tackles and weren't very sharp. If some of the players say we worked them hard during those two weeks, what they probably mean is that we worked on fundamentals. We went back to fundamentals, and they probably remember that. Sometimes you get caught up in X's and O's and forget the basics.

"I knew we were better than we played.

"One thing about that team that's interesting was our abundance of talent at quarterback. We had Dewey Warren returning and Charley Fulton playing behind him. Charley was more versatile, so we thought we could get a lot done with Dewey at quarterback and having Charley as backup there and be available for tailback and wingback. We also had Bubba Wyche. We had three kids who were pretty good. Charley was very knowledgeable about what was going on.

"He had savvy for the game. You needed more than one tailback for the I formation. We had not only Fulton but Walter Chadwick, who was a good runner. When Dewey got hurt, we had Charley to fill in at quarterback.

"And when both of them were hurt, we had Wyche. Bubba played two important games, against Alabama and LSU. Sports Illustrated called him the world's greatest third-string quarterback. Bubba had good maturity about him and was our number-one quarterback in 1968. We didn't require the quarterback to carry the game the way some offenses do today. We had a balanced offense throwing and running and probably threw the ball 25 or 30 times a game.

"We had good camaraderie on that team, a good bunch of guys. Auburn to us was what Florida is today. Tennessee–Auburn games were played in Birmingham, and so there was a lot of travel by fans of both schools.

"Auburn, Alabama, and Ole Miss were games I inherited where there were established, great coaches—

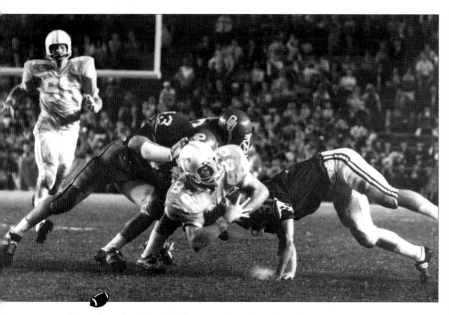

Sure-handed Ken DeLong, whose brother Steve and nephew Keith were All-America Vols, was a standout tight end during the 1967 season.

Shug Jordan at Auburn, Bear Bryant at Alabama, and Johnny Vaught at Ole Miss. The Auburn rivalry was an excellent series.

"We had a very productive defensive day against Auburn. The 1967 and 1969 Tennessee teams were quite comparable and probably a little better than our 1968 team."

Vols 24, Georgia Tech 13

The outlook was dark, indeed, for the Vols in the first period against Georgia Tech. A situation was developing that gave no hint Tennessee would emerge with a 24–13 victory over the Yellow Jackets in one of the most exciting chapters in the history of the honored rivalry.

For background purposes, one should realize that Charley Fulton was the quarterback for one reason—that regular signal-caller Dewey Warren had been injured in the Auburn game and wasn't available. Fulton was borrowed from the tailback position.

In the first period of the Tech contest, with no score on the board, Fulton suffered a cracked rib, leaving quarterback chores in the hands of native Atlantan Bubba Wyche. Coach Doug Dickey proved himself brilliant once more in having his reserve quarterbacks ready when their number was called.

After the game, a writer asked Bubba if he minded being called a third-string quarterback. Wyche answered: "No, because that's what I am." He certainly didn't perform like a third-teamer unless third-teamers are supposed to play a nearly flawless game.

Statistically, Wyche was sound, completing eight of 16 passes for 121 yards and two touchdowns and adding 33 yards on the ground. But it was his mastery of the strategic situations that earned the UT junior postgame raves from coaches and the media.

By the time Tech scored, the Vols under Wyche had run up a 24–0 lead, having tallied a field goal in the opening period, a touchdown in the second, and two more touchdowns in the third.

Tech coach Bud Carson said in his press conference, "I didn't know how much it would hurt Tennessee when Fulton went out. But Wyche came in and did a great job after Fulton was injured."

The victory moved Tennessee closer to expectations for the season, reflecting a comeback that began after the opening loss to UCLA. The Vols' strength derived not from one particular phase of play but from the fact that they seemed to do everything well, both offensively and defensively.

Georgia Tech	0	0	0	13	13
Tennessee	3	14	7	0	24

UT   Kremser, field goal 22

UT   Flowers, pass from Wyche 6 (Kremser kick)

UT   Flowers, pass from Wyche 50 (Kremser kick)

UT   Chadwick, run 1 (Kremser kick)

GT   Sias, pass from Good 7 (Carmichel kick)

GT   Almond, pass from Good 5 (kick failed)

Charley Fulton Remembers

"I was playing tailback early and for most of the year. But I played some at quarterback. Walter Chadwick and I alternated at tailback that season. Bubba Wyche got more snaps in practice than I did, but they had some plays that were geared to me, more option-type plays.

"The week before the Tech game I spent quite a bit of time at quarterback because Dewey was hurt. My background was that I had started at quarterback as a sophomore until getting hurt in the Ole Miss game. Then in 1966 I played mainly at tailback and stayed pretty healthy. But Dewey had a very good year in 1966 and was the quarterback for 1967 while I was assigned at tailback.

"Jimmy Dunn worked with the quarterbacks, while Coach Dickey went back and forth between offense and defense. He divided his time according to where he felt he needed to be based on how we had done the week before.

"I never did figure out why Georgia Tech had left the SEC, but this was still a very big game. I think if it was to do over again, Georgia Tech wouldn't have left. But I don't know that for sure. Our game was always a sellout, Knoxville or Atlanta. This was in Knoxville in 1967.

"I had my ribs hurt early in the game. I remember Bud

Carson was Tech's coach, and he had a good defense. Bubba was really the second-team quarterback, but they sent me in to do some options and give us more of a running game.

"But Bubba went in against Georgia Tech and did a real good job in a tough game. The line was good, and it was big, especially for that era. Jimmy Dunn was an awfully good assistant coach in working with the quarterbacks. I was really a single-wing tailback, recruited to play there by Jim McDonald. But I knew the single wing was about through as far as the rest of the country was concerned.

"As you know, Dewey was a great quarterback, but people probably don't realize how tough he was. When we were freshmen, Dewey spent almost all his practice time at linebacker. Bubba Wyche fell behind because he had to have knee surgery. When all's said and done, he might have been a better quarterback than Dewey or me either one.

"I later coached for Coach Dickey at Florida. He was a tremendous coach. He was one of the most honest people I've ever been around as far as following the rules is concerned. He never tried to bend any of the NCAA rules. It was always either black or white. In football, I was impressed with his mind. He could coach both sides of the ball equally well. He was a very good administrator, a very good organizer, and you could call him a players' coach."

Authors' Note: The above mention of Dickey coaching at Florida refers to his stint as head coach of his alma mater after he resigned from the UT post following the 1969 season. Dickey returned to UT as athletic director in 1985, serving in that capacity until 2003.

Vols 24, Alabama 13

For 25 consecutive games, Alabama hadn't suffered a loss, so when Tennessee prevailed, 24–13, it must have been for Tide fans quite traumatic, to use a word that wasn't tossed around as loosely then as it is now.

Two giants of southern coaching, Alabama's Paul Bryant, left, and Tennessee's Doug Dickey, meet on the field during pregame warm-ups.

Circumstances were such that sportswriters compared the victory to other orange-letter Tennessee triumphs, such as the 1951 Cotton Bowl, the 1956 Georgia Tech win, and the 1959 upset of LSU.

But this one, coming as it did against the superb Alabama coach, Paul Bryant, didn't need any extra hype, to use another trite expression. It was truly monumental because it sent Tennessee's stock sky-high in the quest for a national championship.

Bubba Wyche, replacing the injured Dewey Warren and Charley Fulton at quarterback for the second straight game, again directed the offense to near perfection. Stealing Bubba's thunder a little bit, however, was a defensive back who had received little publicity until the critical showdown with the Crimson Tide.

Albert Dorsey, a senior from Tampa, Florida, and a hard-working member of the UT secondary, intercepted three Alabama passes in the fourth quarter, an unbelievable feat that won him first-team All-America honors.

The third of Albert's thefts broke Alabama's back, coming while the Tide trailed by only four points, 17–13. A minute and 20 seconds were left when Dorsey got the range on a Kenny Stabler pass, pulled the ball from the air, and made a sensational 31-yard run for the touchdown that nailed down the victory.

Almost as important from a strategic standpoint, Jack Reynolds broke up a two-point conversion try after Alabama's second touchdown. Without Hacksaw's huge play, the Crimson Tide would have needed only a field goal to win the game.

Tennessee heroes, in addition to Wyche, Reynolds, and Dorsey, included defensive back Jimmy Weatherford, who was assigned to cover star receiver Dennis Homan; Steve Kiner, the other phenomenal sophomore linebacker; Karl Kremser, the deadly placekicker; and Richmond Flowers, a standout pass receiver who also covered kicks.

Tennessee	7	0	10	7	24
Alabama	7	0	0	6	13

UT	Chadwick, run 1 (Kremser kick)
UA	Stabler, run 6 (Davis kick)
UT	DeLong, pass from Chadwick 11 (Kremser kick)
UT	Kremser, field goal 41
UA	Morgan, run 1 (pass failed)
UT	Dorsey, interception return 31 (Kremser kick)

Albert Dorsey Remembers

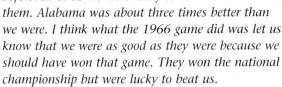

"Every time we played Alabama, it was a big game, and it didn't have anything to do with the fact that we lost a heartbreaker on a missed field goal the year before. In 1965 we were lucky to tie them. Alabama was about three times better than we were. I think what the 1966 game did was let us know that we were as good as they were because we should have won that game. They won the national championship but were lucky to beat us.

"It was interesting how much respect Coach Bear Bryant had for the University of Tennessee, even when we weren't doing very well. That's something that traced back to General Neyland, but it had carried on through the years. It was a hard-hitting, hard-fought series, one that created and deserved great respect.

"The reason so many passes were thrown in my direction was that Kenny Stabler and Dennis Homan were about it for Alabama when it came to passing. Jimmy Weatherford played the opposite halfback from me. We flip-flopped a lot, but Weatherford was assigned to take Homan, and we had Mike Jones backing him up. The rest of the field was left to me.

"They tried to get the ball to Homan but realized it wasn't going to work. From that point on, at the end of three quarters, they decided to try the other side. My side. I think the last of the three interceptions I had, Danny Ford [later coach at Clemson and Arkansas] was playing tight end and was the intended receiver.

"If Bubba Wyche didn't have bad knees, he might have been the most famous quarterback who ever played at Tennessee. His knees were terrible. If he was walking down the street, he might just fall down right there on the spot. He probably had a better overall arm than Dewey Warren. Dewey was good at staying in the pocket until the last second.

"Charley Fulton cracked some ribs against Georgia Tech and was out for a month. But we didn't care who played quarterback. We were just trained to go out and do our jobs. Dewey was a better athlete than people realized.

"Legion Field back then was the stadium in the South. I remember in 1965 going on the field at Birmingham. I never heard such a roar as when Alabama came onto the field. It was a big deal to beat Alabama, not just ending their streak.

"We were a real team, in that every week there was a different star. If somebody got hurt, a second-teamer came on and did a great job. We had one of the best offensive lines that ever played at Tennessee—Bob Johnson, Charles Rosenfelder, Elliott Gammage, John Boynton, and Joe Graham. Gammage came to UT as a tight end. He could really run.

"Defensively, imagine having Steve Kiner and Jack Reynolds at linebacker at the same time. If you meet Kiner or Reynolds or Frank Emanuel now, you'd say, he's the nicest guy in the world. But they weren't that way back then.

"This was the game that established Tennessee as a national power again. The shame of that season was that

Doug and JoAnne Dickey share a table with Alabama's Paul Bryant.

we lost to Oklahoma in the Orange Bowl. We put in a different defense for them in the first half, but it didn't work. We went back to our regular defense in the second half, trailing 19–0, and almost won it.

"We always had great respect for Coach Dickey, who was a man that if you did what he asked, you would win."

Vols 17, LSU 14

In an exchange of field goal tries that settled the outcome in the last minute, Karl Kremser made his, while Roy Hurd missed his. The result was a 17–14 Tennessee victory over LSU.

Tennessee was thrilled to exit Neyland Stadium with any win at all, after seeing its once-healthy 14–0 lead evaporate in the face of a spirited Bengals comeback. After the surefooted Kremser reasserted Tennessee's superiority by rifling through a three-pointer from 20 yards out, the Vols had to brace themselves for the final LSU charge.

Only 59 seconds remained on the clock, so Coach Dickey ordered a squib kick after Kremser's crucial score. UT's skipper wanted to avoid the sight of Sammy Grezaffi streaking down the sidelines 100 yards for an LSU game-winning touchdown.

The speedy defensive back had done just that on a kickoff to inaugurate LSU's comeback bid in the third period. Dickey's strategy backfired a little, however, when LSU's up man caught the ball and brought it back into good field position.

The Tigers drove quickly to the Volunteers' 20 but had no timeouts remaining. Coach Charlie McClendon opened himself up for the grandstand quarterbacks to second-guess him when he elected to go for the field goal with 34 seconds left. He later explained that he wanted no clock-caused foul-up that would cost LSU a chance at the field goal.

But luck was on Tennessee's side. Hurd's kick, 37 yards in length but squarely in front of the goal post, missed the mark, and Tennessee walked off the field still unbeaten since the opening-game loss to UCLA.

Back at quarterback for the Vols, Dewey Warren was widely credited with leading the Tennessee charge. Walter Chadwick and Richard Pickens contributed some outstanding runs to the victory.

Defensively, the tackling of linebackers Jack Reynolds and Steve Kiner and ends Jim McDonald and Vic Dingus was critical to the Tennessee cause. Perhaps the most important play of the game came at the end of the first half, when Jimmy Glover's interception precluded a near-certain LSU field goal that would have given the Tigers momentum at intermission.

LSU	0	0	7	7	14
Tennessee	0	7	7	3	17

UT	Warren, run 7 (Kremser kick)
UT	Chadwick, run 6 (Kremser kick)
LSU	Grezaffi, kickoff return 100 (Hurd kick)
LSU	Stokely, run 14 (Hurd kick)
UT	Kremser, field goal 33

Karl Kremser Remembers

"I felt like the kid in the candy store, getting to come to Tennessee as a walk-on kicker after playing soccer. Coming back to campus has been an eye-opening experience for me. I look at my teammates, and it's just one classy guy after another. You start with our captain, Bob Johnson, and include, really, all of them. It was so much fun.

"I can't say enough about Coach Dickey. I don't think I ever met a man who ran a finer program or was organized better and was a better example of a coach and leader.

"At West Point I was probably the worst cadet in the history of the academy. I got myself in a whole bunch of academic trouble. Then I heard about Tennessee's track program, and with high jumping my second love and hearing about Richmond Flowers, I decided that was the place for me. I finished second one year in the high jump in the NCAA championships. Somebody talked me into also going out for football as a kicker, and I'm glad I did.

"The coaches decided after we went ahead on my field goal late in the LSU game to go for the squib kick. Usually it will take a little hop and go over somebody's head. We sure didn't want Sam Grezaffi returning another one for a touchdown. But the short man took it and returned it for pretty good field position.

"Fortunately, Roy Hurd missed the field goal, and we won the game. Hurd, incidentally, was a real good kicker. LSU was afraid to wait any longer because they were afraid the clock would run out on them. At that time, the coaches would ask me if I thought I could make it, and I told them I believed I could. With my good fortune of having Bob Johnson as snapper and Dewey Warren as holder, I was able to get that one through there.

"Dewey was a real character, a leader because he loosened everybody up. All the players had confidence in Dewey. We had a bunch of guys on that team who wanted the ball a little bit.

"I missed the dinner for Coach Dickey during the 2001 season because the soccer team I coached at Florida International University had a match, and I couldn't get to Knoxville at that time. But I would love to have been there to honor him and be with my teammates again. Coach Dickey was even-tempered. After the Cotton Bowl rout the next year, he told us if we were around long enough, there were going to be games like that one. And don't let it get us down."

After three straight pressure-packed outings against rugged foes, the Vols were happy to help dedicate Tampa's spiffy new football stadium by slapping the Spartans around, 38–0.

"The game was about what I expected, as far as our play was concerned," Doug Dickey said after the game. "but I have to admit Tampa's play surprised me some. They came after us hard, made us get everything the hard way and played what I thought was a fine football game."

The highlight of the afternoon, other than the dedicatory ceremonies before a crowd of 26,500, was a 65-yard touchdown run by Walter Chadwick, UT's fine tailback. Karl Kremser's field goal with 12 minutes left in the opening period turned out to be all the points the Vols would need in the shutout victory.

The other 35 points didn't come easily against the Spartans, who brought momentary glee to their fans by stopping the Vols on their first possession and then moving the ball into Tennessee territory.

After Kremser kicked his field goal, Tennessee made it 10–0 following a blocked punt by Jimmy Glover. Richard Callaway raced across from seven yards out.

Dewey Warren and Bubba Wyche made for a nifty one-two quarterback punch for the Vols, who scored their second touchdown when Wyche hit tight end Ken DeLong for four yards, culminating a drive that began when Steve Carroll recovered a fumble at the Tampa 35.

Chadwick's touchdown run came on Tennessee's second play from scrimmage in the second half. Walter raced down the east sideline after breaking a tackle at midfield with a powerful lunge.

Offensive coordinator Jimmy Dunn praised Chadwick's effort: "Walter did a great job there. He not only broke a good tackle, but he used a downfield blocker, Bob Johnson, real well along the sideline. He slowed up enough so Bob could help him, and he saved enough so he could outrun the last two Tampa defenders."

Tampa's best scoring chance went awry. Late in the second period, the Spartans reached the Tennessee 7-yard line, at which point the defense stiffened. Roy Tice missed the short field goal, which all but brought down the curtain on the Tampa offense.

Tennessee	10	7	14	7	38
Tampa	0	0	0	0	0

UT	Kremser, field goal 32
UT	Callaway, run 6 (Kremser kick)
UT	DeLong, pass from Wyche 4 (Kremser kick)
UT	Chadwick, run 65 (Kremser kick)
UT	Gooch, pass from Warren 11 (Kremser kick)
UT	Gooch, pass from Warren 27 (Kremser kick)

Steve Kiner Remembers

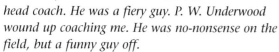

"The University of Tampa had tried to recruit me, since I lived in Tampa, but it came down to Tennessee, Florida State, and Alabama. Vince Gibson recruited me for Tennessee. After my first year at Tennessee, he went to Kansas State as head coach. He was a fiery guy. P. W. Underwood wound up coaching me. He was no-nonsense on the field, but a funny guy off.

"I was a sophomore in 1967, and Bob Johnson was a senior and the captain. Johnson was my mentor, like some of the other seniors. There was a lot of leadership on that squad, which partly explains why we played so well. Johnson wasn't very vocal, but he had a great work ethic and led by example. He set the benchmark, and everybody had to work at that level or better.

"We had gone through a tough two weeks after the opening loss to UCLA.

"Walter Chadwick was the biggest personality on the team, because he was funny. Walter was hilarious. Elliott Gammage, Ron Jarvis, Chadwick—they were all funny. I looked on all of them, and Johnson, as seniors I admired.

> "Bob Johnson was my mentor, like some of the other seniors. There was a lot of leadership on that squad, which partly explains why we played so well."
>
> —Steve Kiner

"It was a big deal for me opening the stadium in Tampa. It was the first opportunity I had to play in front of my high school coaches and hometown fans. I was really disappointed that we were playing Tampa. It was great, though, for me to come back to Tampa. But we were better than Tampa. I would love to have been playing Florida, Miami, FSU, any of them. It was just a cakewalk. They couldn't line up with us.

"I always remembered Tom McEwen, the sports editor at Tampa. In fact, I still have lunch with him when I go back to Tampa. He always wrote good things about me. If I ever got in trouble or anything, he didn't write that stuff. They tore the stadium down. It's a parking lot now. But it was a nice stadium, a great facility.

"Walter Chadwick's long run was down the east sideline. Walter was the best running back in the SEC his senior year. He was patient with the ball and could find his holes. He was big, a punishing runner and had good speed. I still see Walter all the time. Since his car accident in 1970, Chadwick's family has done a great job with him, and so has Elliott Gammage off our team. Walter's memory is good. He still gets fired up about games and plays. Tell me a better running back than Walter.

"P. W. Underwood, my coach, was a hell of guy. He was rough. He was mean as a snake. Doug Knotts, our coordinator, *was all business when he was around me. One day in practice, we were walking off the field with P. W. and George Cafego. P. W. had busted my ass all the way through practice. He would grab you by the facemask and then hit you in the head with his damn forearm and almost knock you out.*

"I yelled at him when I walked by. He and Cafego were carrying on, laughing, huh, huh, huh, ho, ho, ho. I said, 'P. W.' He said, 'What in the hell do you want?' I told him, 'If it wasn't for Cafego, you'd be the ugliest son of a bitch in the whole world.' P. W. started running after me.

"Speaking of Cafego, he was a great guy. They were all good guys. He cranked out punter after punter after punter, year after year after year.

"Dickey? He was the CEO. He was on the tower. That's where you wanted him. If his ass came down on the field, things weren't going well. I loved Dickey. I didn't think of Dickey as aloof although he might have come across that way. To me, he was just all business. He didn't want any grab-ass. He was very intense.

"There was great rapport with that team. When we came up for Dickey's retirement dinner in 2001, I realized that was what it was all about. The guys who lined up next to me were an important part of my life.

"Jim Bates was another character. He came here as a walk-on. He played a little minor league football in Knoxville and then went up to Sevierville as coach. He's had a great career. Now he's the defensive coordinator for the Dolphins."

Vols 35, Tulane 14

Walter Chadwick, who had been a disappointment in his junior season, continued the torrid pace of his senior campaign by leading the Vols past Tulane, 35–14. A multitalented player who also threw two touchdown passes for the Vols,

Described by one Knoxville sportswriter as the best thing to come out of Germany since Marlene Dietrich, placekicker Karl Kremser followed a circuitous route to Tennessee.

the tailback from Georgia accounted for Tennessee's first two touchdowns on runs of 1 and 7 yards, part of a 93-yard total he reeled off against the visiting Green Wave.

Chadwick and Richard Pickens, when they combined with the injured Charley Fulton, were said to give the Vols their most dynamic running game since the days of Hank Lauricella, Andy Kozar, Dick Ernsberger, and Herky Payne back in 1951.

Getting ready for the next week's game against powerful Ole Miss at Memphis was the top priority for Tennessee, which methodically destroyed Tulane by scoring one touchdown in the first quarter and three in the second and then allowing reserves to take over for the rest of the game.

Karl Kremser, the placekicker from across the sea whom the *Knoxville Journal's* Ben Byrd referred to as the greatest thing to come out of Germany since Marlene Dietrich, drew extra attention because of the nature of the rout taking place at Neyland Stadium. The sturdy Kremser consistently kicked off into the end zone and at one point boomed one 80 yards, striking the base of the south-end horseshoe.

Dewey Warren continued to do the things that had made him a force since his return from the injury list. "I felt great out there," he said. "I felt quick. You know, I almost got away a time or two. I don't worry about my knee anymore when I'm running."

Team unity marked this edition of the Volunteers, as noted in Warren's postgame comment: "This team has unity, and it has togetherness. I've felt all along we could be great, and I think we are just now reaching our peak." That boast would be tested the following week when the Vols would challenge tradition-steeped Ole Miss at Liberty Bowl Memorial Stadium in Memphis.

Tulane	0	7	0	7	14
Tennessee	7	21	7	0	35

UT	Chadwick, run 1 (Kremser kick)
UT	Chadwick, run 7 (Kremser kick)
UT	Warren, run 1 (Kremser kick)
UT	Gooch, pass from Wyche 3 (Kremser kick)
TU	Pizzolatto, pass from Duhon 19 (Pontius kick)
UT	Flowers, pass from Warren 11 (Kremser kick)
TU	Duhon, run 3 (Pontius kick)

Dick Williams Remembers

"We had a top-notch running-back corps of Charley Fulton, Walter Chadwick, Richard Pickens, and Ron Jarvis. Chadwick had a big game against Tulane, which wasn't surprising. He had running skills, the ability to jump over the line, and he had some power. Pickens bench-pressed 450 pounds and was considered the most powerful back in the Southeastern Conference. Charley Fulton—you couldn't catch him. Old Thunder Head Jarvis would flat run over you.

"They were a tough bunch. The offense scored on its first possession of just about every game in 1967. That puts a tremendous burden on your opponent. I didn't realize it until 1968 when we had our first meeting of the fall, and Coach Dickey pointed that out. It obviously was a very important statistic to him.

"I haven't ever heard of another team doing that. That offensive line had a mixture of serious and light-hearted guys. But they got together and got the job done.

Elliott Gammage and Joe Graham were the clowns who kept everybody entertained.

"Those guys and Dewey Warren would carry on. I remember one time Dewey got clobbered pretty badly. He limped back in the huddle and hollered, 'Don't throw any more lookout blocks for me.' Of course, Dewey never lacked confidence.

"We had an extremely young defense. We grew up quickly after the UCLA game. I never worked as hard in my life as I did during those two weeks. Frank Yanossy was a guy, our other tackle, who never got the credit he deserved.

"The thing I remember about the Tulane game was that there was a big celebration down on Cumberland Avenue that night because everybody thought we were going to be ranked number one. Turns out we weren't. But people were riding up and down Cumberland on top of cars. A man fell off one, hit his head on the street, and was killed.

"I thought we should have been first, because of all we had accomplished since our first game. Tulane had a good team, especially its running attack. They had just gotten out of the SEC.

"Coach Dickey was highly respected by all of us. That's the way it is with great coaches, and Coach Dickey was a great coach. Doug Knotts coached us tackles, George McKinney the secondary, and P. W. Underwood had the linebackers.

"We were a real close team. We would go out on Saturday night together and pal around all the time."

Vols 20, Mississippi 7

Their offense bolstered by the return of Charley Fulton to action after a five-game absence because of an injury, the Vols posted a landmark 20–7 victory over Ole Miss at Memphis.

The "landmark" description fits for two reasons: (1) The triumph came against a foe with the best chance of derailing Tennessee, which had a six-game winning streak going after the opening loss to UCLA; and (2) it got the monkey of consecutive losses to Ole Miss off the Vols' back.

The Rebels had posted eight straight wins over Tennessee, dating back to 1958, a terribly long time to endure an opponent's dominance in a neighborhood rivalry. When the Vols finally would prevail in 1967, there wasn't much suspense in the game, and in the second half it came down mainly to the Vols running out the clock.

Walter Chadwick, who with Fulton gave Tennessee a potent one-two haymaker punch at tailback, had a hand in the first touchdown, but it didn't come on the ground. The Vols engaged in a bit of trickery by having the left-handed Chadwick fire a 10-yard, left-handed pass to Terry Dalton early in the second quarter.

Although Tennessee was in control the rest of the way, the game began with a scare for the UT defense. The second time Ole Miss had the ball, it marched to the UT 38. On fourth down the Rebels went for it and barely missed. Jimmy Weatherford, an All-America defensive back, slapped down a sideline pass, allowing the Vols to take over.

Defense was the big story throughout the afternoon for Tennessee. Savage tackling by Steve Kiner; alert play by tackle Dick Williams, with two fumble recoveries; and stifling coverage by the secondary, resulting in four interceptions, kept the talent-laden Ole Miss offense at bay.

Abetting the running of Chadwick and Fulton was the deft ball-handling of quarterback Dewey Warren, who by this stage of the season had mastered the art of making the choice between keeping the ball and pitching out.

"Our offense went out there and got the first touchdown," Coach Dickey said. "After that, the defense got us a couple more. Fumbles may be breaks, but I think you could say the defense made the breaks for us."

Tennessee	0	17	3	0	20
Mississippi	0	0	7	0	7

UT	Dalton, pass from Chadwick 10 (Kremser kick)
UT	Chadwick, run 9 (Kremser kick)
UT	Kremser, field goal 42
UM	Wade, run 1 (Keyes kick)
UT	Kremser, field goal 30

Richmond Flowers Remembers

"As an Alabama boy, the only tradition I really knew about concerned the series with Alabama. I learned a lot about UT's tradition as things moved along. At that stage all we wanted to do against Ole Miss was win the game, keep our victory streak going, and win the SEC championship. By that time, we had a lot of pride in ourselves and weren't much concerned about anybody else's victory streak.

"When we beat Alabama that year, we considered ourselves the cock of the walk. Any jinx we might have been under against Ole Miss paled in comparison with what we had overcome against Alabama. That was the jinx that dominated our thinking, and once we got past it, there was no stopping us.

"Charles Rosenfelder was about as tough a player in the offensive line as Bob Johnson was. John Boynton was terrific. Then there was Elliott Gammage, who we could count on to say funny things in the huddle. I'll never forget Elliott keeping things loose. He was always yakking, a true character. But we all felt we were pretty tough. Those linemen didn't fear anybody.

"We got Charley Fulton, a great player, back for this game. I wasn't real happy when he was playing quarterback because he wouldn't throw the ball. Next thing I knew, I'd go out for a pass, then I'd have to block. One thing about big Dewey Warren was that he was going to throw the ball, not run it. I preferred to see Dewey at quarterback, but that's not to say Fulton wasn't a good quarterback, because he was a great scrambler. You had to know two different offenses with those two playing, because neither one could do the things the other did.

"Blocking wasn't my favorite activity. I liked going out there and trying to catch the football.

"The thing I remember most about that year and the growth of Coach Dickey as a coach was that he learned not to sit on any points when you were playing Alabama.

"A defensive player I feel didn't get enough credit was Dick Williams. Later he became a team captain, but in 1967, also, he had some really big plays, like the fumble recoveries against Ole Miss. Dick was a person of outstanding character, one of the finest men on the team.

"The 1967 season was the one I enjoyed most. The next season I had my injury in connection with the Olympics and missed the first game. I came back the next week and was moved to tailback. But at 168 pounds I'm not sure how good a running back I was. They just beat me to death.

"Dickey evolved as a coach with us. Players didn't critique coaches the way it seems they do now. Whatever coaches said, went. Coach

A native of Montgomery, Alabama, Richmond Flowers was an example of a two-sport athlete: an All-America hurdler and All-America receiver.

Dickey must have been a pretty good coach, considering we are listed by the NCAA as a national champion team. I still haven't got my ring."

Vols 17, Kentucky 7

Lexington, a graveyard for many a strong Tennessee team in the past, nearly became the burial site for the 1967 Volunteers, who were happy to leave the Bluegrass with their eight-game winning streak intact, 17–7.

Sparked by the crafty Dewey Warren and the multitalented Charley Fulton, the Vols jumped out ahead, 14–0, but then spent the second half fending off one threat after another from the Wildcats. Warren threw two touchdown passes, and Fulton engineered a vital time-killing drive in the final period.

Under the leadership of the gifted Dicky Lyons on offense and Dick Palmer on defense, Kentucky threatened to do as so many of their predecessors wearing blue and white had done in years past: take heavily favored Tennessee to the woodshed.

Once Tennessee scored its two touchdowns, the second registered as the first quarter was ending, the momentum switched in Kentucky's favor. The Big Blue was within a play or two of pulling off what might have been recorded as college football's upset of the season.

Led by Palmer, the Wildcats gave the Vols the most ferocious rush they had experienced all season. Kentucky's defense was so unyielding that the Tennessee ground attack was held to a paltry 68 yards, the low mark for the season.

Lyons, one of the South's top backs, scared Tennessee when he accounted for the lone Kentucky touchdown in the third period. He broke loose on a 68-yard run to the 3, and two plays later blasted across for the score.

Tennessee put the game out of reach when Mike Jones intercepted a Kentucky pass in the closing minutes and Karl Kremser sent a 20-yard field goal sailing through the uprights with 1:48 remaining, evoking a sigh of relief among the UT fans at Stoll Field.

"I don't think we were ready to play our best game," said Coach Dickey after the game. "But that takes nothing away from Kentucky. We won the game, and we beat a good football team in doing it. One thing it did for us was win at least a share of the SEC championship, and I am proud of that."

Tennessee	14	0	0	3	17
Kentucky	0	0	0	7	7

UT	Baker, pass from Warren 8 (Kremser kick)
UT	Flowers, pass from Warren 29 (Kremser kick)
UK	Lyons, run 3 (Lyons kick)
UT	Kremser, field goal 30

Nick Showalter Remembers

"We came off a 1966 season in which we had beaten a good Syracuse team in the Gator Bowl and were optimistic about our chance to have a really fine year in 1967. The UCLA game stunned us a little bit, but we had been members of a 1965 freshman class that newspapers had called one of the best ever at Tennessee, and we started 1967 with optimism.

"In fact, our intention was to win the national championship. We beat Alabama in Birmingham, and I guess we felt invincible at the time we played Kentucky. I had played middle linebacker against UCLA and was moved back to defensive end, where I belonged.

"But Kentucky gave us a hard time. By that point of the season, we had some tendencies and thought we could move the ball against anybody, even if they knew our tendencies. We went into the game confident we could beat them and got ahead 14–0. We knew we could beat them, but didn't have the stinger we would have had against Alabama or Georgia Tech.

"Kentucky had eight or nine guys in the box and did everything they needed to do to stop us.

"We knew Dicky Lyons was good at returning punts. We were an arrogant bunch, and we felt that, yeah, he's good, but we're going to knock his butt off. We played pretty well on defense. When we let a team get down close, we had a way of stopping them. We didn't give up a hell of a lot of points [141].

"Sharing the SEC title as of the Kentucky game didn't mean a lot to us because we were wanting the national title. The Alabama game was the watershed, and anything beyond that was anticlimactic.

"When you played Kentucky you knew they were going to hit you, and you knew it was their bowl game. So what you had to do was line up and get the job done. Those are the games you wind up winning, but sort of just go through the motions.

"We knew if we beat Vanderbilt the following week, we win the title outright. We beat the fire out of Vanderbilt. You respected Kentucky, but it's like now. You know you are supposed to beat them.

"Coach Dickey had a meeting with us in the fall of two-a-days. He had a printout of what to expect from your opponent in every situation. Dickey was aloof. He would be close to you in a way, but there was always that separation. No doubt, he was the man. Vince Gibson [the defensive coordinator] was like my daddy, wild as a March hare. He kept us out there until it was dark, in August and September, when it doesn't get dark early. He taught us tremendously well and made me the player I was. He made Paul Naumoff into an All-America linebacker.

The switch to defensive end of Nick Showalter, here intercepting a pass, was a key move in the Vols' 1967 turnaround after the loss to UCLA.

"We had an awful lot of good coaches while I was at Tennessee—Jimmy Dunn, Charlie Coffey, George McKinney, Ray Trail, just to mention a few. And, of course, Dickey was a great leader.

"I always felt in any game that Dickey and his guys had us prepared to win. And Dickey was interested in us as people. I was enrolled in pre-med, and he showed a lot of interest in what I was studying for."

Vols 41, Vanderbilt 14

Tennessee just did more of the same things that had worked for it since the UCLA game—playing opportunist on offense, putting up a stiff defense and in general letting its talent enjoy a free rein in the curtain-closer, a 41–14 rout of Vanderbilt at Neyland Stadium.

From the moment Dewey Warren completed a 64-yard gem of a pass to Richmond Flowers, putting the ball at the visitors' three, there wasn't much suspense in the Southeastern Conference match-up, at least after Walter Chadwick had negotiated the last nine feet for the six points.

Things went Tennessee's way, as seems appropriate for a team with national-championship aspirations, all the way through the first and second quarters. Vanderbilt uncorked

a solitary drive, but when it failed to produce points, Vols fans seemed content with a 24–0 halftime advantage.

Richard Pickens, the burly fullback from Knoxville, ground out most of the yardage on the second touchdown drive, but it was left to tailback Charley Fulton to maneuver the final 13 yards. The third touchdown resulted from a 70-yard drive that featured a pair of Fulton-to-Flowers passes. Chadwick covered the final three yards.

Old Automatic, Karl Kremser, accounted for the last three points of the half with a 38-yard field goal.

A 24-point deficit was a lot to ask Vanderbilt to overcome, but the Commodores gave it a game try. A beautifully executed onside kick to start the second half led to a touchdown, making the score 24–7. Vanderbilt tried it again, but after much discussion, the officials decided a Commodore had touched the ball too soon, so possession was awarded to Tennessee.

Instead of Vanderbilt trying to cut the Tennessee lead to 24–14, the Vols mounted a scoring drive of their own, with Bubba Wyche directing the team smartly downfield and carrying the ball across from the three.

With Tennessee on top by 31–7, that was that as far as any suspense was concerned. Crowned national champion by Litkenhous ratings, UT turned its thoughts toward the Orange Bowl and an opportunity to convince AP and UP pollsters they had made a mistake in ranking Southern California number one.

Vanderbilt	0	0	7	7	14
Tennessee	14	10	10	7	41

UT	Chadwick, run 3 (Kremser kick)
UT	Fulton, run 13 (Kremser kick)
UT	Chadwick, run 3 (Kremser kick)
UT	Kremser, field goal 38
VU	Valput, run 1 (Meriwether kick)
UT	Wyche, run 2 (Kremser kick)
UT	Kremser, field goal 31
VU	Noel, pass from May 10 (Meriwether kick)
UT	Patterson, run 5 (Wright kick)

Dewey Warren Remembers

"We were an opportunist team all season. We had a bunch of great players who took a mistake or a turnover and turned it into something positive. We had a high percentage of taking opportunities and getting points off them. We thrived on that. I think that was one of the reasons we could have such a good season.

"We had people to step up like Bubba Wyche did when Charlie Fulton and I were hurt. The chemistry was so good on that team that we never bogged down because somebody was hurt. I got my job back against LSU. Against Alabama, with Bubba in the game, I could have played, but there was no reason for me to go in since he was playing so well.

"Richmond Flowers didn't much like it when Fulton was playing quarterback because Charley didn't throw the ball much. Richmond liked to catch a bunch of passes, and he had a better chance to do it when Bubba and I were playing quarterback and Charley was the tailback.

"We had some characters on that team that made it fun—guys like Elliott Gammage. Elliott up on the line of scrimmage would talk to Joe Graham, also on the line, while

A boosters' luncheon in Greeneville, Tennessee, which featured Bob Neyland Jr. as a speaker, attracted five members of the 1967 team: from left, Dick Williams, Jim McDonald, Neal McMeans, Richard Pickens, and Nick Showalter.

I was trying to call plays. Elliott was a comedian, but you could always count on him. He would do his part.

"There was a time at Memphis, against Army, that a Cadet kept jumping offsides and hitting Gammage. Finally, Elliott told him, 'Look, this guy next to me is an All-America, Bob Johnson. Start hitting on him and leave me alone.'

"One time—it may have been in the Vanderbilt game—the line gave me a lookout block. They yelled, 'Watch out, Rat; here they come.' And the whole defense swarmed me. When Dickey saw the film and asked for an explanation, they told him they did it just to keep me honest.

"Looking back, though, I wouldn't trade those guys for anybody. When you win championships, it starts in the offensive and defensive lines. The receivers were great, too. They had been for years—guys like Johnny Mills and Hal Wantland, who weren't there in 1967.

"Dickey and all the coaches knew how to get the chemistry right. Everybody had one goal, and that was to win. We weren't two separate units, offense and defense. We were unified. Jimmy Dunn was a riverboat gambler and a pleasure to play for.

"We had no superstars. We had guys who wanted to win.

"In the Vanderbilt game all three quarterbacks played. That was another thing that made the team so good. There was no greed, no selfishness. Vanderbilt had some good individual players but didn't have the speed or depth we did.

"Vanderbilt and Kentucky always fought and scrapped because that was their bowl game. You had to buckle your chinstrap against them. We knew just like they do today we had to approach each week one game at a time.

"We had a great mixture, young and old, veterans and inexperienced players. Of course, it was great to have Bob Johnson at center. We never had a bad quarterback exchange. He was smart. Going through the university in four years in engineering. It didn't surprise me at all that Paul Brown wanted Bob as the first player drafted by the Bengals to build their team around."

> "Vanderbilt and Kentucky always fought and scrapped because that was their bowl game. You had to buckle your chinstrap against them."
>
> —Dewey Warren

Oklahoma 26, Vols 24 (Orange Bowl)

You couldn't ask for a much better scenario for the Vols to prove their right to a number-one ranking, but a close call on a final field goal attempt went Oklahoma's way, preserving the Sooners' 26–24 margin over Tennessee in the 1968 Orange Bowl.

Karl Kremser, a giant among placekickers and Mr. Dependable throughout the season, missed on a 43-yard try that would have given the Vols an improbable one-point win over the Big Eight champion Sooners. Coach Doug Dickey put things in perspective with his postgame comment: "If it hadn't been for Karl Kremser, we wouldn't have been here tonight."

That the game came down to an opportunity for the Vols to stage a rally with last-moment heroics was a tribute to the talent and fighting quality of Dickey's team. Barely resembling the outfit that had captured fans' imagination in the weeks since the opening loss to UCLA, Tennessee dug itself into a messy little hole by halftime.

The normally stalwart defense was porous as a sieve during an uncharacteristic opening 30 minutes, giving up three touchdowns on drives of 68, 80, and 80 yards. A defensive adjustment at halftime stopped the option cold and set the stage for the Vols to mount a gallant comeback. Unfortunately, however, it came up short.

Trailing 19–0 at the start of the third period because of productive work by Oklahoma quarterback Bob Warmack, the Vols gave the bowl's Most Valuable Player a fit as they forged their way back into the contest. Jimmy Glover and Jimmy Weatherford both came up with timely interceptions that translated into two touchdowns.

A Kremser field goal and a Dewey Warren running burst put Tennessee's scoring total at 24. But in the meantime, the decisive play of the game came when the Big Red's Bob Stephenson intercepted a Warren pass and returned it for a touchdown.

A goofy call by Oklahoma gave the Vols their last chance. The Sooners unwisely went for it on fourth down around midfield. The Vols stopped the play, forcing Oklahoma to endure more suspense than was probably necessary.

"We made too many mistakes at the beginning," Dickey told reporters in the dressing room. "But I admire the team for the way in which it fought back and came within one kick of winning. Oklahoma had perfect execution in the first half."

Tennessee	0	0	14	10	24
Oklahoma	7	12	0	7	26

OU	Warmack, run 7 (Vachon kick)
OU	Hinton, pass from Warmack 20 (kick failed)
OU	Owens, run 1 (kick failed)
UT	Glover, interception return 36 (Kremser kick)
UT	Fulton, run 5 (Kremser kick)
OU	Stephenson, interception return 25 (Vachon kick)
UT	Kremser, field goal 26
UT	Warren, run 1 (Kremser kick)

Bob Johnson Remembers

"We really laid an egg in the first game of the season, at UCLA. We had a good run in the middle of the season and thought we were pretty good. Whether

Vols mentor Doug Dickey, in his official Athletic Department photo.

1967
T

we should have been number one in the polls or not, I don't know. A lot of us looked at the season and realized we did it to ourselves because of that first game.

"I didn't think we played very well against Oklahoma. We lost our edge from the time the season ended until we played in the Orange Bowl. We were in Miami. I had just gotten married. Dewey had just gotten married. And so had Jimmy Hahn.

"There were stars in people's eyes, being at the Orange Bowl. A lot of hoopla that caused us to lose our focus. Our senior year really went awfully well until the bowl game. We just didn't start the game ready to play.

"At halftime, it was about as harshly as Coach Dickey ever talked to us. As I remember, he was about as non-low-key as I ever saw him. He was scolding the team pretty well. We played better the second half, partly because we were embarrassed.

"We had a lot of young players who may have gotten a little full of themselves. The bowl had about 15 or 20 convertibles for the team, and it wasn't easy to handle.

"I snapped on Kremser's kick. It was a good hold, and Karl hit it good.

"In the second half, we pursued like crazy on defense and had a bunch of guys around the ball. It has to do with intensity and hustling to the ball.

"I was surprised that Oklahoma went for it on fourth down. It was like a gift. That was a strange decision.

"The closeness of our teams was evident when we held a reunion during the 2001 season to honor Coach Dickey, and a couple hundred of his old players turned out.

"Jack Reynolds was the Pete Rose of college football. He only knew one gear, and that was all-out.

"I would classify Coach Dickey and Paul Brown as being cast in the same mold. To everybody else, they seemed a bit aloof. But when you're in the heat of battle, you get less aloofness and more emotion from them than the public sees.

"When it was time to play, Coach Dickey's blood would get roaring, too. You don't play the game of football relaxed.

My definition of heroes has changed. When you get out of school, you realize that coaches like Dickey want the very best to make the team as good as it can be. You get yelled at or your friend gets demoted or you get made fun of.

"Later you say the reason Coach Dickey or Paul Brown did the things they did was because they were absolutely convinced those things would make the team better.

"The regret—and it happens on every team—is that we lost our focus going into the bowl."

1967 National Review

John McKay's Southern California Trojans battled to the national championship in both wire-service polls, edging out Tennessee, which never erased the negative fallout from a season-opening loss to UCLA in Los Angeles.

Southern Cal and UCLA fought it out all season long for supremacy on the West Coast. The issue was settled in the curtain-dropping clash at the Los Angeles Coliseum where the Trojans nipped UCLA, 21–20.

Like Tennessee, USC's record wasn't perfect. After disposing of such traditional powers as Texas, Michigan State, and Notre Dame, the Trojans stumbled against Oregon State, 3–0. But they nailed down the top position in both the writers' and coaches' polls by coming back a week later to claim the crucial win over UCLA.

UCLA likewise faltered against Oregon State, winning its first six games before settling for a 17–17 tie against the Beavers. The Bruins' stock suffered further damage in consecutive losses to Southern Cal and Syracuse as the season came to a close. A consolation prize went UCLA's way, however, when Gary Beban, the Bruins quarterback, won the Heisman Trophy by edging out USC running back O. J. Simpson.

A strong case could have been made for Oklahoma as a national-title contender. As far as the polls were concerned, however, Chuck Fairbanks's Sooners fell from contention when they dropped a 9–7 decision to Texas in the third game of the season. A key game for Oklahoma was a 21–14 win against Nebraska, but even a decision over the Cornhuskers couldn't elevate the Sooners over Southern Cal and Tennessee in the final polls.

Coach-of-the-year honors went in 1967 to John Pont, who guided his Indiana Hoosiers to a 9–1 record before suffering a 14–3 loss to Southern Cal in the Rose Bowl.

Other teams that experienced success in 1967 included Notre Dame (8–2) and Alabama (8–2–1).

A highlight was the return of Southwest Conference champ Texas A&M to the Cotton Bowl after a 26-year absence. When the Aggies, coached by Gene Stallings, defeated Alabama in the bowl game at Dallas, Crimson Tide coach Paul (Bear) Bryant helped carry Stallings off the field. Bryant had coached Stallings at Texas A&M.

The 1998 Vols

Chapter 6

1998

Tennessee fans, to whom worry comes easy, were more than customarily troubled at the start of the 1998 season, attributable largely to the loss of the great All-America quarterback Peyton Manning.

With gifted—and underrated—Tee Martin facing the thankless task of succeeding the supremely popular Manning, the outlook wasn't brilliant for the Volunteers heading into the opening game.

But when Tennessee squeaked by Syracuse and Florida bowed to the Vols in an overtime thriller at Neyland Stadium, fans were ready to name a street after Martin just as they had done a year earlier for Manning.

Like dominos, the remainder of the schedule fell into place week by week, thrusting the Vols into the first-ever official national championship game. An estimated 20,000 Tennessee fans made the trip to Tempe, Arizona, to watch the orange forces go up against Florida State to decide who would rightfully claim number one for 1998.

As revered play-by-play announcer John Ward declared when the game ended: "The national championship is clad

The 1998 coaching staff. Seated, from left, are Kurt Roper, Dan Brooks, David Cutcliffe, Head Coach Phillip Fulmer, John Chavis, Steve Caldwell, and Steve Jameson. Standing, from left, are John Stucky, Roger Frazier, David Blackburn, Mike Barry, Kevin Ramsey, Pat Washington, Randy Sanders, Mark Bradley, Condredge Holloway, and Mike Rollo.

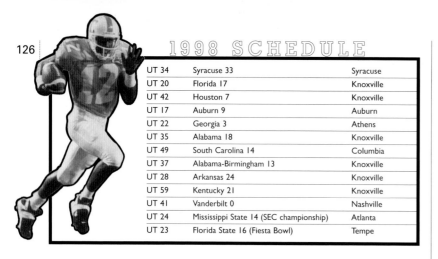

UT 34	Syracuse 33	Syracuse
UT 20	Florida 17	Knoxville
UT 42	Houston 7	Knoxville
UT 17	Auburn 9	Auburn
UT 22	Georgia 3	Athens
UT 35	Alabama 18	Knoxville
UT 49	South Carolina 14	Columbia
UT 37	Alabama-Birmingham 13	Knoxville
UT 28	Arkansas 24	Knoxville
UT 59	Kentucky 21	Knoxville
UT 41	Vanderbilt 0	Nashville
UT 24	Mississippi State 14 (SEC championship)	Atlanta
UT 23	Florida State 16 (Fiesta Bowl)	Tempe

in Big Orange." Yes, the Tennessee Vols of Coach Phillip Fulmer were the undisputed champions of college football following a 23–16 victory over the Seminoles.

No other member of college football's top 10 finished the season undefeated except seventh-ranked Tulane. The result was that every voter in both the media and coaches' polls listed Tennessee first.

Fulmer attributed the title run to a work ethic that permeated the entire squad and allowed the Vols to handle success in a mature and even-keeled manner. "That attitude is essential for a team that hopes to reach all its goals," Fulmer said. "We were fortunate all season that the players listened to their coaches and did as they were told."

The championship was especially sweet for Fulmer, a native of Winchester, Tennessee, who had grown up with a choice to make between playing football for the Alabama Crimson Tide or for his home-state UT Volunteers. He eventually cast his lot with Doug Dickey's Tennessee squad, serving in the offensive line and becoming team captain in 1971.

Fulmer's coaching career brought him back to Knoxville in 1980 as an assistant to Johnny Majors, whom he succeeded as head coach in 1992. After UT clinched both the SEC and national titles in 1998, Fulmer was named national coach of the year. For several years he has ranked among the top U.S. coaches for total won-lost record.

Vols 34, Syracuse 33

A seasoned Syracuse offense, led by multitalented quarterback Donovan McNabb, gave Tennessee as much as it could handle before succumbing to a scoring drive in the closing moments of a 34–33 victory for the Vols.

An opening-day crowd of almost 50,000 watched in the Carrier Dome as the Vols marched downfield behind the quarterbacking of Tee Martin to set up Jeff Hall's 27-yard field goal for the winning margin.

Connecting for the game-deciding points came naturally for the poised and collected Hall, who had won the Georgia game with a last-second kick during his freshman season in 1995.

Tennessee's defense found McNabb's wizardry hard to overcome, but an amazing day by linebacker Al Wilson limited the damage Syracuse could inflict. The senior, who had been the spiritual leader of the Vols throughout his career, recorded 13 tackles, caused a fumble, and included a sack and lost yardage play among his tackles.

Other statistical leaders for the Vols played huge roles in the victory. Tailback Jamal Lewis carried 20 times for 140 yards, and wide receiver Peerless Price numbered two touchdowns among the six passes he caught for 87 yards.

Tennessee went into the fray ranked number 10 in the nation by the AP poll. Syracuse was ranked number 17 but hoped to bridge the gap against the Vols by having the home-field advantage breaking in its favor.

McNabb, whose running ability limited the kind of pass rush Tennessee could mount, scrambled around enough to help him complete 22 out of 28 passes. He accounted for 300 yards and two touchdowns through the air.

The Vols' Martin, making his debut as a starter, made up in clutch situations for what he may have lacked in passing accuracy. He completed only nine of 26 tosses but managed to post two touchdowns and gain 143 yards.

Tennessee	7	7	10	10	34
Syracuse	0	10	3	20	33

UT	Price, pass from Martin 12 (Hall kick)
SU	Brominski, pass from McNabb 10 (Trout kick)
UT	Martin, run 1 (Hall kick)
SU	Trout, field goal 38
UT	Lewis, run 2 (Hall kick)
UT	Hall, field goal 18
SU	Johnson, pass from McNabb 17 (run failed)
SU	McNabb, run 6 (McIntosh run)
UT	Price, pass from Martin 8 (Hall kick)
SU	Trout, field goal 41
SU	Trout, field goal 19
UT	Hall, field goal 27

Coach Phillip Fulmer Remembers

"I was confident Jeff Hall would make the winning field goal, especially when Syracuse called timeout and he came over to the sidelines. I could see the look in his eyes and the smile on his face. I patted him on the rear, hugged his neck, and I said, 'Jeff, make Winchester proud of you.' [Author's Note: Like Fulmer, Hall hailed from Winchester, Tennessee.] And he did. A perfect snap, perfect hold, and perfect kick. It started a very special season.

"Jeff had kicked one like that against Georgia when he was a freshman. Jeff was one of the most consistent kickers in practice we ever had. I would say he and Fuad Reveiz were the two guys who were always ready in practice, no matter what the weather was like. He exuded confidence.

"A lot of people asked me about that play and quite a few others. There were probably 100 plays during the season that affected the course of the year, and it would be hard to isolate one as more important than others. Jeff's kick and the ensuing celebration in the locker room bonded a team that had a real good chemistry.

"Donovan McNabb may have been the best player we have gone against in my 10 years as head coach at Tennessee. For us to get it done against McNabb and at their place was a tremendous accomplishment. He was a phenomenal football player. He maybe didn't get the credit in college he deserved.

"I thought Tee Martin would get better as the season went along. His level of confidence and competence improved with every practice. He had an air about him that was the mark of a winning player. That whole team had confidence and ability and had a way of making the plays it needed to.

"The best thing that team did was truly take one game at a time. After the Arkansas game, they saw what they could accomplish. We were able to beat Kentucky and Vanderbilt, then win the SEC title game against Mississippi State. Then for the national championship game, it was just one big effort to get it done.*

> *"I thought Tee Martin would get better as the season went along. His level of confidence and competence improved with every practice."*
>
> *—Phillip Fulmer*

An array of trophies attests to the Vols' 1998 championship.

"But in the Syracuse game we were still finding ourselves. The confidence and chemistry came later. There were a lot of unsung heroes that year, guys like Jeff Coleman, Steve Johnson, Travis Henry, and Travis Stephens, not to mention the defense coming through after Al Wilson got hurt.

"That team was fun to coach. They weren't thinking about a national championship. They were thinking about being the best they could be. Everything you told them soaked in. They didn't have other agendas. They practiced to be the best. The 1999 team might have been more talented than the 1998 team, but they came up a play or two short."

Vols 20, Florida 17

If Tee Martin was lucky enough to pass the Syracuse test with a near-miracle finish, then surely Florida, the Volunteers' longtime nemesis, would give the new signal-caller his comeuppance in the home opener two weeks later.

Not quite. The game at Neyland Stadium went into overtime deadlocked, 17–17. In the first (and only) extra period, Martin made a play that allowed Jeff Hall the opportunity to kick a field goal for a 20–17 victory, the Vols' first decision over Florida since 1992.

The dependable Hall delivered the winning kick from the 31-yard line. The key play was Martin's scramble from the 38 on third down. Weaving his way through the Florida defense, he reached the 24, from which point the poised Hall methodically did his job.

Florida's last try to win or at least tie went down the tube on a final field goal attempt that drifted off to the left. Sealing the Gators' defeat, the errant shot set off one of those wild celebrations that mark landmark victories.

A 70-yard touchdown pass allowed Florida to knot the game in the third quarter, setting the stage for a nip-and-tuck final period that ended with neither team registering points. Tennessee's most noteworthy plays before Hall's game-winner were a 57-yard scoring burst by Shawn Bryson and a 29-yard touchdown pass from Martin to Peerless Price.

The defense struck some great licks, embodying a virtuoso performance by Al Wilson, who caused three fumbles, had a sack, deflected a pass, and registered nine tackles along with three assists. No previous Tennessee defender had forced three cough-ups in a single contest.

Deon Grant used his long arms and exceptional leaping ability to intercept a Florida pass in the fourth quarter that looked for all the world as though it were glory-bound. A record crowd, 107,653, watched the proceedings.

Florida's misfire on the field goal in overtime came on a 32-yard attempt. It was the second consecutive game against an SEC team in which the Vols had held the opposition to negative yardage on the ground. The Gators were 13 under the zero mark.

Florida	3	7	7	0	0	17
Tennessee	7	3	7	0	3	20

UF	Cooper, field goal 21
UT	Bryson, run 57 (Hall kick)
UT	Hall, field goal 39
UF	Taylor, pass from Palmer 8 (Cooper kick)
UT	Price, pass from Martin 29 (Hall kick)
UF	McGriff, pass from Palmer 70 (Chandler kick)
UT	Hall, field goal 41

Will Overstreet Remembers

"I was a true freshman that year, and it was a great experience for me—stepping up to a new level after high school and seeing the pressure mount game by game as we fought for the national championship. It was a tough year, but something I'll always cherish.

"I had been told that if I played as a freshman I wouldn't necessarily make all the right plays, but that it was important that I always try as hard as I can. So I was determined to report in good shape and that I would make it a point to always be near the ball. I would always try my best and be one of the hardest workers.

"In the Syracuse game I was in on special teams and for one defensive play, behind Corey Terry at right end. In the Florida game coaches used me a whole lot. The first impression was the magnitude of everything. It was the first time I had ever seen a game at Neyland Stadium. I couldn't believe the crowd and the noise. The sight and sound were shocking to me.

"Corey started, and I came in on the second or third series. On the first play, we had a stunt, and nobody blocked me. So I ran dead into the quarterback, Jesse Palmer, causing him to throw a terrible pass. Boy, what a thrill. I figured here I was, an All-America to be. Easy stuff.

"I played about half the snaps that game. Palmer had a pretty good game, but Al Wilson and some of us were causing or getting turnovers. Florida could march up the field, but had trouble scoring. They made great plays, and we had to make greater ones.

"Deon Grant turned a Florida touchdown pass into an interception, and Raynoch Thompson picked up a Florida fumble at our two. Al Wilson caused three fumbles.

"I started thinking we could be a national-championship contender when some of the other teams started getting beat. With our schedule, we knew if we took care of business we could be up there knocking at the championship door.

"In the long run, being on the championship team will rank as one of the great experiences of my life. To have that happen the first year of the BCS was simply amazing. And, of course, the Florida game was one of the best experiences of my life.

"What a day for my first home game at Neyland Stadium. I stayed out on the field as long as I could.

"Al Wilson was a great leader on that team. He came to work every day prepared to do whatever it took."

Vols 42, Houston 7

In contrast to the two nail-biters that preceded it, games that were settled in the closing moments, Tennessee went to work early against Houston, seized command quickly, and rolled to a 42–7 triumph over the Cougars.

Tee Martin, whose first two games as starting quarterback revealed a tendency to overthrow his targets, improved his accuracy at the expense of Houston and came off the field with a reputation as an adequate marksman, both short- and long-range. Martin threw early and often, hitting for 214 yards and four touchdowns, including one to Cedrick Wilson in the first quarter from the three. Two more scores in the second quarter lifted the game out of the suspense category and allowed Coach Fulmer to substitute liberally in quest of depth that would be useful late in the season.

Sharing the stage with Martin was tailback Jamal Lewis. The sophomore speedster took in one touchdown pass from Martin and broke loose on a 59-yard scoring run in the third quarter to put the game out of reach.

The avalanche of six touchdowns erased any lingering doubts that Tee Martin could direct a top-drawer offense with splendid results, especially with Lewis in the backfield sharing the brunt of the running attack with the multitalented quarterback. (It was a theory that would be put to a stern test a couple of games later.)

Six touchdowns was impressive, indeed, considering one touchdown was called back for a rules infraction and that the game ended with the Vols perched on the Cougar 1.

In addition to firing a touchdown pass to Lewis, Martin connected for scores to Wilson (33 yards), Shawn Bryson (63 yards), and Peerless Price (22 yards). Reserve quarterback Burney Veazey found tight end John Finlayson for a 21-yard touchdown pass in the fourth period. Houston's lone score came on a 19-yard pass play in the last quarter.

Aggressive defensive play by the Vols wrecked Houston's offense. Eight tackles for losses and three sacks highlighted Tennessee's performance, in which Eric Westmoreland, Raynoch Thompson, Chris Ramseur, and Deon Grant provided leadership. Lewis finished with 135 yards on the ground, while Price led the receiving effort, grabbing seven passes for 76 yards and the last Tennessee score before the reserves took over late in the game.

Houston	0	0	7	0	7
Tennessee	7	14	7	14	42

UT	Wilson, pass from Martin 33 (Hall kick)
UT	Lewis, pass from Martin (Hall kick)
UT	Bryson, pass from Martin 63 (Hall kick)
UH	Regimbald, pass from McKinley 19 (Waddell kick)
UT	Lewis, run 59 (Hall kick)
UT	Price, pass from Martin 22 (Hall kick)
UT	Finlayson, pass from Veazey 21 (Hall kick)

Coach Dan Brooks Remembers

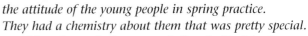

"I knew we had a lot of good players in 1998, but being a coach I worried about how we would adjust to the loss of two bell-cows like Peyton Manning and Leonard Little. I liked the attitude of the young people in spring practice. They had a chemistry about them that was pretty special.

"Our players had a strong feeling for Tee Martin, realizing he was a very talented guy who had waited here all those years for his opportunity. They rallied around him and wanted him to be successful. And I heard that he said that summer we were going to win the national championship.

"Going into the Houston game, after tremendous battles with Syracuse and Florida, you worry about whether the team respected its opponent that week. If we showed up and did what we were expected to do, we would be okay. But it was a worry because Houston was a respectable football team.

"With this team, they did what had to be done. They showed up for Houston and played a decent game. All year long somebody was going to do something that had to be done. We missed Leonard Little, but he was such a dedicated player, he had left something for the others to live up to—guys like Shaun Ellis.

"The closeness of the team was best exhibited in the Arkansas game. People may forget we blocked a field goal that might have put it out of reach from our standpoint. But after the block, we didn't score. Still, nobody was complaining.

"Over on the sideline, I heard Billy Ratliff tell Martin to keep his head up, that the defense wouldn't be out there long. And sure enough, they gave the offense one more chance. Travis Henry took the ball downfield for all the yardage and got us the winning points. They had a great confidence in themselves.

"Against Houston, we made progress offensively, and defensively we played a very solid game.

"We had four good players at tackle that year, and we decided to play them all. We didn't care who was in the game at a given moment. You had Darwin Walker, who is still playing; Billy Ratliff, who was as good as any tackle we've ever had except for injuries; Jeff Coleman, who was our starter out of Gaffney, South Carolina; and Ron Greene, another outstanding player.

"That year we started talking about our Carolina Connection. All four starters in the defensive line from the Carolinas: Shaun Ellis from Anderson, South Carolina; Jeff Coleman from Gaffney, South Carolina; Darwin Walker from Walterboro, South Carolina; and Corey Terry, from Warrenton, North Carolina. We should have kept our mouths shut, because when we had the national championship team with that many guys from the Carolinas, it got to be harder and more competitive to recruit.

"The ends were Corey Terry, a great running back in high school, and Ellis, who turned out to be a first-round draft choice. He was a man playing this game. During the Houston game, Will Overstreet really emerged and was a starter from that time on. DeAngelo Lloyd also played a lot.

"Some things have to go right to win a championship, and that's what happened."

Vols 17, Auburn 9

Tennessee paid a steep price—the loss of Jamal Lewis for the rest of the season—but the Vols managed to stave off repeated Auburn rallies and hang on for a 17–9 victory at Jordan-Hare Stadium.

Defensive end Shaun Ellis made the play early that in retrospect perhaps did more than anything else to settle the issue in UT's favor. In the opening period, Auburn moved the ball smartly into Tennessee territory.

Somehow Ellis managed to step between the quarterback and the Auburn running back on a pitch play. He looked dangerously close to running out of gas, but the big lineman managed to sprint 90 yards for the touchdown that turned the game around.

Still in the first period, Lewis, Tennessee's sensational tailback, broke loose on a 67-yard touchdown run that was Tennessee's final six-pointer of the afternoon. A short time later, Jeff Hall closed out UT's scoring with a 46-yard field goal.

From that point, a 17–0 first-quarter lead, Tennessee spent the rest of the game fending off one Auburn offensive try after another. UT's clutch play reached its zenith in the second quarter when Auburn picked up a first down at the Tennessee 1. Four straight times the Tigers tried without success to dent the UT line.

Raynoch Thompson, an all-star linebacker, made the stop on fourth down, delivering a devastating blow to Auburn's hopes of upsetting the defending Southeastern Conference champions.

Spencer Riley–to–Tee Martin was a perfect team for the center-to-quarterback snap.

The game marked Tennessee's first appearance at Auburn since 1990, and it was the team's first victory there since 1980. Playing without All-America linebacker Al Wilson, the Vols managed seven lost-yardage tackles and two sacks. Against the spirited Tennessee defense, Auburn could manage only a trio of field goals, scored from 40, 44, and 45 yards. Though stunned by the Vols' first-quarter blitz, Auburn never let up and was firing for a touchdown as the game ended.

Tennessee	17	0	0	0	17
Auburn	0	3	3	3	9

UT	Ellis, interception return 90 (Hall kick)
UT	Lewis, run 67 (Hall kick)
UT	Hall, field goal 46
AU	Bironas, field goal 40
AU	Bironas, field goal 44
AU	Bironas, field goal 45

Spencer Riley Remembers

"When Jamal got hurt, the rest of the team knew we needed to rally around Travis Stephens, who moved up to first team at tailback. We had an experienced line—Fred Weary, Chad Clifton, Jarvis Reado, Cosey Coleman, and Mercedes Hamilton.

"Jarvis and Mercedes were both seniors. We were a good, tight bunch of guys. Travis did a great job for us. We knew we just had to open up some holes for him.

"That year we were playing with Tee Martin as quarterback moving up after the graduation of Peyton Manning. They were different-type quarterbacks. Peyton was pretty much detail-oriented while Tee was wind-up, let her fly.

But Tennessee's victory came with the loss of the talented Lewis for the next eight games, including a bowl. The sophomore speedster, who accrued 140 yards on 18 carries against Auburn, went out late in the game with a knee injury that would end his participation for the rest of the season.

1998

T

"With Peyton, you knew pretty well he was going to throw the football. With Tee, you really didn't know if he was going to run or throw. If the receivers were covered, he could tuck the ball in and set sail.

"Tee showed his ability in the Nebraska game the year before. The Syracuse game really let us know what he was capable of doing.

"The Auburn team of 1998 was more well rounded defensively than the 1997 team we beat in the SEC championship game. They had a good game plan and were really fired-up playing us at Jordan-Hare Stadium.

"I've played about everywhere in the SEC, and that was one of my favorite places. Their fans were real supportive of their team. My mom and dad and my wife, Beth, were all at the game.

"Al Wilson missed the game with an injury, but our defense was very good. Al was a vocal leader toward the defense and how they played. With the offense, he didn't say much even though he was captain. He knew we would do our job.

"It's a great feeling to have played on the national championship team. I'll never forget it. We players have stayed close."

Vols 22, Georgia 3

Tennessee fans were in a pessimistic frame of mind after the Vols barely hung on for a victory over Auburn and then received the news that their star running back was out for the season.

As Phillip Fulmer often suggested, someone needed to step forward in the squad's hour of need. That's what sophomore Travis Stephens did as he replaced the injured Jamal Lewis and led the Vols to a 22–3 victory over the Bulldogs.

Tennessee's ground game was far from impotent as Stephens carried 20 times in a workhorse performance and dented the Georgia defense for 107 yards, allaying fears that without Lewis the Vols would be limited only to what they could produce through the air.

Another Travis, a young man from Florida with the last name of Henry, added 53 yards as a backup tailback. Both Travises would establish themselves as fan favorites long before they finished their eligibility at Tennessee. Tee Martin was sharp with his passing, ripping the Bulldogs for a pair of short touchdown throws to Cedrick Wilson and Peerless Price.

After Tennessee and Georgia swapped field goals in the first quarter, the Vols took command in the second period and led 9–3 at the half on two more field goals. They then sealed the victory with two touchdowns in the third period.

Jeff Hall, the Vols' dependable placekicker, hit on field goals of 27, 39, and 43 yards, accounting for all of UT's scores in the first half.

Deon Grant, the free safety, earned Southeastern Conference defensive-player-of-the-week honors with a masterful performance that included six tackles, an interception, a pass broken up, and a recovered fumble.

Fiery linebacker Al Wilson chipped in with six tackles, a tackle for loss, and a sack. Derrick Edmonds, substituting for the injured Fred White at strong safety, had eight tackles and an interception.

Tennessee	3	6	13	0	22
Georgia	3	0	0	0	3

UT	Hall, field goal 27
UGA	Hines, field goal 48
UT	Hall, field goal 39
UT	Hall, field goal 43
UT	Wilson, pass from Martin (run failed)
UT	Price, pass from Martin 3 (Hall kick)

<u>Travis Stephens Remembers</u>

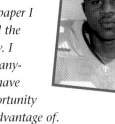

"When I learned from the newspaper I would be the starter, I welcomed the opportunity to prove I could play. I wasn't nervous—nothing more, anyway, than the nervousness you have with every game. It was an opportunity that I was determined to take advantage of.

"I knew even when Jamal Lewis became the starter I eventually would get the chance to play. For one thing, Jamal made the statement that he was going to leave after his junior year.

"The coaches made their decision to have Jamal start, and if I hadn't felt sure I would get a chance eventually, I would have transferred. We have to make our decisions the same way the coaches make theirs.

"I remember going into the Georgia game the broadcasters on TV thought we were going to lose. But fans look at things differently than the players and coaches. I understand why the fans were down. We had lost the big-time running back, and Georgia was supposed to be coming along with Quincy Carter at quarterback.

"They didn't know how well we would be able to replace Jamal. But the fans back in my hometown of Clarksville knew what I could do, and I did, too.

"Like I said, I found out in the newspaper I would start against Georgia. But I was second man on the depth chart, so I figured I would move up. I am glad I later redshirted because I wanted to have a full year as a starter.

"It was all worth it. The national championship. There was nothing like it."

Vols 35, Alabama 18

As Tennessee posted a crucial 35–18 victory over old foe Alabama, Peerless Price turned in the most memorable play of the game, a 100-yard kickoff return that nullified the Crimson Tide's bid for a comeback.

Price's heroics came at just the right time to take the starch out of the Red Elephants, who had cut UT's margin to 21–11 on Shaun Alexander's 44-yard touchdown run and a subsequent two-point conversion.

All the to-do came in the third period when Alexander's lengthy excursion fueled Bama's hopes of mounting a rally that would deny Tennessee a fourth consecutive victory in the South's most storied football rivalry.

The Vols distributed their scoring neatly, with single touchdowns in each of the first three quarters and a pair of tallies in the final quarter. The first two TDs came on Tee Martin runs of three and five yards.

Travis Henry, who had alternated with Travis Stephens in carrying the ball since the loss of Jamal Lewis in the Auburn game, bore the brunt of the load against the Tide, romping for 113 yards on 22 carries. Henry accounted for touchdowns on runs of 1 and 5 yards.

John Chavis's defensive unit was in fine form, standing tall except when Alexander carried. The talented Alabama running back carried 26 times for 132 yards, but Raynoch Thompson with 13 tackles and Al Wilson with eight, were mainly responsible for limiting the Tide to a pair of touchdowns.

Price's kickoff return was only the third such run in UT football history to measure 100 yards. Pete Panuska had made one against Maryland in the 1984 Sun Bowl, while Willie Gault traversed the distance against Pittsburgh in 1980.

UT fans savored the fourth straight win over the Tide. The Tennessee faithful were still trying to get over the dominance Alabama had enjoyed in the series from the early 1960s into the 1990s, with only an occasional letup.

Alabama	3	0	8	7	18
Tennessee	7	7	7	14	35

UT	Martin, run 1 (Hall kick)
UA	Pflunger, field goal 41
UT	Martin, run 5 (Hall kick)
UA	Alexander, run 44 (Jackson, pass from Zow)
UT	Price, kickoff return 100 (Hall kick)
UT	Henry, run 1 (Hall kick)
UA	Zow, run 2 (Pflunger kick)
UT	Henry, run 5 (Hall kick)

After an injury sidelined Jamal Lewis in 1998, Travis Henry performed admirably as Lewis's replacement at tailback.

Coach David Cutcliffe Remembers

"When I came to Tennessee, the Alabama game was the signature game. But when we changed to two divisions in the SEC, the Florida game took on a greater impact, partly because of the surge in the Florida program. In the Eastern Division, Tennessee–Florida became critical.

"But I think with the Tennessee fans, the Alabama game remained more emotional. And the same was true with our players because they knew how the fans and the students feel. That game in October still has a special place.

"When we lost Jamal, we were concerned about a drop in productivity. But we knew we had two talented backs in Travis Henry and Travis Stephens. Jamal had been a combination of breakaway speed and size.

"The way we employed the two Travises was that we would size up our opponent and then fit the game plan with the talents of the two running backs. It may have oversimplified things a bit, but I always told Henry and Stephens they would play according to who took best care of the ball.

1998

T

"Early I was concerned about whether Travis Stephens would hold on to the ball. He later grew somewhat, and by then both of them were dependable as far as securing the ball was concerned.

"It was an interesting year in the SEC, and I remember telling Tee it was vital that he play smart and let the other players do what they can to win games. He didn't have to do it by himself.

"We had a situation in the Georgia game where he was taking too much on his own. He had made some critical mistakes in the first half. Previous to that game, he had played conservatively and done what we asked him.

"I had to sit him down at halftime and tell him he needed to play smarter the second half. If he didn't, somebody else would be playing quarterback. He did like I wanted him to, and he continued to improve that year. He grew up between the Georgia and Alabama games.

"Beating Alabama a fourth consecutive year was very significant. As great as the Alabama-Tennessee rivalry was, it had become a series of streaks, first one and then the other dominating. When you beat a team four years in a row, and their seniors can't remember winning against you, they start wondering if they can ever beat you. It becomes a big thing.

"Coach Fulmer's attention to detail is the first thing I think about when I try to assess his ability. A successful person needs that gift and a good work ethic. He has them both. He loves to compete, and it shows in his football team."

Vols 49, South Carolina 14

Disposing of South Carolina more or less as anticipated, the Volunteers provided an exciting side attraction in the otherwise routine 49–14 victory over the Gamecocks at Columbia.

While fans were noting the dimension of the Tennessee triumph, Tee Martin, unbeknownst to most of the 69,000 spectators, was quietly destroying one of the NCAA's most treasured records: the mark for most consecutive completed passes.

Martin repeatedly hit the bull's-eye—to Peerless Price, to Jermaine Copeland, to Cedric Wilson. Before you knew it, he had completed 23 in a row, making him an NCAA record-holder on two counts.

First, that was the most consecutive completions ever in a single game, with a 10-yard toss to Price as the record-breaker. When combined with Martin's last pass of the Alabama game, a completion, it gave him a total of 24 over more than one game. With 96 percent of its passes completed for the game, Tennessee set an NCAA team record.

The Vols were hitting on all burners against the Gamecocks, accounting for 221 yards on the ground and 340 through the air. Martin hit Price for two touchdowns and Copeland and Wilson for one each.

Shawn Bryson, Phillip Crosby, and Travis Henry registered touchdowns on rushing plays, and Henry paced the ground attack with 96 yards on 12 carries.

Defensively, Billy Ratliff captured the spotlight by blocking a field goal. Al Wilson had the better all-around game, making eight tackles, causing a fumble and recovering one. The Vols had a 49–0 lead before South Carolina tallied its two touchdowns.

Cedrick Wilson got Tennessee off to a roaring start by recovering a fumble that led to a touchdown. The win moved Tennessee's advantage in the series to 13–2–2. Ratliff's block of the field goal was the first by a Tennessee player since 1996.

Tennessee	7	14	21	7	49
South Carolina	0	0	0	14	14

UT	Copeland, pass from Martin 21 (Hall kick)
UT	Wilson, pass from Martin 2 (Hall kick)
UT	Price, pass from Martin 13 (Hall kick)
UT	Price, pass from Martin 71 (Hall kick)
UT	Bryson, run 5 (Hall kick)
UT	Crosby, run 1 (Hall kick)
SC	Davis, pass from Petty 24 (Leavitt kick)
UT	Henry, run 1 (Hall kick)
SC	Kelly, pass from Petty 14 (Leavitt kick)

Al Wilson Remembers

"Being a part of the team when Tee Martin set the consecutive pass record will always be one of my biggest thrills. Of course, it had never occurred to any of us that anything like that could happen. I didn't even realize he was close to any kind of a record until somebody picked up on it over on the sideline.

"It was great for Tee, and it was great for the team. That was a day he was hitting on all cylinders. You know, Tee told me before the season started that we were going to win the national championship. That was his prediction. I told him at the time, you lead us, and we will ride your coattails.

"As one of the team captains that year, I took it on myself to assume the leadership role that had been vacated when Peyton Manning and Leonard Little graduated. Nobody knew for sure who would step up and take over. I decided I was going to lead the team to be the best we could be.

"We were a team. We weren't separated by offense and defense. My role was to help lead the entire team, not just

the defense. It was my job to go out there and lead by example with the hope the entire team would feed off it. With Peyton and Leonard gone, we really didn't have any stars, so what we did was to jell and play as a unit.

"To me, it didn't click in that we might win the national championship until late in the season. But then when we got by Vanderbilt and played for the SEC championship, I realized we had a shot at winning it. We came from behind in several games. We fought for one another and wouldn't quit until the last click of the clock.

"A lot of people ask me about the Florida game and what winning against the Gators meant to me. In that game I was credited with causing three fumbles. Even though we took our opponents one at a time, I remember being in some

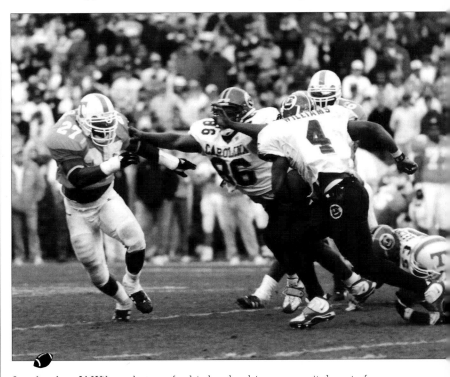

Linebacker Al Wilson, known for his leadership, was a vital part of the 1998 national championship campaign.

1998

T

kind of a zone that particular day. I wasn't aware of anything out there except me and the guy carrying the ball.

"But the whole season was a highlight of my life, not that one game especially. That season and that team gave me so many great memories that Tennessee will always be a special place for me.

"The coaches treated me as a leader. We trusted one another. I told them what I thought would work in a situation, and if they thought so, too, we would use it. We worked off one another."

Vols 37, Alabama–Birmingham 13

It went in the books as a 37–13 victory over Alabama-Birmingham—no surprise there—but the aftershocks by Saturday night had national reverberations.

Two events happened that day to make the decision over UAB highly consequential in the overall picture of college football. First, of course, was the win over the Blazers, a triumph that cast both the offense and defense in a favorable light.

It would have been written and talked about as only another string in Tennessee's succession of consecutive 1998 victories, bringing the count to eight, the first time the Vols held a streak that long since 1956. But Big Ten action completely changed the picture and catapulted the Vols to the forefront of national rankings.

Ohio State's loss to Michigan the same day elevated the Vols to number one in both the AP and coaches' polls and gave Tennessee the top spot also in the Bowl Championship Series rankings, positions they would maintain from that point on.

The Vols spread their scoring in a workmanlike manner, with 10 points in the first quarter, 14 in the second, 10

in the third, and three in the fourth. Phillip Fulmer played his reserves liberally in the latter part of the game.

On offense, credit went to Travis Henry, who pounded out 104 yards on 17 carries, and to Tee Martin, whose hot hand connected on 18 of 25 passes for 274 yards and a touchdown, a 28-yard toss to Cedrick Wilson.

Defensive stalwarts included linebackers Al Wilson, Raynoch Thompson, and Eric Westmoreland, who combined for 29 tackles. Westmoreland provided two of the most telling plays, knifing twice through the UAB line to nail runners behind the line of scrimmage.

The Vols got through the game without once requiring David Leaverton to hoist a punt. Winning the battle of first downs by a substantial 27–15 margin, Tennessee posted 447 yards total offense.

UAB	0	3	3	7	13
Tennessee	10	14	10	3	37

UT	Hall, field goal 39
UT	Henry, run 18 (Hall kick)
UAB	Gallego, field goal 20
UT	Stephens, run 11 (Hall kick)
UT	Martin, run 1 (Hall kick)
UT	Wilson, pass from Martin 28 (Hall kick)
UAB	Gallego, field goal 36
UT	Hall, field goal 20
UT	Hall, field goal 37
UAB	Jolly, run 32 (Gallego kick)

Jeff Hall Remembers

"Moving up to number one in the polls didn't mean much to us at the time because Coach Fulmer talked to us

about how the wind blows hardest at the top of the flagpole. For most of that season, we had been underdogs and knew that we truthfully had to take them one at a time.

"Another reason we didn't celebrate was that we were to play Arkansas the following week, and the Razorbacks were undefeated, too. So there really wasn't anything to get too excited about. We knew it was midseason and the rankings meant nothing.

"We all avoided the press's questions about that kind of thing, and that allowed us to keep our perspective. The whole season was made of heroes, and we had different heroes as we went along. The biggest turning point for us in the season was the Arkansas game, when we recovered the fumble and then drove the remaining yards for the winning touchdown. When we won that game the way we did, we knew something special was going on.

"I treated all field goals the same, whether it was in a game like UAB or the Syracuse or Florida games. I was always wound up, knowing it was critical for me to get out there and score the points. I was prepared for every game, no matter who we played.

"Coach Fulmer and I were from the same home town and played for the same school, Franklin County High School. My dad was two years ahead of him in school, and my mom was right behind him. There were a lot of similarities in background as far as circle of friends was concerned. I had, and still have, great respect for him. There is nobody I would rather have played for."

Vols 28, Arkansas 24

One of the most memorable comebacks in Tennessee football history, one that wasn't complete until only 20 seconds showed on the game clock, allowed the Vols to skip past Arkansas, 28–24, on a rainy afternoon at Neyland Stadium.

Two teams ranked in the top 10 swapped apparent knockout blows, Arkansas thinking it had delivered the

Arkansas quarterback Clint Stoerner's fumble, caused by Billy Ratliff, was a key to Tennessee's 1998 championship. The Vols edged the Razorbacks, 28–24.

haymaker when it went ahead 21–3 in the second quarter. But it was Tennessee that landed the KO when Travis Henry plunged across from the 1-yard line in the final minute.

Trailing 24–22, with the Razorbacks trying to run out the clock, Tennessee got a reprieve on an Arkansas fumble with 1:43 left. Billy Ratliff recovered Clint Stoerner's bobble. Film replays indicated that it was Ratliff's charge on the snap that caused the fumble.

Given the break they had to have, the Vols entrusted their fortunes to Henry, who would end the game with 197 yards on 32 carries. Five times Henry carried the ball against the Arkansas defenders until he ripped across from the 1 at the end of a 43-yard drive.

Stoerner had been the workhorse of the Arkansas attack, passing for 274 yards on 17 completions in 34 attempts. Three tosses went for touchdowns. One covered 62 yards.

Tennessee signal-caller Tee Martin was down a bit in his passing percentages, connecting on only 10 of 27. One of his throws accounted for a touchdown, a 26-yarder to Peerless Price.

Statistically, the game was pretty much a wash, with each team amassing 21 first downs and the Vols enjoying a 22-yard advantage in total yards, 377 to 355.

Jeff Hall's field goals of 41 and 21 yards contributed to the victory as did a safety charged against the Razorbacks after an errant snap from center on a punt attempt. The Arkansas kicker wisely booted the ball through his end zone, giving Tennessee two points but not field position.

Arkansas	7	14	3	0	24
Tennessee	0	10	10	8	28

UA	Smith, pass from Stoerner 14 (Latourette kick)
UA	Lucas, pass from Stoerner 62 (Latourette kick)
UT	Hall, field goal 41
UA	Lucas, pass from Stoerner 8 (Latourette kick)
UT	Price, pass from Martin 36 (Hall kick)
UA	Latourette, field goal 33
UT	Martin, run 4 (Hall kick)
UT	Hall, field goal 21
UT	Safety, ball kicked out of end zone
UT	Henry, run 1 (Run failed)

Billy Ratliff Remembers

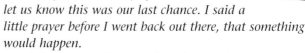

"We hadn't given up over on the side-lines. Just before we went back out there on defense, Al Wilson came over to urge us on. Al was out of the game because of a shoulder injury. But he let us know this was our last chance. I said a little prayer before I went back out there, that something would happen.

"There was still quite a bit of time left on the clock. The offensive lineman I was playing against was the best I had seen all year. But I had noticed the last two series I had been able to push him back a little bit. I was surprised that Arkansas ran a play-action at that time. I expected them to strictly keep the ball on the ground and run out the clock.

"I realized the only way I could make a big play was to push the lineman into either the quarterback or the running back, whoever had the ball. On that play I pushed and pushed until it seemed as though Stoerner tripped over the lineman's leg. I looked down, and there was the football on the ground.

1998

T

> *"I don't think Arkansas realized there had been a fumble. After the recovery, the whole defensive unit stood on the sidelines and hollered to the offense that we needed some scoring."*
>
> *—Billy Ratliff*

"It must have been there three seconds, at least, and I was lucky enough to recover it. That was a long time. I don't think Arkansas realized there had been a fumble. After the recovery, the whole defensive unit stood on the sidelines and hollered to the offense that we needed some scoring. Travis Henry and the rest of the offense took care of business the rest of the way.

"I guess that fumble and recovery amounted to the biggest play of my career. Up to then, my favorite play had been the time I sacked Danny Wuerffel my freshman season. That made my season.

"We made a lot of big defensive plays we needed in order to have an undefeated season. I still have a lot of friends from that group: Al Wilson, Shaun Ellis, Darwin Walker, Corey Terry, Buck Buxton, Ron Green, Raynoch Thompson, Will Overstreet. I stay close to those guys. We are a family.

"We didn't expect Arkansas to come after us through the air the way they did. They were primarily a running team, but it was Stoerner's passing that gave us so much trouble that day. They were undefeated at the time we played them and were ranked in the top 10.

"Believe it or not, the Florida State game was about our easiest game that year. We had heard so much Florida State this and Florida State that that we were ready to take them on when we got there."

Vols 59, Kentucky 21

Shawn Bryson, a pulverizing blocker at fullback, showed the sprinter side of his football skills in scoring two touchdowns and leading the Vols to a convincing 59–21 victory over Kentucky.

A crowd of 107,252 watched Tennessee in its final Neyland Stadium performance in a season that would culminate in a national championship. Following a momentary jolt, in which Kentucky seized the lead briefly late in the first period, the Vols took command and held a 41–7 lead at the half.

Bryson was normally content to apply the block that allowed Travis Henry or Travis Stephens to set sail from tailback. But against the Wildcats he increased his repertoire to account for touchdowns on runs of 1 and 58 yards and a two-point conversion on a pass from Tee Martin.

The ever-dependable Jeff Hall came through as a kick artist, notching three field goals and six conversion kicks. His 15 points made him the Southeastern Conference's all-time scoring champion with 371 points.

Travis Stephens, another resourceful Tennessee tailback, carries for yardage against Kentucky..

Henry, Stephens, and Phillip Crosby scored on short runs. Martin broke free for a 33-yard touchdown run and added another score on a 55-yard pass play to Cedrick Wilson. The win over the Wildcats clinched the Eastern Division berth in the SEC championship game.

Kentucky's All-America passer, Tim Couch, was introduced rudely to Tennessee defensive end Will Overstreet, who had two sacks as one of the highlights of his rookie season in college. Overstreet's teammates added four other sacks at Couch's expense.

Martin completed 13 of 20 passes for 189 yards, while Couch's numbers for the game were 36 completions on 55 tries for 337 yards and two touchdowns.

Eric Westmoreland was conspicuous from his linebacker post, chalking up three plays for lost yardage among the nine tackles he made during the game. In addition to six sacks, the Vols had five other tackles for losses.

Kentucky	7	0	7	7	21
Tennessee	14	24	14	7	59

UT	Hall, field goal 37
UT	Hall, field goal 32
UK	Mickelson, pass from Couch 3 (Hanson kick)
UT	Bryson, run 1 (Bryson, pass from Martin)
UT	Wilson, pass from Martin 55 (Hall kick)
UT	Bryson, run 58 (Hall kick)
UT	Hall, field goal 47
UT	Crosby, run 1 (Hall kick)
UK	Homer, run 1 (Hanson kick)
UT	Henry, run 2 (Hall kick)
UT	Martin, run 33 (Hall kick)
UT	Stephens, run 1 (Hall kick)
UK	Mickelson, pass from Couch 3 (Hanson kick)

David Leaverton Remembers

"We were talking about championships because that was our goal at the beginning of the season. We were talking more in terms of the SEC championship because we knew we had Kentucky and Vanderbilt left on the schedule. Those were games that Tennessee didn't lose very often.

"We had beaten the giants of the conference and had those two games left. We saw the SEC championship as a very attainable goal at that point. The coaches did a good job every week taking the team that we were playing and making them sound like the best team in the league.

"We were ready for Kentucky, but we knew with Tim Couch at quarterback, Kentucky was the kind of team that could score 60 points on us in a matter of seconds. They had put up about 500 yards of offense the previous year. We definitely couldn't take them lightly.

"The defense showed the leadership that was based on the idea that Tim Couch wouldn't be allowed to take over the game. Guys like Al Wilson weren't going to let that happen. They wouldn't let Couch get out of hand. He had a number of great weapons, good receivers. You are usually going to score a pretty good number of points on Kentucky.

"Shawn Bryson, who made a big run in this game, had an incredible game. The run that stands out in my mind by Shawn came in the Florida game when he ran right up the middle and kept going and going. From that point on, I knew Shawn was a weapon and anytime he got hold of the ball, something special would happen. This was his last home game, and I know it was an exciting time for him and his family. He wanted to go out and say goodbye to all the Tennessee fans with a dominating performance, and he succeeded in doing that. He was an incredible player with great ability. Unfortunately, the fullback position at Tennessee doesn't provide an opportunity for great glory, but he made the most of that position as anybody Tennessee has had.

"Will Overstreet had a couple of sacks in this game. From the day he walked on campus, I could tell this guy was mentally focused. He was an incredible player. Somewhat undersized—compared to people like Leonard Little. But the man has a motor like no other. I've met with a lot of guys in the NFL who played against Will Overstreet, and they agree to a man, he never quits.

"There are some things you cannot teach, and that is something Will has inside his heart. He's going to work harder than you every single play. He gets the most out of what God has given him. It was neat in this game to see a glimpse of what he would one day become. He became a player on our team that every opponent had to account for on every play.

"My freshman year was the toughest time in my life. I really wanted to quit the football team and pursue some other interests. It was a tough thing to sit through that freshman year, but to stick around and win the national championship made it all worthwhile. It was reward, it was redemption, from the low point of my career as a freshman. All those tough times sort of faded into the background.

"I think the key to our national championship, first of all, we played as a team. We did not care who was going to get the credit or blame. It was a team who had lost most of our superstars, and we knew we couldn't depend on the marquee players anymore. This wasn't the most talented team in the history of Tennessee football, but it was one of the most hardworking and unified teams I had ever been around."

Vols 41, Vanderbilt 0

Wrapping up an undefeated campaign, pending postseason activity, the Vols put Vanderbilt away, 41–0, to give themselves the outright Eastern Division championship of the Southeastern Conference.

The week before, Tennessee had nailed down the Eastern representative role in the SEC championship game. A full house at Vanderbilt watched the orange forces ring up their 19th consecutive regular season victory against an error-prone Vanderbilt squad that suffered four interceptions and two lost fumbles.

One fumble in particular haunted the Commodores. Tennessee linebacker Chris Ramseur darted into the end zone after scooping up the dropped ball at the 12. Deon Grant, Fred White, Dwayne Goodrich, and Derrick Edmonds accounted for the interceptions. Darwin Walker had the other fumble recovery.

After a 22-yard field goal by Jeff Hall put Tennessee ahead—accounting for the only points of the first period—the Vols got into their rhythm, posting 17 points in the second quarter, seven in the third, and 14 in the fourth.

Vanderbilt simply couldn't get its offense untracked in the face of a Tennessee defense determined to post the Vols' first shutout since 1995. The Commodores ended the day with 11 first downs, 91 yards on the ground, and 83 through the air.

After Hall's first-period field goal, the Vols added two touchdowns in the first half, quarterback Tee Martin and receiver Peerless Price hooking up on a 67-yard pass play to get things started. The pass itself was relatively short, but Price did some fancy footwork to take the ball to pay dirt. He broke away from three Commodore defenders and converted a short gain into a scintillating touchdown run.

Then, Travis Henry, continuing his outstanding work as the replacement for Jamal Lewis at tailback, scored from 12 yards out. The pair of touchdowns, followed by another Hall field goal, pushed Tennessee's advantage at halftime to 20–0.

Martin completed 13 of 20 passes for 241 yards, which combined with the Vols' net of 189 yards by ground to make the total offensive production hit 430 yards. Price reached a career high 189 yards as a receiver.

Tennessee	3	17	7	14	41
Vanderbilt	0	0	0	0	0

UT	Hall, field goal 22
UT	Price, pass from Martin 67 (Hall kick)
UT	Henry, run 12 (Hall kick)
UT	Hall, field goal 42
UT	Ramseur, fumble return 12 (Hall kick)
UT	Martin, run 1 (Hall kick)
UT	Stephens, run 1 (Hall kick)

Coach John Chavis Remembers

"Our defense was one with a lot of capabilities. We had sustained some heavy losses from 1997, both on offense and defense. We had plenty of talent, but the key thing we had was attitude. Those guys played as one. They cared about each other. That's what made us a special unit all season.

"Our defense that year felt it had to take up a little slack for the offense, which had lost Peyton Manning. Peyton was one of the all-time Volunteers, but the defensive players liked Tee Martin, too, and wanted him to be successful.

"In this game, we realized Vanderbilt had given people problems all season. It's one where you throw out the records. More times than not, a few key plays will be the difference in the ball game. They had a nice scheme, but we were ready.

"Then, just before the game, Raynoch Thompson tells me he can't go at linebacker with an ankle injury. Raynoch is one of the toughest guys I know, so one of our top players can't make it.

"But Al Wilson and Eric Westmoreland stepped it up. Talking about Al Wilson, in 23 years of coaching I haven't been around a better leader than he was. He had a gift of talking, and people liked to listen to him.

"More important than that, though, was the way he practiced. He called on his teammates to go all out in practice. His leadership wasn't some kind of a game-time show. That was Al Wilson. He loved to compete, and he loved to win. He was the one who tied us together.

"That was a game in Nashville where we had exceptional fan support. It was truly like a home game that day. There was a lot of orange, and it made it great for our team.

"We played an aggressive style all season. We are better when we turn them loose and let them play. We're a team that's always on the edge, and that makes us better.

"Of course, looking back on the season, people still ask me about the Arkansas game and the way our defense provided one last opportunity for the offense to score and pull out the victory. The character of our team really showed up. There was little more than a minute left. Our defense showed how much confidence it had when Billy Ratliff told Tee Martin as Tee was coming off the field, 'Keep your helmet on; we'll just be out there a minute.' It was a bold statement, but showed Billy's will to win.

"They created an opportunity. We expected Arkansas to run some time off by sending the quarterback wide. Billy was so quick off the football he knocked the center back into the quarterback, causing the quarterback to stumble. It was a play we needed."

Vols 24, Mississippi State 14

An electrifying atmosphere prevailed at the Georgia Dome in Atlanta as the Volunteers went after their second straight league title before a capacity crowd. Everything happened just right for the Tennessee Volunteers on December 5, not

the least of which was making the winning rally that pulled the fat out of the fire against Mississippi State in the Southeastern Conference championship game.

Another concern vanished when UCLA and Kansas State, two other undefeated teams competing with Tennessee for invitations to the Bowl Championship Series national title game, dropped by the wayside with losses to Miami and Texas A&M, respectively.

The SEC match-up between the Eastern and Western Division regular-season survivors was touch and go until the final nine minutes. Exactly 8:43 remained, in fact, when Tee

As the season drew to a close, the Vols gathered at the Georgia Dome for the 1998 SEC championship game against Mississippi State.

Martin hit Peerless Price with a 41-yard pass to put Tennessee ahead for keeps.

Moments later, after a Mississippi State fumble, Martin connected with Cedrick Wilson for a 26-yard touchdown strike that wrapped up the scoring in the 24–14 Tennessee triumph.

The heroics of Martin, Price, and Wilson, as well as that of some of their talented teammates, became vital earlier in

1998
T

the fourth period when Kevin Prentiss's punt return for 83 yards, a dazzling bit of open-field maneuvering, put Mississippi State into the lead at 14–10.

Tennessee had moved out to a 10–7 halftime advantage, overcoming a 7–0 State lead, on a two-yard touchdown run by Travis Stephens and a 31-yard field goal by Jeff Hall. The victory, bringing Tennessee's record to 12–0, provided the Vols a second consecutive SEC championship.

Other than the fourth-quarter punt return and an interception return for a touchdown, Tennessee kept close reins on the Bulldogs. State was able to produce only 65 yards rushing and 84 yards passing.

The Vols, meanwhile, were able to win despite a subpar performance by Martin in the first three quarters. But with the game on the line, Tee's two passing gems more than made up for any previous disapproval his aerials might have caused.

Mississippi State	7	0	0	7	14
Tennessee	0	10	0	14	24

MSU Bean, interception return 70 (Hazelwood kick)

UT Stephens, run 2 (Hall kick)

UT Hall, field goal 31

MSU Prentiss, punt return 83 (Hazelwood kick)

UT Price, pass from Martin 41 (Hall kick)

UT Wilson, pass from Martin 26 (Hall kick)

Peerless Price Remembers

"The offense felt we could come from behind in the fourth quarter when Mississippi State went ahead. It had happened throughout the season,

Peerless Price's touchdown on a pass from Tee Martin gave Tennessee a huge lift in the Fiesta Bowl victory over Florida State.

against Syracuse and Arkansas in particular. In the Florida game, we had to go into overtime.

"We had been there before, and this was for all the marbles to have a chance to win the national title. Kansas State and UCLA lost that day, to assure us we would be in the BCS final. We knew UCLA had lost, but we didn't know about Kansas State.

"But that gave us extra motivation. You don't need extra motivation, really, though, because you're playing to prove yourself the best in your conference.

"We lost Peyton Manning, but we knew Tee Martin could handle the job. We didn't know he would be that good and lead us to a championship, but we knew he would put us in position to win games.

"Tee must have learned from Peyton. Peyton asked more of you while Tee went out there and used his athletic ability. Peyton was a more accurate passer, but Tee threw a bullet and had good accuracy. The players liked both Peyton and Tee an awful lot.

"We played this game indoors, but the only problem was the lights sort of bothered you. I liked playing indoors, but after I joined the Buffalo Bills and experienced the cold weather, I got used to it. When you come to Buffalo as a rookie, it kind of shocks you.

"After the touchdown that put us ahead, Corey Terry recovered a fumble on the very next play. Coach Fulmer decided to take a shot and see if we could put it out of reach. I ran the post, and Cedrick Wilson ran the post corner.

"On my pass, the 41-yarder from Martin, we ran a 62-X takeoff. My job was to run as hard as I could toward the goal. I had to make a pretty good catch because the defender was right with me. But I caught it in the corner.

"It wasn't hard for Coach Fulmer to get us to keep our focus for this game."

Vols 23, Florida State 16 (Fiesta Bowl)

The 23–16 victory over Florida State in the BCS championship game clinched the 1998 national championship for the Vols—with no ifs, ands, or buts about it.

For the first time ever, college football recognized a champion at the end of the season, and despite controversy concerning BCS methods, the unbeaten Vols were the undisputed champions.

The game was played under a bright Arizona moon and three nights into the new millennium. Vice President Al Gore was among the celebrants in the Tennessee dressing room at Sun Devil Stadium in Tempe. The first-ranked Volunteers and second-ranked Seminoles sparred through a defensive struggle that was highlighted by Dwayne Goodrich's interception return, a methodical 88-yard scoring drive, and a 79-yard touchdown pass from Tee Martin to Peerless Price.

Tennessee exploded for a pair of touchdowns early in the second period, giving the Vols a strategic advantage they exploited through the tense give-and-take of the second half.

As the second quarter got under way, Martin fired a four-yard touchdown pass to fullback Shawn Bryson from the 4, marking the end of an 88-yard drive. Florida State, trying to even the count, lofted a pass that Goodrich intercepted and lugged back 54 yards, staking UT to a 14–0 advantage.

Punter David Leaverton's tackle of Florida State's Peter Warwick helped insure Tennessee's Fiesta Bowl triumph.

The Seminoles countered with a touchdown and field goal, reducing their deficit to 14–9 at halftime. From that point, the game evolved into a mostly defensive chess match. Price's touchdown on Martin's pass covered 79 yards and ended Tennessee's scoring.

The game represented the debut of Randy Sanders as offensive coordinator, replacing David Cutcliffe, who had moved on to the head coaching job at Ole Miss. Martin's performance for his new leader was a winner in all respects. Tee completed 11 of 18 passes for two touchdowns and 278 yards.

The Vols gained 392 yards while holding Florida State to 253. Al Wilson was in on nine tackles. The other two linebackers, Raynoch Thompson and Eric Westmoreland, registered some valuable tackle-for-loss plays.

Florida State	0	9	0	7	16
Tennessee	0	14	0	9	23

UT	Bryson, pass from Martin 4 (Hall kick)
UT	Goodrich, interception return 54 (Hall kick)
FSU	McCray, run 1 (kick failed)
FSU	Janikowski, field goal 34
UT	Price, pass from Martin 79 (kick failed)
UT	Hall, field goal 23
FSU	Outzen, run 7 (Janikowski kick)

Tee Martin Remembers

"Going into the game, we felt we were disrespected. We were undefeated, Florida State had lost a game, and still they were favored over us. Everybody said we were going to lose to them because they were Florida State. We wanted to prove to everybody we were the new bullies on the block. But we never doubted we could beat them. We wanted them to know how we play football in the SEC.

"Their quarterback did a good job, but our defense took things away from them they wanted to do. We did a good job of covering Peter Warrick, who was about 75 percent of their offense.

"We knew the game would come down to making big plays and not letting Florida State make them. We had made our mistakes early on. Peerless and I had a good relationship all season. Coach Sanders gave us the opportunity to make a play, and we did.

"The play on fourth and 1, the pass to Bryson, was something we had worked on. We knew they would expect us to run the ball. That showed we had done a good job of game-planning. They were geared to stop the run. But I put it out there to Shawn Bryson. We knew Shawn had good hands and that he would get the job done.

"The fact that Coach Sanders would call it in his first game as coordinator showed how much faith and confidence he had in us. We didn't want to go down with bullets in our gun. We wanted to shoot all the bullets. Coach Sanders said he was going to call an aggressive game and that what he wanted from us was that we play hard and we play smart.

"Coach Sanders helped me grow a lot, especially my senior year, 1999. Coach Cutcliffe was very instrumental also in my growth. He was a strong disciplinarian who wanted us to be perfect at quarterback. And that's the way you need to be, as least as far as your focus is concerned. He made sure we were ready every game.

"I felt good going into the season partly because we had success against Nebraska in the Orange Bowl when I had the chance to play late in the game. I had practiced with the first team for that game and didn't realize until a few days earlier I wouldn't start.

"But I had a chance to play late in the game. We moved downfield and scored a touchdown, which gave me great confidence coming into the 1998 season. That

summer, I had told everyone I knew that we would win the championship—the national championship, not just the SEC.

"We had a close call in our first game, against Syracuse at the Carrier Dome. We got an interference call to give us a chance late in the game. It was blatant interference on Syracuse. The guy tore up the carpet getting to Cedrick Wilson. It was in the open, and everybody could see it. That was a great game and a test of our character.

"The Florida game was another big one. We had to win that game.

"As you might figure, Coach Fulmer had everything to do with our success that season. He is a clean-cut guy. He practices what he preaches. He's a player's kind of coach. He says what he means and doesn't go behind your back saying something else.

> "As you might figure, Coach Fulmer had everything to do with our success that season. . . . He practices what he preaches. He's a player's kind of coach."
>
> —Tee Martin

"Coach is a family man, always has his wife and kids with him, and is the kind of man you like to play hard for.

"The camaraderie on that team is still good. We all talk to each other and see each other. Everybody sticks together. I talk to some from the previous teams. I still talk to Peyton and Joey Kent, for instance.

"That's part of what Coach Fulmer does. He wants the players to have fun, and he sees to it that everybody gets along. That's a big part of why Tennessee does so well."

The Vols were national champions—undisputed. With the Bowl Championship Series in place, college football for the first time was able to crown one team—and one team only—as best in the nation.

The Sears national championship trophy was presented to Coach Phillip Fulmer after the Fiesta Bowl victory over Florida State.

1998
T

Aside from Tennessee and Tulane, no other school had gone through its entire schedule unscathed. The Green Wave, apparently because its schedule was judged less severe, was awarded seventh place in both final polls despite a spotless record.

Up until the final day of the season, no one knew for sure that Tennessee would be in the title game. Fortunately for Tennessee—and for the reputation of the BCS—things fell into place on December 5, averting what would undoubtedly have been a nasty situation.

It happened that Tennessee and two other teams—in addition to Tulane—had reached the final day of the campaign with perfect records. Although the Vols were ranked number one, Tennessee fans worried that a narrow win over Mississippi State in the SEC title game, coupled with impressive victories the same day by UCLA and Kansas State, might cost UT a berth in the national-title game at the Fiesta Bowl.

The potential snub by the BCS didn't occur, thanks in part to the Miami Hurricanes and the Texas A&M Aggies. Miami cruised past UCLA in a game that had been postponed from earlier in the season because of bad weather in Miami.

And in the Big 12 title game, the other unbeaten power, Kansas State, went down to defeat at the hands of Texas A&M, which, interestingly, was quarterbacked by a transfer from Tennessee, Branndon Stewart.

With the stock of UCLA and Kansas State reduced, and Tennessee firmly listed as number one in the polls, the scramble began to choose UT's foe in the Fiesta Bowl. There were several once-defeated teams from which to choose. The contenders were Florida State, Ohio State, UCLA, and Kansas State.

The BCS polls and computers came up with Florida State. Some surmised it was largely because the Seminoles' only defeat had occurred earlier in the season than any of the others.

So, in a game at Tempe, Arizona—which came about as close to an "official" national championship as college football has ever produced—the Vols defeated Bobby Bowden's Seminoles, 23–16.

In the postseason AP poll, the top 10, in order, were Tennessee, Ohio State, Florida State, Arizona, Florida, Wisconsin, Tulane, UCLA, Georgia Tech, and Kansas State. The Heisman Trophy went to running back Ricky Williams of Texas, who was followed in the voting by Kansas State quarterback Michael Bishop and UCLA quarterback Cade McNown. 🏈

NORBERT ACKERMANN, center from Louisville, Kentucky, was a businessman in Atlanta, Georgia.

DOUG ATKINS, defensive end and All-America from Humboldt, Tennessee, played for 17 years in the NFL and was inducted into the Halls of Fame of both college and professional football.

BILL BARNES, blocking back from Memphis, Tennessee, coached under Red Sanders at UCLA, where he later became head coach.

DAN BROOKS is the defensive line coach at the University of Tennessee. He is a graduate of Western Carolina University.

JOHN CHAVIS is defensive coordinator and linebackers coach at the University of Tennessee. He is a UT graduate and former member of the football team.

ED CIFERS, end from Kingsport, Tennessee, played professional football and was president of a hosiery mill in Lenoir City, Tennessee.

LEONARD COFFMAN, fullback from Greeneville, Tennessee, coached at the University of Wyoming and Greeneville (Tennessee) High School. He later farmed in Greeneville, dealing mainly in livestock.

DAVID CUTCLIFFE, former offensive coordinator and quarterbacks coach at UT, is now head coach at the University of Mississippi.

TED DAFFER, defensive guard and All-America from Norfolk, Virginia, was involved in business for a flooring service and an athletic equipment company. He also managed mobile home parks in Florida.

BOB DAVIS, center from Bluefield, West Virginia, coached football and worked in athletics administration at the University of Tennessee after serving as head coach at Carson-Newman College.

DOUG DICKEY was head coach of the University of Tennessee Volunteers from 1964 through 1969. He served as athletics director at UT from 1985 through 2003 and was inducted into the College Football Hall of Fame.

ALBERT DORSEY, defensive back and All-America from Tampa, Florida, is in the cast iron business in McMinnville, Tennessee, and lives in Brentwood, Tennessee.

DICK ERNSBERGER (deceased), fullback from Richmond, Virginia, was an educator and founded a sports apparel firm.

GENE FELTY, center from Bristol, Tennessee, coached high school football prior to owning and operating an insurance company in Bristol.

RICHMOND FLOWERS, wingback and All-America from Montgomery, Alabama, played professional football and is now in the commodity business, living in Birmingham, Alabama.

MACK FRANKLIN, defensive end from Madisonville, Tennessee, became an educator, serving as a principal and assistant superintendent of schools in Hamilton County, Tennessee.

PHILLIP FULMER has been head coach of the University of Tennessee Volunteers since 1992, compiling a record that ranks him number two among the nation's active coaches.

CHARLIE FULTON, tailback and quarterback from Memphis, Tennessee, coached at the University of Florida and later was in business with a chemical company in Gainesville, Florida.

RAY GRAVES, center from Knoxville, Tennessee, played professional football and later was head coach and athletic director at the University of Florida.

JOHN GRUBLE, offensive end from Mount Airy, North Carolina, was in the insurance business in Dallas, Texas, and served on the Cotton Bowl selection committee.

JIMMY HAHN, blocking back from Newport News, Virginia, and a two-time winner of Jacobs Blocking Trophy in the Southeastern Conference, served as a United States Army officer and was in the land development business in Virginia.

JEFF HALL, placekicker from Winchester, Tennessee, played professional football and works for an investment firm in Knoxville, Tennessee.

JIM HASLAM, offensive tackle from St. Petersburg, Florida, was founder and CEO of Pilot Oil Corporation, which operates travel centers and truck stops throughout the nation.

JIMMY HILL (deceased), defensive back from Maryville, Tennessee, played NFL football for five years and owned and operated a clothing store in Maryville.

HAROLD JOHNSON, kicking game specialist from Jackson, Tennessee, practices law. He also served as a Southeastern Conference football and basketball official.

BOB JOHNSON, center and All-America from Cleveland, Tennessee, played professional football and owns an adhesive manufacturing company in Cincinnati, Ohio.

VINCE KASETA, offensive end from Brockton, Massachusetts, became vice president of the Agfa Division of the Bayer Company in Massachusetts.

STEVE KINER, linebacker and All-America from Tampa, Florida, played professional football and is a mental health counselor in Atlanta, Georgia.

ANDY KOZAR, fullback from St. Michael, Pennsylvania, was a recipient of the NCAA Silver Anniversary Award and served on the faculty and administration at the University of Tennessee.

KARL KREMSER, placekicker from Levittown, Pennsylvania, coaches soccer at Florida International University.

HANK LAURICELLA, tailback and All-America from New Orleans, Louisiana, served in the Louisiana legislature and was a general partner in his family's real estate business, the Lauricella Land Company. He was enshrined in the National Football Foundation and Hall of Fame.

DAVID LEAVERTON, punter from Midland, Texas, played professional football and returned to Knoxville, Tennessee, to enter business.

TEE MARTIN, quarterback from Mobile, Alabama, played professional football with the Pittsburgh Steelers and is now with the Oakland Raiders.

JOHN MICHELS, offensive guard and All-America from Philadelphia, Pennsylvania, coached at Texas A&M, in the Canadian Football League, and for 27 years with the Minnesota Vikings.

GENE MOELLER (deceased), linebacker from Davenport, Iowa, retired as a lieutenant colonel from the U.S. Army and served as an administrator in the University of Tennessee Athletic Department.

ED MORGAN, wingback from Hendersonville, North Carolina, was a design engineer for numerous projects, including work for the Kennedy Space Center.

ANDY MYERS (deceased), defensive tackle from Knoxville, Tennessee, was in the real estate business in his hometown.

WILL OVERSTREET, defensive end from Jackson, Mississippi, plays professional football with the Atlanta Falcons.

HAROLD (HERKY) PAYNE, tailback from Pensacola, Florida, coached and taught at Farragut High School in Knoxville, Tennessee.

BILL PEARMAN, defensive tackle and All-America from Charlotte, North Carolina, founded the Touchdown Club of Memphis and worked for Browning-Ferris Industries.

IKE PEEL, halfback from Dyersburg, Tennessee, coached at the University of Tennessee and later farmed in West Tennessee.

GORDON POLOFSKY, linebacker from Cranston, Rhode Island, played NFL football and was later in the wholesale liquor business in Knoxville.

PEERLESS PRICE, wide receiver from Dayton, Ohio, played professional football with the Buffalo Bills and is currently with the Atlanta Falcons.

BILLY RATLIFF, defensive tackle from Magnolia, Mississippi, works in the office of the Knox County Trustee in Knoxville, Tennessee.

BERT RECHICHAR, wingback and safety from Belle Vernon, Pennsylvania, played professional football and held the field-goal distance record in the NFL. He was in business in Pennsylvania.

SPENCER RILEY, center from New Market, Tennessee, is a teacher and coach at Karns High School in Knoxville.

CHARLES ROSENFELDER, offensive guard from Humboldt, Tennessee, is in the petroleum business and lives in Knoxville.

PAT SHIRES, tailback and placekicker from Hinton, West Virginia, worked for Proctor and Gamble Pharmaceuticals in Knoxville, Tennessee.

NICK SHOWALTER, monster man from Kingsport, Tennessee, is a dentist in Knoxville.

TRAVIS STEPHENS, tailback from Clarksville, Tennessee, plays professional football with the Houston Texans.

VAN THOMPSON (deceased), quarterback from Jackson, Tennessee, operated a retail shoe store in Jackson.

MURRAY WARMATH, former line coach at Tennessee, was head coach at Mississippi State and Minnesota.

DEWEY WARREN, quarterback from Savannah, Georgia, played professional football and coached. He now conducts a sports radio show in Knoxville, Tennessee.

DICK WILLIAMS, defensive tackle from Greeneville, Tennessee, is in the insurance business in Crossville, Tennessee.

AL WILSON, linebacker and All-America from Jackson, Tennessee, plays professional football with the Denver Broncos.

Team Rosters & Coaching Staffs

1938

SQUAD: Norbert Ackermann, Robert Andridge, Pryor Bacon, John Bailey, William Barnes, Sam Bartholomew, Lloyd Broome, George Cafego, Edward Cifers, Boyd Clay, Leonard Coffman, James Coleman, James Cowan, Cheek Duncan, Ralph Eldred, Robert Foxx, Gerald Hendricks, Carl Hubbuck, George Hunter, Melvin Lampley, Joseph Little, William Luttrell, William McCarren, Delbert Melton, Edward Molinski, James Rike, Edwin Sellers, Calvin Sexton, Abe Shires, Jack Siphers, Thomas Smith, Robert Sneed, Max Steiner, Robert Suffridge, Larry Turner, Al Thomas, Van Thompson, Joe Wallen, Buist Warren, Nick Weber, Hodges West, Clay Whitehead, Walter Wood, Robert Woodruff, Bowden Wyatt

COACHES: Robert Neyland, John Barnhill, Bill Britton, Hugh Faust, William Murrell, Murray Warmath

1940

SQUAD: Norbert Ackermann, Robert Andridge, James Aurelia, Mike Balitsaris, Lloyd Broome, Robert Broome, Earle Brown, William Bryson, Johnny Butler, Edward Cifers, James Coleman, Don Edmiston, Fay Farris, Harry Ford, Robert Foxx, Ray Graves, Webster Hubbell, Al Hust, Emil Hust, Byron Hutchison, William King, Owen Lloyd, William Luttrell, Edward Molinski, William Meek, Richard Mulloy, Henry Noel, William Nowling, Fred Newman, Bernard O'Neil, Edd Osborne, Elwood Powers, Ike Peel, Chester Robertson, Dave Romine, James Schwartzinger, Marshall Shires, Leonard Simonetti, Robert Suffridge, Max Steiner, Van Thompson, Willis Tucker, Warren Vick, Nick Weber, Buist Warren, Hodges West, Eugene Young

COACHES: Robert Neyland, John Barnhill, Bill Britton, Hugh Faust, John Mauer, William Murrell

1950

SQUAD: Frank Alexander, Doug Atkins, Donald Bordinger, Frank Boring, Earl Campbell, George Carter, W. C. Cooper, Ted Daffer, Bob Davis, Kenneth Donahue, Basil Drake, Jody Ellis, Dick Ernsberger, Carl Eschenback, Gene Felty, Charles Flora, Bill Ford, Bill Fulton, Grady Gentry, John Gruble, Jimmy Hahn, James Haslam, Jimmy Hill, Francis Holohan, Joe Hughes, Bill Jasper, Harold Johnson, Tommy Jumper, Vince Kaseta, Andy Kozar, Gil Kyker, Dan Laughlin, Hank Lauricella, Vernon Lyons, Joe Maiure, Jerry Malach, James Markelonis, David Markloff, Charles Meyer, John Michels, Gene Moeller, Ed Morgan, Jerry Morris, Andy Myers, Bobby Neyland, Harold Payne, Bill Pearman, Gordon Polofsky, Kenneth Pruett, Bert Rechichar, Roger Rotroff, J. W. Sherrill, Bud Sherrod, Pat Shires, Bernie Sizemore, Roy Smith, Charles Stokes, Jack Stroud, Francis Stupar, Francis Trubits, Tom Twitty, Roger Vest

COACHES: Robert Neyland, Chan Caldwell, Ralph Chancey, William Hildebrand, Al Hust, L. B. Johnson, Ike Peel, Harvey Robinson, Hodges West

1951

SQUAD: Ralph Adams, Bill Addonizio, Frank Alexander, Doug Atkins, Bill Barbish, Bill Blackstock, Don Bordinger, Frank Boring, Dan Butler, Ray Byrd, Earl Campbell, Bob Cloninger, Larry Crowson, Billy Cunningham, Ted Daffer, Bob Davis, John Davis, Dick Emsberger, Bob Fisher, Mack Franklin, Bill Fulton,

Hugh Garner, Jimmy Hahn, Jim Haslam, Gary Herrmann, Frank Holohan, Harold Hubbard, Jerry Hyde, Bill Jasper, Tommy Jumper, Vince Kaseta, Joel Kinley, Vic Kolenik, Andy Kozar, Dan Laughlin, Hank Lauricella, Lamar Leachman, Vernon Lyons, Joe Maiure, Ray Martin, Charles Meyer, John Michels, Gene Moeller, Ed Morgan, Colin Munro, Andy Myers, Bobby Neyland, Ed Nickla, Martin Paris, Bob Patterson, Harold Payne, Bill Pearman, Gordon Polofsky, Bert Rechichar, Roger Rotroff, Dan Sekanovich, Jay Sentell, Pat Shires, Charles Stokes, Roger Vest, Jimmy Wade, Paul Walker, Wayne Watson, Oaka Williams

COACHES: Robert Neyland, Chan Caldwell, Ralph Chancey, Al Hust, L. B. Johnson, Ike Peel, Harvey Robinson, Hodges West

1967

SQUAD: Bill Baker, Jim Bates, Tommy Baucom, John Boynton, John Brozowski, Richard Callaway, Tom Callaway, Steve Carroll, Walter Chadwick, Benny Dalton, Terry Dalton, Ken DeLong, Vic Dingus, Albert Dorsey, Dick Ellis, Dave Filson, Richmond Flowers, Charles Fulton, Elliott Gammage, Jimmy Glover, Mike Gooch, Jeff Gorin, Joe Graham, Jimmy Hahn, Jerry Holloway, Ron Jarvis, Tom Jernigan, Bob Johnson, Mike Jones, Rusty Kidd, Steve Kiner, Gary Kreis, Karl Kremser, Kelley LaCoste, Rick Marino, Jim McDonald, Chick McGeehan, Neal McMeans, Gary Melton, J. B. Merritt, Jim Mondelli, David Murphy, Mitch Mutter, Bobby Patterson, Richard Pickens, Mike Price, Jack Reynolds, Charles Rosenfelder, Nick Showalter,

Clifton Stewart, Jimmy Thomas, Dewey Warren, Derrick Weatherford, Jim Weatherford, Herman Weaver, Dick Williams, Gary Wright, Bubba Wyche, Frank Yanossy, Bill Young

COACHES: Doug Dickey, Bill Battle, George Cafego, Bob Davis, Jimmy Dunn, Jack Kile, Doug Knotts, George McKinney, Ray Trail, P. W. Underwood

1998

SQUAD: Roger Alexander, Mikki Allen, Miles Atherton, Will Bartholomew, Matt Blankenship, Clay Bostic, Travis Brown, Shawn Bryson, Ed Butler, Josh Campbell, Toby Champion, Chad Clifton, Jeff Coleman, Cosey Coleman, Jermaine Copeland, Phillip Crosby, Eric Diogu, Derrick Edmonds, Shawn Ellis, Justin Emert, John Finlayson, Buck Fitzgerald, Teddy Gaines, Tad Golden, Bernard Gooden, Matt Goodin, Dwayne Goodrich, Bobby Graham, Tyrone Graham, Deon Grant, Judd Granzow, Ron Green, Kevin Gregory, Gerald Griffin, Jeff Hall, Mercedes Hamilton, Travis Henry, Bill Hurst, Bernard Jackson, Andre James, Neil Johnson, Shawn Johnson, Steve Johnson, Austin Kemp, David Leaverton, Jamal Lewis, DeAngelo Lloyd, Andre Lott, Robert Loudermilk, David Martin, Tee Martin, Ethan Massa, Willie Miles, Will Overstreet, Eric Parker, Antron Peebles, Peerless Price, Chris Ramseur, Billy Ratliff, Jarvis Reado, Spencer Riley, Diron Robinson, Benson Scott, Tim Sewell, Bobby Starks, Travis Stephens, Dominique Stevenson, Kevin Taylor, Corey Terry, Raynoch Thompson, Josh Tucker, Burney Veazey, Darwin Walker, Fred Weary, Eric Westmoreland, Fred White, Al Wilson, Cedrick Wilson

COACHES: Phillip Fulmer, Mike Barry, David Blackburn, Mark Bradley, Dan Brooks, Steve Caldwell, John Chavis, David Cutcliffe, Condredge Holloway, Kevin Ramsey, Randy Sanders, John Stucky, Pat Washington